1995 Introductions, including: Bebox, Javascript, Virtual Boy, Xena, Microsoft Bob, Pentium Pro, Sega Nomad, Is-95, Microsoft Agent, Frappuccino, Apple Bandai Pippin, Initial D, Dan Hibiki, Smartmedia, System Management Bus, 3d Movie Maker, Rapi:t, .ci

Hephaestus Books

Contents

Articles

BeBox

BeBox

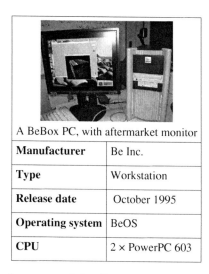

A BeBox PC, with aftermarket monitor	
Manufacturer	Be Inc.
Type	Workstation
Release date	October 1995
Operating system	BeOS
CPU	2 × PowerPC 603

The **BeBox** was a short-lived dual processor PC, offered by Be Inc. to run the company's own operating system, BeOS. Notable aspects of the system include its CPU configuration, I/O board with "GeekPort", and "Blinkenlights" on the front bezel.

The BeBox made its debut in October 1995 (BeBox Dual603-66). The processors were upgraded to 133 MHz in August 1996 (BeBox Dual603e-133). Production was halted in January 1997 [1], following the port of BeOS to the Macintosh, in order for the company to concentrate on software. Be sold around 1000 66 MHz BeBoxes and 800 133 MHz BeBoxes.

CPU Configuration

Initial prototypes were equipped with two AT&T Hobbit processors and three AT&T 9308S DSPs.

Production models used two PowerPC 603 processors running at 66 or 133 MHz to power the BeBox. Prototypes having dual 200 MHz CPUs or four CPUs exist, but these were never publicly available.

I/O board

- Four serial ports (9-pin D-shell)
- One mouse port, PS/2-type
- Two joystick ports (15-pin D-shell)
- Two MIDI out ports
- Two MIDI in ports
- Three infrared (IR) I/O ports (6-pin mini DIN)
- One internal CD audio line-level input (5-pin strip)
- One internal microphone audio input (4-pin strip)
- One internal headphone audio output (4-pin strip)
- Two line-level RCA inputs (L/R)
- Two line-level outputs (L/R)
- One microphone input 3.5 mm stereo phono jack
- One headphone output 3.5 mm stereo phono jack
- A 16-bit stereo sound system @ 48 and 44.1 kHz
- One "GeekPort" (37-pin D-shell)

    - An experimental-electronic-development oriented port, backed by three fuses on the mainboard.
    - Digital and analog I/O and DC power connector, 37-pin connector on the ISA bus.
    - Two independent, bidirectional 8-bit ports
    - Four A/D pins routing to a 12-bit A/D converter
    - Four D/A pins connected to an independent 8-bit D/A converter
    - Two signal ground reference pins
    - Eleven power and ground pins:

        - Two at +5 V, one at +12 V, one at -12 V, seven ground pins.

"Blinkenlights"

Two yellow/green vertical LED arrays, dubbed the "blinkenlights", were built into the front bezel to illustrate the CPU load. The bottommost LED on the right side indicated hard disk activity.

External links

- The BeBox Zone [2]
- BeBox Photo Gallery (Joseph Palmer: Be HW Engineer) [3]
- Pinout for the GeekPort connector [4]

JavaScript

JavaScript

Paradigm	Multi-paradigm: prototype-based, functional, imperative, scripting
Appeared in	1995
Designed by	Brendan Eich
Developer	Netscape Communications Corporation, Mozilla Foundation
Stable release	1.8.2 (June 22, 2009)
Preview release	1.8.5 (July 27, 2010)
Typing discipline	dynamic, weak, duck
Major implementations	KJS, Rhino, SpiderMonkey, V8, WebKit
Influenced by	Self, C, Scheme, Perl, Python, Java
Influenced	JScript, JScript .NET, Objective-J, TIScript
🕮 JavaScript at Wikibooks	

Filename extension	.js
Internet media type	application/javascript, text/javascript
Uniform Type Identifier	com.netscape.javascript- source
Type of format	Scripting language

This article is part of the JavaScript series.
JavaScript
JavaScript syntax
JavaScript topics

JavaScript is an implementation of the ECMAScript language standard and is typically used to enable programmatic access to computational objects within a host environment. It can be characterized as a prototype-based object-oriented scripting language that is dynamic, weakly typed and has first-class functions. It is also considered a functional programming language like Scheme and OCaml because it has closures and supports higher-order functions.

JavaScript is primarily used in the form of client-side JavaScript, implemented as part of a web browser in order to provide enhanced user interfaces and dynamic websites. However, its use in applications outside web pages is also significant.

JavaScript uses syntax influenced by that of C syntax, also JavaScript copies many Java programming language names and naming conventions; but the two languages are otherwise unrelated and have very different semantics. The key design principles within JavaScript are taken from the Self and Scheme programming languages.

History

Anyway I know only one programming language worse than C and that is Javascript. [...] I was convinced that we needed to build-in a programming language, but the developers, Tim first, were very much opposed. It had to remain completely declarative. Maybe, but the net result is that the programming-vacuum filled itself with the most horrible kluge in the history of computing: Javascript.

Robert Cailliau

JavaScript was originally developed by Brendan Eich of Netscape under the name *Mocha*, which was later renamed to *LiveScript*, and finally to JavaScript. LiveScript was the official name for the language when it first shipped in beta releases of Netscape Navigator 2.0 in September 1995, but it was renamed JavaScript in a joint announcement with Sun Microsystems on December 4, 1995 when it was deployed in the Netscape browser version 2.0B3.

JavaScript very quickly gained widespread success as a client-side scripting language for web pages. As a consequence, Microsoft developed a compatible dialect of the language, naming it JScript to avoid trademark issues. JScript added new date methods to fix the non-Y2K-friendly methods in JavaScript, which were based on java.util.Date [1]. JScript was included in Internet Explorer 3.0, released in August 1996. The dialects are perceived to be so similar that the terms "JavaScript" and "JScript" are often used interchangeably. Microsoft, however, notes dozens of ways in which JScript is not ECMA-compliant.

In November, 1996 Netscape announced that it had submitted JavaScript to Ecma International for consideration as an industry standard, and subsequent work resulted in the standardized version named ECMAScript.

JavaScript has become one of the most popular programming languages on the web. Initially, however, many professional programmers denigrated the language because its target audience was web authors and other such "amateurs", among other reasons. The advent of Ajax returned JavaScript to the spotlight and brought more professional programming attention. The result was a proliferation of comprehensive frameworks and libraries, improved JavaScript programming practices, and increased usage of JavaScript outside of web browsers, as seen by the proliferation of server-side JavaScript platforms.

In January 2009 the CommonJS project was founded with the goal of specifying a common standard library mainly for JavaScript development outside the browser.

Trademark

"JavaScript" is a trademark of Oracle Corporation. It is used under license for technology invented and implemented by Netscape Communications and current entities such as the Mozilla Foundation.

Features

The following features are common to all conforming ECMAScript implementations, unless explicitly specified otherwise.

Imperative and structured

JavaScript supports all the structured programming syntax in C (e.g., if statements, while loops, switch statements, etc.). One partial exception is scoping: C-style block-level scoping is not supported (instead, JavaScript has function-level scoping). JavaScript 1.7, however, supports block-level scoping with the let keyword. Like C, JavaScript makes a distinction between expressions and statements. One syntactic difference from C is automatic semicolon insertion, in which the semicolons that terminate statements can be omitted.

Dynamic

dynamic typing

> As in most scripting languages, types are associated with values, not variables. For example, a variable x could be bound to a number, then later rebound to a string. JavaScript supports various ways to test the type of an object, including duck typing.

object based

> JavaScript is almost entirely object-based. JavaScript objects are associative arrays, augmented with prototypes (see below). Object property names are string keys: obj.x = 10 and obj["x"] = 10 are equivalent, the dot notation being syntactic sugar. Properties and their values can be added, changed, or deleted at run-time. Most properties of an object (and those on its prototype inheritance chain) can be enumerated using a for...in loop. JavaScript has a small number of built-in objects such as Function and Date.

run-time evaluation

> JavaScript includes an eval function that can execute statements provided as strings at run-time.

Functional

first-class functions

> Functions are first-class; they are objects themselves. As such, they have properties and methods, such as length and call(); and they can be assigned to variables, passed as arguments, returned by other functions, and manipulated like any other object. Any reference to a function allows it to be invoked using the () operator.

nested functions

> 'Inner' or 'nested' functions are functions defined within another function. They are created each time the outer function is invoked. In addition to that, the scope of the outer function, including any constants, local variables and argument values, become part of the internal state of each inner function object, even after execution of the outer function concludes.

closures

> JavaScript allows nested functions to be created, with the lexical scope in force at their definition, and has a () operator to invoke them now or later. This combination of code that can be executed outside the scope in which it is defined, with its own scope to use during that execution, is called a closure in computer science.

Prototype-based

prototypes

> JavaScript uses prototypes instead of classes for inheritance. It is possible to simulate many class-based features with prototypes in JavaScript.

functions as object constructors

> Functions double as object constructors along with their typical role. Prefixing a function call with new creates a new object and calls that function with its local this keyword bound to that object for that invocation. The constructor's prototype property determines the object used for the new object's internal prototype. JavaScript's built-in constructors, such as Array, also have prototypes that can be modified.

functions as methods

> Unlike many object-oriented languages, there is no distinction between a function definition and a method definition. Rather, the distinction occurs during function calling; a function can be called as a method. When a function is called as a method of an object, the function's local this keyword is bound to that object for that invocation.

Miscellaneous

run- time environment

> JavaScript typically relies on a run-time environment (e.g. in a web browser) to provide objects and methods by which scripts can interact with "the outside world". In fact, it relies on the environment to provide the ability to include/import scripts (e.g. HTML <script> elements). (This is not a language feature per se, but it is common in most JavaScript implementations.)

variadic functions

> An indefinite number of parameters can be passed to a function. The function can access them through formal parameters and also through the local arguments object.

array and object literals

> Like many scripting languages, arrays and objects (associative arrays in other languages) can each be created with a succinct shortcut syntax. In fact, these literals form the basis of the JSON data format.

regular expressions

> JavaScript also supports regular expressions in a manner similar to Perl, which provide a concise and powerful syntax for text manipulation that is more sophisticated than the built-in string functions.

Vendor-specific extensions

JavaScript is officially managed by Mozilla Foundation, and new language features are added periodically. However, only some non-Mozilla JavaScript engines support these new features:

- property getter and setter functions (also supported by WebKit, Opera, ActionScript, and Rhino)
- conditional catch clauses
- iterator protocol adopted from Python
- shallow generators/coroutines also adopted from Python
- array comprehensions and generator expressions also adopted from Python
- proper block scope via new let keyword
- array and object destructuring (limited form of pattern matching)
- concise function expressions (function(args) expr)
- ECMAScript for XML (E4X), an extension that adds native XML support to ECMAScript

Syntax and semantics

Main article: JavaScript syntax

As of 2009, the latest version of the language is JavaScript 1.8.1. It is a superset of ECMAScript (ECMA-262) Edition 3. Extensions to the language, including partial E4X (ECMA-357) support and experimental features considered for inclusion into future ECMAScript editions, are documented here.

Simple examples

A simple recursive function:

```
function factorial (n){
    if (n == 0)
        return 1;
    else
        return n * factorial(n-1);
}
```

Anonymous function (or lambda) syntax:

```
function add(i, j){

    var add_pri = function(x, y){
                    return x + y
                        };

    return add_pri(i, j);
}
```

Closures:

```
function showclosure(){

    var inc = makeinc(1);

    inc(); //1
    inc(); //2
    inc(); //3
}


function makeinc(initalValue){
```

```
    var count = initalValue

    return function(){
        return count++;
    };
}
```

Variadic function demonstration. This will alert with 1 then 2 then 3. `arguments` is a special variable.

```
function unlimited_args(){

    for( var i = 0; i < arguments.length; i++ ) {
        alert(arguments[i]);
    }
}


unlimited_args(1,2,3);
```

Example - syntax and semantics

This sample code showcases various JavaScript features. The example can be executed with the following steps: (1) Copy the code to a file with extension .html. (2) Use Mozilla Firefox or Google Chrome to open the file.

```
<html>
  <head><title>LCM Calculator</title></head>
  <body style="font-family:'Courier New'">
  <script type="text/javascript">
/* Finds the lowest common multiple of two numbers */
function LCMCalculator(x, y) { // constructor function
    function checkInt(x) { // inner function
        if (x % 1 != 0)
            throw new TypeError(x + " is not an integer"); // exception
 throwing
        return x;
    }
    //semicolons are optional (but beware since this may cause
consecutive lines to be
    //erroneously treated as a single statement)
```

```
        this.a = checkInt(x)
        this.b = checkInt(y)
    }
    // The prototype of object instances created by a constructor is
    // that constructor's "prototype" property.
    LCMCalculator.prototype = { // object literal
        gcd : function() { // method that calculates the greatest common
    divisor
            // Euclidean algorithm:
            var a = Math.abs(this.a), b = Math.abs(this.b), t;
            if (a < b) {
                t = b; b = a; a = t; // swap variables
            }
            while (b !== 0) {
                t = b;
                b = a % b;
                a = t;
            }
            // Only need to calculate gcd once, so "redefine" this method.
            // (Actually not redefinition - it's defined on the instance
    itself,
            // so that this.gcd refers to this "redefinition" instead of
    LCMCalculator.prototype.gcd.)
            // Also, 'gcd' == "gcd", this['gcd'] == this.gcd
            this['gcd'] = function() { return a; };
            return a;
        },
        "lcm" /* can use strings here */: function() {
            // Variable names don't collide with object properties, e.g.
    |lcm| is not |this.lcm|.
            // not using |this.a * this.b| to avoid FP precision issues
            var lcm = this.a / this.gcd() * this.b;
            // Only need to calculate lcm once, so "redefine" this method.
            this.lcm = function() { return lcm; };
            return lcm;
        },
        toString : function() {
            return "LCMCalculator: a = " + this.a + ", b = " + this.b;
```

```javascript
        }
};


// Note: Array's map() and forEach() are predefined in JavaScript 1.6.
// They are currently not available in the JScript engine built into
// Microsoft Internet Explorer, but are implemented in Firefox, Chrome,
 etc.
// They are used here to demonstrate JavaScript's inherent functional
nature.

[[25,55],[21,56],[22,58],[28,56]].map(function(pair) { // array literal
 + mapping function
    return new LCMCalculator(pair[0], pair[1]);
}).sort(function(a, b) { // sort with this comparative function
    return a.lcm() - b.lcm();
}).forEach(function(obj) {
    /* Note: print() is a JS builtin function available in Mozilla's js
 CLI;
     * It is functionally equivalent to Java's System.out.println().
     * Within a web browser, print() is a very different function
     * (opens the "Print Page" dialog),
     * so use something like document.write() or alert() instead.
     */
    // print         (obj + ", gcd = " + obj.gcd() + ", lcm = " +
obj.lcm());
    // alert         (obj + ", gcd = " + obj.gcd() + ", lcm = " +
obj.lcm());
    document.write(obj + ", gcd = " + obj.gcd() + ", lcm = " +
obj.lcm() + "<br>");
});


    </script>
    <noscript>
(Message from JavaScript example) <br>
Your browser either does not support JavaScript, or you have JavaScript
 turned off.
    </noscript>
  </body>
```

```
</html>
```

The following output should be displayed in the browser window.

```
LCMCalculator: a = 28, b = 56, gcd = 28, lcm = 56
LCMCalculator: a = 21, b = 56, gcd = 7, lcm = 168
LCMCalculator: a = 25, b = 55, gcd = 5, lcm = 275
LCMCalculator: a = 22, b = 58, gcd = 2, lcm = 638
```

If Internet Explorer is used, the example will generate an error. Hence the example illustrates the point that the JScript interpreter in Internet Explorer executes code differently from the JavaScript interpreters in other browsers. (See comments in the source code for details on the relevant differences for this example.)

Use in web pages

Main article: Client-side JavaScript

See also: JavaScript engine and Ajax (programming)

The primary use of JavaScript is to write functions that are embedded in or included from HTML pages and that interact with the Document Object Model (DOM) of the page. Some simple examples of this usage are:

- Opening or popping up a new window with programmatic control over the size, position, and attributes of the new window (e.g. whether the menus, toolbars, etc. are visible).
- Validating input values of a web form to make sure that they are acceptable before being submitted to the server.
- Changing images as the mouse cursor moves over them: This effect is often used to draw the user's attention to important links displayed as graphical elements.

Because JavaScript code can run locally in a user's browser (rather than on a remote server), the browser can respond to user actions quickly, making an application more responsive. Furthermore, JavaScript code can detect user actions which HTML alone cannot, such as individual keystrokes. Applications such as Gmail take advantage of this: much of the user-interface logic is written in JavaScript, and JavaScript dispatches requests for information (such as the content of an e-mail message) to the server. The wider trend of Ajax programming similarly exploits this strength.

A JavaScript engine (also known as *JavaScript interpreter* or *JavaScript implementation*) is an interpreter that interprets JavaScript source code and executes the script accordingly. The first JavaScript engine was created by Brendan Eich at Netscape Communications Corporation, for the Netscape Navigator web browser. The engine, code-named SpiderMonkey, is implemented in C. It has since been updated (in JavaScript 1.5) to conform to ECMA-262 Edition 3. The Rhino engine, created primarily by Norris Boyd (formerly of Netscape; now at Google) is a JavaScript implementation in

Java. Rhino, like SpiderMonkey, is ECMA-262 Edition 3 compliant.

A web browser is by far the most common host environment for JavaScript. Web browsers typically use the public API to create "host objects" responsible for reflecting the DOM into JavaScript. The web server is another common application of the engine. A JavaScript webserver would expose host objects representing an HTTP request and response objects, which a JavaScript program could then manipulate to dynamically generate web pages.

Because JavaScript is the only language that the most popular browsers share support for, it has become a target language for many frameworks in other languages, even though JavaScript was never intended to be such a language. Despite the performance limitations inherent to its dynamic nature, the increasing speed of JavaScript engines has made the language a surprisingly feasible compilation target.

Example - use in web pages

A minimal example of a standards-conforming web page containing JavaScript (using HTML 4.01 syntax) would be the following:

```
<!DOCTYPE HTML PUBLIC "-//W3C//DTD HTML 4.01//EN"
"http://www.w3.org/TR/html4/strict.dtd">
<html>
  <head><title>simple page</title></head>
  <body>
    <script type="text/javascript">
      document.write('Hello World!');
    </script>
    <noscript>

Your browser either does not support JavaScript, or you have JavaScript turned off.
    </noscript>
  </body>
</html>
```

Compatibility considerations

Main article: Web interoperability

Since JavaScript runs in widely varying environments, an important part of testing and debugging it is testing across browsers.

The DOM interfaces for manipulating web pages are not part of the ECMAScript standard, or of JavaScript itself. Officially, they are defined by a separate standardization effort by the W3C; in practice, browser implementations differ from the standards and from each other, and not all browsers execute JavaScript.

To deal with these differences, JavaScript authors can attempt to write standards-compliant code which will also be executed correctly by most browsers; failing that, they can write code that checks for the presence of certain browser features and behaves differently if they are not available. In some cases, two browsers may both implement a feature but with different behavior, and authors may find it practical to detect what browser is running and change their script's behavior to match. Programmers may also use libraries or toolkits which take browser differences into account.

Furthermore, scripts may not work for some users. For example, a user may:

- use an old or rare browser with incomplete or unusual DOM support,
- use a PDA or mobile phone browser which cannot execute JavaScript,
- have JavaScript execution disabled as a security precaution,
- use a speech browser due to, for example, a visual disability.

To support these users, web authors can try to create pages which degrade gracefully on user agents (browsers) which do not support the page's JavaScript. In particular, the page should remain usable albeit without the extra features that the JavaScript would have added.

Accessibility

Main article: Web accessibility

Assuming that the user has not disabled its execution, client-side web JavaScript should be written to enhance the experiences of visitors with visual or physical disabilities, and certainly should avoid denying information to these visitors.

Screen readers, used by the blind and partially sighted, can be JavaScript-aware and so may access and read the page DOM after the script has altered it. The HTML should be as concise, navigable and semantically rich as possible whether the scripts have run or not. JavaScript should not be totally reliant on mouse-specific events so as to deny its benefits to users who either cannot use a mouse or who choose to favor the keyboard for whatever reason. Equally, although hyperlinks and webforms can be navigated and operated from the keyboard, accessible JavaScript should not require keyboard events either. There are device-independent events such as onfocus and onchange that are preferable in most cases.

JavaScript should not be used in a way that is confusing or disorientating to any web user. For example, using script to alter or disable the normal functionality of the browser, such as by changing the way the back-button or the refresh event work, is usually best avoided. Equally, triggering events that the user may not be aware of reduces the user's sense of control as do unexpected scripted changes to the page content.

Often the process of making a complex web page as accessible as possible becomes a nontrivial problem where issues become matters of debate and opinion, and where compromises are necessary in the end. However, user agents and assistive technologies are constantly evolving and new guidelines and relevant information are continually being published on the web.

Security

JavaScript and the DOM provide the potential for malicious authors to deliver scripts to run on a client computer via the web. Browser authors contain this risk using two restrictions. First, scripts run in a sandbox in which they can only perform web-related actions, not general-purpose programming tasks like creating files. Second, scripts are constrained by the same origin policy: scripts from one web site do not have access to information such as usernames, passwords, or cookies sent to another site. Most JavaScript-related security bugs are breaches of either the same origin policy or the sandbox.

Cross-site vulnerabilities

Main articles: Cross-site scripting and Cross-site request forgery

A common JavaScript-related security problem is cross-site scripting, or XSS, a violation of the same-origin policy. XSS vulnerabilities occur when an attacker is able to cause a target web site, such as an online banking website, to include a malicious script in the webpage presented to a victim. The script in this example can then access the banking application with the privileges of the victim, potentially disclosing secret information or transferring money without the victim's authorization. A solution to XSS vulnerabilities is to use *HTML escaping* whenever displaying untrusted data.

Some browsers include partial protection against *reflected* XSS attacks, in which the attacker provides a URL including malicious script. However, even users of those browsers are vulnerable to other XSS attacks, such as those where the malicious code is stored in a database. Only correct design of Web applications on the server side can fully prevent XSS.

XSS vulnerabilities can also occur because of implementation mistakes by browser authors.

Another cross-site vulnerability is cross-site request forgery or CSRF. In CSRF, code on an attacker's site tricks the victim's browser into taking actions the user didn't intend at a target site (like transferring money at a bank). It works because, if the target site relies only on cookies to authenticate requests, then requests initiated by code on the attacker's site will carry the same legitimate login credentials as requests initiated by the user. In general, the solution to CSRF is to require an authentication value in a hidden form field, and not only in the cookies, to authenticate any request that might have lasting effects. Checking the HTTP Referrer header can also help.

"JavaScript hijacking" is a type of CSRF attack in which a <script> tag on an attacker's site exploits a page on the victim's site that returns private information such as JSON or JavaScript. Possible solutions include requiring an authentication token in the POST and GET parameters for any response that returns private JSON (even if it has no side effects); using POST and never GET for requests that return private JSON; and modifying the response so that it can't be used via a <script> tag (by, for example, wrapping the JSON in a JavaScript comment).

Misplaced trust in the client

Client-server applications, whether they involve JavaScript or not, must recognize that untrusted clients may be under the control of attackers. Thus any secret embedded in JavaScript could be extracted by a determined adversary, and the application author cannot assume that his JavaScript runs as intended, or at all. Some implications:

- Web site authors cannot perfectly conceal how their JavaScript operates, because the code is sent to the client, and obfuscated code can be reverse-engineered.
- JavaScript form validation only provides convenience for users, not security. If a site verifies that the user agreed to its terms of service, or filters invalid characters out of fields that should only contain numbers, it must do so on the server, not only the client.
- Scripts can be selectively disabled, so JavaScript can't be relied on to prevent operations such as "save image".
- It would be extremely bad practice to embed a password in JavaScript (where it can be extracted by an attacker), then have JavaScript verify a user's password and pass "password_ok=1" back to the server (since the "password_ok=1" response is easy to forge).

Browser and plugin coding errors

JavaScript provides an interface to a wide range of browser capabilities, some of which may have flaws such as buffer overflows. These flaws can allow attackers to write scripts which would run any code they wish on the user's system.

These flaws have affected major browsers including Firefox, Internet Explorer, and Safari.

Plugins, such as video players, Adobe Flash, and the wide range of ActiveX controls enabled by default in Microsoft Internet Explorer, may also have flaws exploitable via JavaScript, and such flaws have been exploited in the past.

In Windows Vista, Microsoft has attempted to contain the risks of bugs such as buffer overflows by running the Internet Explorer process with limited privileges. Google Chrome similarly limits page renderers to an operating-system-enforced "sandbox."

Sandbox implementation errors

Web browsers are capable of running JavaScript outside of the sandbox, with the privileges necessary to, for example, create or delete files. Of course, such privileges aren't meant to be granted to code from the web.

Incorrectly granting privileges to JavaScript from the web has played a role in vulnerabilities in both Internet Explorer and Firefox. In Windows XP Service Pack 2, Microsoft demoted JScript's privileges in Internet Explorer.

Microsoft Windows allows JavaScript source files on a computer's hard drive to be launched as general-purpose, non-sandboxed programs. This makes JavaScript (like VBScript) a theoretically viable vector for a Trojan horse, although JavaScript Trojan horses are uncommon in practice. (See Windows Script Host.)

Uses outside web pages

In addition to web browsers and servers, JavaScript interpreters are embedded in a number of tools. Each of these applications provides its own object model which provides access to the host environment, with the core JavaScript language remaining mostly the same in each application.

Embedded scripting language

- Apple's Dashboard Widgets, Apple's Safari 5 extensions, Microsoft's Gadgets, Yahoo! Widgets, Google Desktop Gadgets, Serence Klipfolio are implemented using JavaScript.
- Adobe's Acrobat and Adobe Reader (formerly Acrobat Reader) support JavaScript in PDF files.
- Tools in the Adobe Creative Suite, including Photoshop, Illustrator, Dreamweaver and InDesign, allow scripting through JavaScript.
- OpenOffice.org office application suite allows for JavaScript as one of its scripting languages.
- The interactive music signal processing software Max/MSP released by Cycling '74, offers a JavaScript model of its environment for use by developers. It allows much more precise control than the default GUI-centric programming model.
- ECMAScript was included in the VRML97 standard for scripting nodes of VRML scene description files.
- Some high-end Philips universal remote panels, including TSU9600 and TSU9400, can be scripted using a JavaScript-based tool called ProntoScript.
- Sphere is an open source and cross platform computer program designed primarily to make role-playing games that use JavaScript as a scripting language.
- The open-source Re-Animator [2] framework allows developing 2D sprite-based games using JavaScript and XML.
- Methabot is a web crawler that uses JavaScript as scripting language for custom filetype parsers and data extraction using E4X.

- The game engine Unity supports three scripting languages: JavaScript, C#, and Boo.
- DX Studio (3D engine) uses the SpiderMonkey implementation of JavaScript for game and simulation logic.
- Maxwell Render provides an ECMA standard based scripting engine for tasks automation.
- Google Docs Spreadsheet has a script editor which allows users to create custom formulas, automate repetitive tasks and also interact with other Google products such as Gmail.

Scripting engine

- Microsoft's Active Scripting technology supports JScript as a scripting language. This is often considered compatible with JavaScript, but Microsoft lists many JScript features that are not compliant with ECMA standards.
- The Java programming language, in version SE 6 (JDK 1.6), introduced the javax.script package, including a JavaScript implementation based on Mozilla Rhino. Thus, Java applications can host scripts that access the application's variables and objects, much like web browsers host scripts that access the browser's Document Object Model (DOM) for a webpage.
- The Qt C++ toolkit includes a QtScript module to interpret JavaScript, analogous to javax.script.
- Late Night Software's JavaScript OSA (aka JavaScript for OSA, or JSOSA), is a freeware alternative to AppleScript for Mac OS X. It is based on the Mozilla 1.5 JavaScript implementation, with the addition of a MacOS object for interaction with the operating system and third-party applications.

Application platform

- ActionScript, the programming language used in Adobe Flash, is another implementation of the ECMAScript standard.
- The Mozilla platform, which underlies Thunderbird, Firefox and some other web browsers, uses JavaScript to implement the graphical user interface (GUI) of its various products.
- Adobe Integrated Runtime is a JavaScript runtime that allows developers to create desktop applications.
- webOS uses the WebKit implementation of JavaScript in its SDK to allow developers to create stand-alone applications soley in JavaScript.
- CA, Inc.'s AutoShell cross-application scripting environment is built on JavaScript/SpiderMonkey with preprocessor like extensions for command definitions and custom classes for various system related tasks like file i/o, operation system command invocation and redirection and COM scripting.
- GNOME Shell, the shell for the GNOME 3 desktop environment. The Seed, Gjs [3] (from Gnome) and Kjsembed [4] (from KDE) packages are aimed to utilize that needs.

Development tools

Within JavaScript, access to a debugger becomes invaluable when developing large, non-trivial programs. Because there can be implementation differences between the various browsers (particularly within the Document Object Model) it is useful to have access to a debugger for each of the browsers that a web application targets.

Script debuggers are available for Internet Explorer, Firefox, Safari, Google Chrome, and Opera.

Three debuggers are available for Internet Explorer: Microsoft Visual Studio is the richest of the three, closely followed by Microsoft Script Editor (a component of Microsoft Office), and finally the free Microsoft Script Debugger which is far more basic than the other two. The free Microsoft Visual Web Developer Express [5] provides a limited version of the JavaScript debugging functionality in Microsoft Visual Studio.

Web applications within Firefox can be debugged using the Firebug add-on, or the older Venkman debugger. Firefox also has a simpler built-in Error Console, which logs and evaluates JavaScript. It also logs CSS errors and warnings.

Opera includes a set of tools called DragonFly.

WebKit's Web Inspector includes a JavaScript debugger in Apple's Safari.

Some debugging aids are themselves written in JavaScript and built to run on the Web. An example is the program JSLint, developed by Douglas Crockford, currently senior JavaScript architect at Yahoo! who has written extensively on the language. JSLint scans JavaScript code for conformance to a set of standards and guidelines. Web development bookmarklets [6] and Firebug Lite [7] provide variations on the idea of the cross-browser JavaScript console.

MiniME [8] is an open source JavaScript minifier, obfuscator and code checking tool for the .NET platform.

Versions

See also: ECMAScript#Dialects and ECMAScript#Version correspondence

Version	Release date	Equivalent to	Netscape Navigator	Mozilla Firefox	Internet Explorer	Opera	Safari	Google Chrome
1.0	March 1996		2.0		3.0			
1.1	August 1996		3.0					
1.2	June 1997		4.0-4.05					
1.3	October 1998	ECMA-262 1st edition / ECMA-262 2nd edition	4.06-4.7x		4.0			

1.4			Netscape Server					
1.5	November 2000	ECMA-262 3rd edition	6.0	1.0	5.5 (JScript 5.5), 6 (JScript 5.6), 7 (JScript 5.7), 8 (JScript 5.8)	6.0, 7.0, 8.0, 9.0, 10.0	3.0, 3.1, 3.2, 4.0, 5	1.0
1.6	November 2005	1.5 + Array extras + Array and String generics + E4X		1.5				
1.7	October 2006	1.6 + Pythonic generators + Iterators + let		2.0				6
1.8	June 2008	1.7 + Generator expressions + Expression closures		3.0				
1.8.1		1.8 + Native JSON support + Minor Updates		3.5				
1.8.2	June 22, 2009	1.8.1 + Minor updates		3.6				
1.8.5	July 27, 2010	1.8.1 + ECMAScript 5 Compliance		4	9			

Related languages and features

Since the acceptance of JavaScript as a popular language, several languages and features have developed from it.

Objective-J is a strict superset of JavaScript that adds traditional inheritance and Smalltalk/Objective-C style dynamic dispatch and optional pseudo-static typing to pure JavaScript.

TIScript is a superset of JavaScript that adds classes, namespaces and lambda expressions.

JSON, or JavaScript Object Notation, is a general-purpose data interchange format that is defined as a subset of JavaScript.

Mozilla browsers currently support LiveConnect, a feature that allows JavaScript and Java to intercommunicate on the web. However, Mozilla-specific support for LiveConnect is scheduled to be phased out in the future in favor of passing on the LiveConnect handling via NPAPI to the Java 1.6+ plug-in (not yet supported on the Mac as of March 2010).

JavaScript and Java

A common misconception is that JavaScript is similar or closely related to Java. It is true that both have a C-like syntax, the C language being their most immediate common ancestor language. They are both object-oriented, typically sandboxed (when used inside a browser), and are widely used in client-side Web applications. In addition, JavaScript was designed with Java's syntax and standard library in mind. In particular, all Java keywords are reserved in JavaScript, JavaScript's standard library follows Java's naming conventions, and JavaScript's Math and Date objects are based on classes from Java 1.0.

But the similarities end there. Java has static typing; JavaScript's typing is dynamic (meaning a variable can hold an object of any type and cannot be restricted). Java is loaded from compiled bytecode; JavaScript is loaded as human-readable source code. Java's objects are class-based; JavaScript's are prototype-based. JavaScript also has many functional features based on the Scheme language.

See also

- Client-side JavaScript
    - Ajax
    - Comparison of JavaScript frameworks
    - Dynamic HTML
- Comparison of layout engines (ECMAScript)
- Comparison of JavaScript-based source code editors
- ECMAScript
- JavaScript engine (Discussion of JavaScript engines (interpreters) with list of engines)
- JavaScript OSA - A system-level scripting language for the Apple Macintosh
- JavaScript syntax
- JSAN
- JScript
- JSDoc
- JSLint
- JSON
- List of ECMAScript engines
- Server-side JavaScript
- Unobtrusive JavaScript

Further reading

- Bhangal, Sham; Jankowski, Tomasz (2003). *Foundation Web Design: Essential HTML, JavaScript, CSS, PhotoShop, Fireworks, and Flash.* APress L. P.. ISBN 1-59059-152-6.
- Burns, Joe; Growney, Andree S. (2001). *JavaScript Goodies.* Pearson Education. ISBN 0-7897-2612-2.
- Duffy, Scott (2003). *How to do Everything with JavaScript.* Osborne. ISBN 0-07-222887-3.
- Flanagan, David; Ferguson, Paula (2002). *JavaScript: The Definitive Guide* (4th ed.). O'Reilly & Associates. ISBN 0-596-00048-0.
- Flanagan, David (2006). *JavaScript: The Definitive Guide* (5th ed.). O'Reilly & Associates. ISBN 0-596-10199-6.
- Goodman, Danny; Markel, Scott (2003). *JavaScript and DHTML Cookbook.* O'Reilly & Associates. ISBN 0-596-00467-2.
- Goodman, Danny; Eich, Brendan (2001). *JavaScript Bible.* John Wiley & Sons. ISBN 0-7645-3342-8.
- Harris, Andy (2001). *JavaScript Programming for the Absolute Beginner.* Premier Press. ISBN 0-7615-3410-5.
- Heinle, Nick; Koman, Richard (1997). *Designing with JavaScript.* O'Reilly & Associates. ISBN 1-56592-300-6.
- McDuffie, Tina Spain (2003). *JavaScript Concepts & Techniques: Programming Interactive Web Sites.* Franklin, Beedle & Associates. ISBN 1-887-90269-4.
- McFarlane, Nigel (2003). *Rapid Application Development with Mozilla.* Prentice Hall Professional Technical References. ISBN 0-13-142343-6.
- Powell, Thomas A.; Schneider, Fritz (2001). *JavaScript: The Complete Reference.* McGraw-Hill Companies. ISBN 0-07-219127-9.
- Shelly, Gary B.; Cashman, Thomas J.; Dorin, William J.; Quasney, Jeffrey J. (2000). *JavaScript: Complete Concepts and Techniques.* Cambridge: Course Technology. ISBN 0-7895-6233-2.
- Watt, Andrew H.; Watt, Jonathan A.; Simon, Jinjer L. (2002). *Teach Yourself JavaScript in 21 Days.* Pearson Education. ISBN 0-672-32297-8.
- Vander Veer, Emily A. (2004). *JavaScript For Dummies* (4th ed.). Wiley Pub.. ISBN 0-7645-7659-3.

External links

- Douglas Crockford's video lectures on JavaScript [9]
- FAQ for Usenet's comp.lang.javascript [10]
- Mozilla Developer Center
  - Mozilla's Official Documentation on JavaScript [11]
  - References for Core JavaScript versions: 1.5+ [12]
  - overview over new features in JavaScript [13]
  - List of JavaScript releases: versions 1.5+ [14]
  - Re-Introduction to JavaScript [15]
- JavaScript - Opera Developer Community [16]

Virtual Boy

Virtual Boy

Manufacturer	Nintendo
Type	Video game console
Generation	Fifth generation era
Retail availability	• [JP] July 21, 1995 • [NA] August 14, 1995
Discontinued	• [JP] December 22, 1995 • [NA] March 2, 1996
Units sold	770,000
Media	Game Pak (cartridge)
CPU	NEC V810

Nintendo's **Virtual Boy** (バーチャルボーイ *Bācharu Bōi*) (also known as the **VR-32** and **V**irtual **U**topia **E**xperience during development) was the first video game console capable of displaying "true 3D graphics" out of the box. Whereas most video games use monocular cues to achieve the illusion of three dimensions on a two-dimensional screen, the Virtual Boy creates an illusion of depth through the effect known as parallax. In a manner similar to using a head-mounted display, the user looks into an eyepiece made of neoprene on the front of the machine, and then an eyeglass-style projector allows viewing of the monochromatic (in this case, red) image.

It was released on July 21, 1995 in Japan and August 14, 1995 in North America at a price of around US$180. It met with a lukewarm reception that was unaffected by continued price drops. Nintendo discontinued it the following year.

Overview

Technical information

The Virtual Boy system uses a pair of 1×224 linear arrays (one per eye) and rapidly scans the array across the eye's field of view using flat oscillating mirrors. These mirrors vibrate back and forth at a very high speed, thus the mechanical humming noise from inside the unit. Each Virtual Boy game cartridge has a yes/no option to automatically pause every 15–30 minutes so that the player may take a break.

Monochrome display

The Virtual Boy is iconic for its monochromatic use of red LED pixels; they were used due to being the least expensive, the lowest drain on batteries, and for being the most striking color to see. During development, a color LCD was experimented with but was found to cause users to see double instead of creating the illusion of depth. In addition, LCDs at the time had low refresh rates, and were often blurry. They also consumed more power than LEDs.

The Virtual Boy, which uses an oscillating mirror to transform a single line of pixels into a full field of pixels, requires high-performance LEDs in order to function properly. Because each pixel is only in use for a tiny fraction of a second (384 pixels wide, 50.2 Hz scan rate = approximately 52 μs per scanline), high peak brightness is needed to make the virtual display bright and comfortable for the user to view. The two-screen system demanded a fast refresh rate, unlike the original Game Boy which had blurry motion, so using an LCD was not an option.

Controller

The Virtual Boy, being a system with heavy emphasis on three-dimensional movement, needed a controller that could operate along a Z axis. The Virtual Boy's controller was an attempt to implement dual digital "D-pads" to control elements in the aforementioned 3D environment.

The controller itself is shaped like an "M" (similar to a Gamecube controller). One holds onto either side of the controller and the part that dips down in the middle contains the battery pack. There are six buttons on the controller (A, B, Start, Select, L and R), the two D-pads, and the system's

The Virtual Boy controller

"on/off" switch. The two directional pads are located on either side of the controller at the top. The "A"

and "B" buttons are located below the pad on the right side and the "Start" and "Select" buttons are located in the same spot on the left side. What would normally be called "shoulder buttons" ("L" and

"R") are located behind the area where the pads are, on the back of the controller, functioning more as triggers.

One of the unique features of the controller is the extendable power supply that slides onto the back. It houses the six AA batteries required to power the system. This can be substituted with a wall adapter, though a "slide on" attachment is required for the switchout. Once the slide on adapter is installed, a power adapter can be attached to provide constant power.

Extension port

The system's EXT (extension) port, located on the underside of the system below the controller port, was never officially supported since no official multiplayer games were ever published, nor was an official link cable released. (Although Waterworld and Faceball were going to use the EXT port for multiplayer play, the multiplayer features in the former were removed [1] and the latter was cancelled.) At Planet Virtual Boy there is a tutorial [2] on how to make a multiplayer cable for the Virtual Boy by modifying a couple of standard Nintendo Composite cables. Currently, only a few games support the link cable.

Specifications

Hardware specifications

Processor	NEC V810 (P/N uPD70732) 32-bit RISC Processor @ 20 MHz (18 MIPS) 1 KB instruction cache
Memory	128 KB dual-port VRAM 128 KB of DRAM 64 KB WRAM (PSRAM)
Display (× 2)	Reflection Technologies Inc. (RTI) Scanning LED Array (SLA) P4 1 × 224 pixel resolution (when scanned; 384 x 224) 2-bit monochromatic (black + 3 shades of red) 50.2 Hz Horizontal Scan Rate
Power	6 AA Batteries or DC10V 350mA AC Adapter/Tap (third-party Performance Adaptor DC 9V 500mA)
Sound	16-bit Stereo
Controller	4 buttons and 2 Direction pads uses NES controller protocol
Serial Port	8 pin cable

Hardware Part Numbers	VUE-001 Virtual Boy Unit VUE-003 Stand VUE-005 Controller VUE-006 Game Pak VUE-007 Battery Pack VUE-010 Eyeshade VUE-011 AC Adapter Tap ("Use With Super NES AC Adapter No. SNS-002 Only") VUE-012 Eyeshade Holder VUE-014 Red & Black Stereo Headphones
Weight	750 grams
Dimensions	8.5"H × 10"W × 4.3"D

Cartridge specifications

128 megabit addressable ROM space (4–16 megabit ROM used in released games)
128 megabit addressable RAM space (0–8 kilobyte Battery Backed RAM in released games)
128 megabit addressable expansion space (unused in any released games)
Expansion interrupt available to the cartridge
Left and right audio signals pass through cartridge
60-pin connector

Development

The console was designed by Gunpei Yokoi, inventor of the Game & Watch and Game Boy handhelds, as well as the *Metroid* franchise. While compact and seemingly portable, Virtual Boy was not intended to replace the Game Boy in Nintendo's product line, as use of the system requires a steady surface and completely blocks the player's peripheral vision. According to David Sheff's book *Game Over*, Yokoi never actually intended for the console to be released in its present form. However, Nintendo pushed the Virtual Boy to market so that it could focus development resources on the Nintendo 64.

Reception

"Powered by a 32-bit processor, the Virtual Boy produced very impressive 3-D effects, although the monochromatic graphic style proved to limit the appeal of the visuals."

The commercial demise of the Virtual Boy was considered to be the catalyst that led to Yokoi being driven from Nintendo, yet it was maintained that Yokoi kept a close relationship with Nintendo despite Yokoi having later created a rivalling handheld system for Bandai. According to *Game Over*, the company laid the blame for the machine's faults directly on the creator. Nintendo quickly discontinued the Virtual Boy in late 1995 in Japan and in early 1996 in North America.

In 2007 the system was listed as number five in PC World's "The Ugliest Products in Tech History" list. TIME Magazine's website listed the Virtual Boy as one of the worst inventions of all time.

Because Nintendo only shipped 800,000 Virtual Boy units worldwide, it is considered a valuable collector's item.

Marketing

Voice-overs for some advertisements were done by Dylan Bruno. There were several in-store promotional videos created for various games (as well as the Virtual Boy itself), and the system was actively marketed in magazines and on TV. The marketing slogan was "A 3D Game for a 3D World".

Games

Main article: List of Virtual Boy games

Due to the short lifespan of the system, only 22 games were released. Of them, 19 games were released in the Japanese market, while only 14 were released in North America.

See also

- List of Virtual Boy demos
- Nintendo 3DS

References

- Kent, Steven L. (2001). *The Ultimate History of Video Games*. Roseville, California: Prima. ISBN 0-7615-3643-4.
- "Virtual Boy Is Born at Shoshinkai November, 1994" [1] (JPEG). *Nintendo Power* (68): 52–53. January 1995. Retrieved 2006-07-19.

External links

- Virtual Boy [2] at Nintendo.com (archived versions [3] at the Internet Archive Wayback Machine)
- List of Virtual Boy games [4] at GameFAQs
- Virtual Boy [5] at the Open Directory Project
- Virtual Boy Hardware Specifications [6] at Planet Virtual Boy
- Virtual Boy Programmers Manual [7] at Planet Virtual Boy
- Performance Adapter Set [8] at virtual-boy.org

Xena

Xena

Lucy Lawless as **Xena**	
First appearance	"The Warrior Princess"
Last appearance	"A Friend in Need, part 2"
Created by	Robert Tapert
Portrayed by	Lucy Lawless Hudson Leick
Species	Human
Gender	Female
Occupation	Warrior for good, formerly Warlord and Destroyer of Nations
Affiliation	Gabrielle, Ares, Hercules, Borias, Caesar, Alti, Lao Ma, Ephiny, Joxer, Eve, the Amazons, Solan

Xena is a fictional character from Robert Tapert's *Xena: Warrior Princess* franchise. She commonly wore a tight brown, skirted, leather outfit. She first appeared in the 1995–1999 television series *Hercules: The Legendary Journeys*, before going on to appear in *Xena: Warrior Princess* TV show and subsequent comic book of the same name. The character has also appeared in the spin-off animated movie *The Battle for Mount Olympus*, as well as numerous non-canon expanded universe material, such as books and video games. Xena was played by New Zealand actress Lucy Lawless, and occasionally by Hudson Leick, during the series second season.

Xena is the protagonist of the story, and the series depicts her quest to seek redemption for her past sins as a ruthless warlord by using her formidable fighting skills to help people. In *Hercules*, during her two first episodes, Xena was an outlaw, but in the third (and last), she joins Hercules to defeat Darphus, who had taken her army. Aware that the character of Xena had been very successful among the public, the producers of the series decided to create a spin-off series based on her adventures. The character Gabrielle, introduced in the first episode, becomes Xena's greatest ally; her initial naïveté helps to balance Xena and assists her in recognizing and pursuing the "greater good". Lauren Chapluk would stunt-double for the actress in heavily demanding scenes that required extensive acrobatics and physical skill.

Appearances

Hercules

Xena originally appears as an outlaw in the *Hercules* episode "The Warrior Princess"; about ten years into her career of pillaging and marauding, Xena meets Hercules. Initially, she sets out to kill him. In "The Gauntlet", her army turns against her because of warlord Darphus' lust for power and believing Xena has become weak after she stops her lieutenant Darphus from killing a child in a sacked village. She runs a gauntlet, and survives, becoming the only person ever to survive the gauntlet. She then fights Hercules, in the hope that she will regain her army if she can bring back his head. Xena seems to be getting the upper hand until Hercules' cousin Iolaus intervenes, giving him the moment to regain composure and defeat her. However, Hercules refuses to kill Xena, telling her, *"Killing isn't the only way of proving you're a warrior."* Touched and inspired by Hercules' integrity, and by the fact that he too suffered the loss of blood kin as she did and yet chooses to fight in honor of them, she decides to join him and defeat her old army. In "Unchained Heart", Hercules tells Xena that there is goodness in her heart, and the two of them share a brief romantic relationship, before Xena decides to leave and start making amends for her past.

Xena: Warrior Princess

Xena returned in Robert Tapert's television series *Xena: Warrior Princess*, for all of the show's 134 episodes. In season one (1995–96), Xena, haunted by her past, determines to end her warrior ways. As she stripped off her armor and weaponry and buried them in the dirt, she saw a group of village girls attacked by a band of warriors. Among the girls is a young woman named Gabrielle (played by Renée O'Connor). Xena saves the girls, leaving Gabrielle in awe of the Warrior Princess' abilities. Gabrielle begs to be Xena's traveling companion, and over time, Gabrielle becomes Xena's dearest friend. In the Season Two (1996)-(1997), Xena meets Solan, the son she gave to the Centaurs to raise, and help them in a battle against Dagnine, an old enemy of hers, who has used the power of the Ixion Stone to transform himself into the most powerful centaur ever known. During the episode *Intimate Stranger*, Ares, the god of war, put Xena's soul inside Callisto's body, and Callisto's soul inside Xena's body. Hudson Leick playing Xena was done to cover for the lack for Lucy Lawless after her riding accident while taping *The Tonight Show with Jay Leno* on October 8, 1996. The episode originally had the two switching bodies back at the end, but was adapted to incorporate the body switch at the last minute. Ares broke the exchange in the next episode, *Ten Little Warlords*, when Xena helps him regain his immortality.

In Season Three (1997–98), while Xena was helping to defend Britannia against Caesar, Gabrielle comes into contact with an evil cult that tricks her into killing one of its priestesses, Meridian. Using her, the dark god Dahak impregnates Gabrielle just as Xena rescues her. Over the next two weeks, the child grows inside Gabrielle, and eventually she gives birth to a girl. Even though she is the seed of evil, Gabrielle tells Xena that she is also a part of her and that there must be some good in her as well; naming her Hope. Fearing that the child will become a danger to the world and be used as a pawn for her evil father, Xena wants to kill her, but unbeknownst to Xena, Gabrielle saves her daughter by putting her in a basket and sending her downriver. A few months later, Gabrielle finds Hope again, now looking like a 9 year old and already in the process of helping her father by implementing his plan to take over the world. Hope allies herself with Callisto, and in revenge for Xena's attempt to kill her as a baby, she murders Xena's son, Solan. This forces Gabrielle to accept that Hope is indeed dangerous. She kills her daughter by giving her poison, an act that continues to haunt Gabrielle throughout the series. Gabrielle holds herself responsible for Solan's death, as well as for betraying Xena a second time, even after reconciliation with Xena is achieved through the musical journey in the Land of Illusia. Therefore, when she once again encounters Hope, Gabrielle sacrifices herself to save Xena by jumping into a lava pit and taking Hope down with her. At the time, Hope was pregnant with Ares' child, the first Destroyer. It is later revealed that Ares teleported to an inner ledge inside the lava pit and saved Hope and Gabrielle, hoping to use the latter as a bargaining chip against Xena.

Xena begins Season 4 (1998–99) going to Hades looking for Gabrielle's soul. He tells her she is in the Amazon Land of the Dead. While there, Xena discovers an old ally, Alti, has enslaved the souls of an Amazon tribe, and kills her. Meanwhile, Alti plagues Xena with disturbing visions of her and Gabrielle being crucified, which convinced Xena that Gabrielle is alive. In the episode *A Family Affair*, Xena and her friend, Joxer, go to Potidaea, where Hope ultimately gives birth to the Destroyer. Impersonating Gabrielle, she returns to Gabrielle's hometown Potidaea. Xena later returns to Potidaea and is reunited with "Gabrielle". With news of a wild beast brutally murdering animals at night, Xena finds the Destroyer and barely escapes with her life. Discovering that she is dealing with Dahak's grandson, Xena deduces that "Gabrielle" is really Hope. After finding the real Gabrielle, they devise a plan to kill Hope and the Destroyer. Gabrielle finds the Destroyer, who, thinking she is its mother, hugs her. Xena uses this moment to stab it in the back with her sword, fatally wounding it. When Hope runs out to help her child, the Destroyer thinks she has betrayed it and stabs her before realizing how it has been tricked by Xena and Gabrielle. Crying, it hugs its mother as the two die in each other's arms. Later in *Between The Lines*, during a journey to India, Xena and Gabrielle meet the mysterious Naiyima, a mystical wise woman who reveals to Gabrielle that both she and Xena are destined to live many lives throughout the ages and that they are both bound to each other through a spiritual connection of karmic reincarnation. During this journey, they also encounter Alti once again, but with Naima's help, they are able to defeat her. Late in the season, during The Ides of March episode, Xena and Gabrielle are crucified by the Romans, as Caesar is betrayed and killed by Brutus. They are later revived by a mystic named Eli with the spiritual aid of Callisto, who by that time had become an angel.

In the Season 5 (1999–2000), Eve, the miracle child Xena conceives after her resurrection (again through the efforts of the redeemed Callisto), is prophesied to bring about the Twilight of the Olympian gods. To escape the gods' persecution, Xena and Gabrielle fake their deaths. Their plan goes awry when Ares buries them in an ice cave where they sleep for 25 years. During that time, Eve is adopted by the Roman nobleman Octavius and grows up to become Livia, the Champion of Rome, and a ruthless persecutor of Eli's followers. After her return, Xena is able to turn Livia to repentance, and Livia takes back the name Eve and becomes the Messenger of Eli.[22] After Eve's cleansing by baptism, Xena is granted the power to kill gods as long as her daughter lives. In a final confrontation, the Twilight comes to pass when Xena kills most of the gods to save her daughter, and is herself saved by Ares when he gives up his immortality to heal the badly injured and dying Eve and Gabrielle.

In the final Season (2000-2001), Xena's quest for redemption ends when she sacrifices herself to kill Yodoshi, and decides to stay dead so the souls of the 40,000 she killed years ago could be released into a state of peace. However, her spirit is seen with Gabrielle in a ship shortly afterward. As noted in Season 4 by Naima, this is not the end of Xena's journey as she will eventually be reborn into a new life and identity to continue furthering the cause of good over evil.

It is safely assumed Gabrielle then travels to "the land of the pharaohs" which is in need of "a girl with a chakram". This now applies to Gabrielle instead of Xena, for by the end of the last episode, Gabrielle can use the chakram. In a symbolic gesture, she throws the chakram and catches it on its ricochet.

In other media

Xena has appeared in all of the series spin-offs, usually as the lead character. The animated movie *Hercules and Xena: The Battle for Mount Olympus* marks the first appearance of Xena outside of the television series. She also appears in the comics series *Xena: Warrior Princess*, originally released by Topp and Dark Horse Comics. In 2007, Dynamite Entertainment acquired the rights to the book upon discovering the show still had many fans.

Xena is a playable character in the videogames *Xena: Warrior Princess*, and a selectable character in *The Talisman of Fate*. In 1999, Lucy Lawless also appeared in the animated television show *The Simpsons* dressed as her Xena character. In the movie *Hamlet 2*, the character Xena appears in the introduction.

Reception

Main article: Xena: Warrior Princess in popular culture

Xena: Warrior Princess has been referred to as a pop cultural phenomenon and feminist and lesbian icon. The television series, which employed pop culture references as a frequent humorous device, has itself become a frequent pop culture reference in video games, comics and television shows, and has been frequently parodied and spoofed.

Xena: Warrior Princess has been credited by many, including *Buffy the Vampire Slayer* creator Joss Whedon, with blazing the trail for a new generation of female action heroes such as Buffy, Max of *Dark Angel*, Sydney Bristow of *Alias*, and Beatrix Kiddo a.k.a. the Bride in Quentin Tarantino's *Kill Bill.*. The director Quentin Tarantino is also a fan of Xena.

Xena and Gabrielle's relationship (*see Influence on the lesbian community*) has been cited as one of the reasons why the series has been so popular, coupled with the denials of her character's lesbianism from Lawless while the series was running.

External links

- *Xena: Warrior Princess* [1] at the Internet Movie Database
- *Xena: Warrior Princess* [2] at TV.com

[on YouTube [3]]

Microsoft Bob

Microsoft Bob

Microsoft Bob

Developer(s)	Microsoft
Stable release	1.00a / August 30, 1995
Development status	Discontinued
Operating system	Windows 3.1 and 95
Type	GUI
License	Proprietary
Website	http://www.microsoft.com

Microsoft Bob was a Microsoft software product, released in March 1995, which provided a new, nontechnical interface to desktop computing operations. Despite its ambitious nature, *Bob* was one of Microsoft's more visible product failures. Microsoft's Steve Ballmer mentioned Bob as an example of a situation "where we decided that we have not succeeded and let's stop".

Origins

Microsoft Bob was designed for Windows 3.1x and Windows 95 and intended to be a user-friendly interface for Microsoft Windows, supplanting the *Program Manager*. At one point, the project was managed by Melinda French, who at the time was Bill Gates' girlfriend (the two later married). At the time French left Microsoft, she was Product Unit Manager for a group which included *Bob* and three other Microsoft titles. The project leader for Bob was Karen Fries, a Microsoft researcher. The design was based on research by Professors Clifford Nass and Byron Reeves of Stanford University. Microsoft originally owned the domain name bob.com [1], but traded it to Bob Kerstein for the windows2000.com [2] domain name.

Applications

Bob included various office suite programs such as a finance application and a word processor. The user interface was designed to simplify the navigational experience for novice computer users.

The main interface is portrayed as the inside of a house, with different rooms to correspond to common real-world room styles such as kitchen and family room. Each room can contain decorations and furniture, as well as icons that represent applications. Bob offers the user the option of fully customizing the entire house. The user has full control over decorating each room, and can add, remove, or reposition all objects. The user can also add or remove rooms from the house and change the destinations of each door. There is also a feature in which Bob offers multiple themes for room designs and decorations, such as contemporary and postmodern.

The applications built into Bob are represented by matching decorations – for example, clicking on a clock opens the calendar, while a pen and paper represent the letter writer. The user can also add shortcuts to applications on his or her computer. These shortcuts display the icon inside various styles of decorations such as boxes and picture frames.

Bob features "Assistants": cartoon characters which can help the user navigate the virtual house or perform tasks in the main interface or within the built-in applications.

Bob's install images are used as "padding" on the original *Windows XP* install CDs as an anti-piracy measure.

Negative awards

Despite being discontinued before Windows 98 was released, Microsoft Bob continued to be severely criticized in reviews and popular media.

Bob received the 7th place in PC World Magazine's list of the 25 worst products of all time, a spot in Time Magazine's list of the 50 Worst Inventions and number ten worst product of the decade by CNET.com.

External links

- Microsoft Bob Review [3]
- Extensive info in Bob in D2CA's Microsoft Bob Exhibit [4]
- Information about Microsoft Bob version 1.0 for Windows [5]
- The GUI Gallery: Microsoft Bob [6], Examining Bob in the context of other graphical user interfaces
- A short computing history (story and slideshow) of Bobs from Microsoft Bob to Bob Metcalfe to Alice & Bob. [7]
- A more in-depth article about Microsoft Bob (German) [8]

Pentium Pro

Pentium Pro

Produced	November 1, 1995
Common manufacturer(s)	• Intel
Max. CPU clock rate	150 MHz to 200 MHz
FSB speeds	60 MHz to 66 MHz
Min. feature size	0.35 μm to 0.50 μm
Instruction set	x86
Microarchitecture	P6
Cores	1
Socket(s)	• Socket 8

The **Pentium Pro** is a sixth-generation x86 microprocessor developed and manufactured by Intel introduced in November 1995. It introduced the P6 microarchitecture (sometime referred as i686) and was originally intended to replace the original Pentium in a full range of applications. While the Pentium and Pentium MMX had 3.1 and 4.5 million transistors, respectively, the Pentium Pro contained 5.5 million transistors. Later, it was reduced to a more narrow role as a server and high-end desktop processor and was used in supercomputers like ASCI Red. The Pentium Pro was capable of both dual- and quad-processor configurations. It only came in one form factor, the relatively large rectangular Socket 8. The Pentium Pro was succeeded by the Pentium II Xeon in 1998.

Microarchitecture

Summary

Belying its name, the Pentium Pro had a completely new microarchitecture, a departure from the Pentium rather than an extension of it. It has a decoupled, 12 stage, superpipelined architecture which uses an instruction pool. The Pentium Pro (P6) featured many advanced concepts not found in the Pentium, although it wasn't the first or only x86 processor to implement them (see NexGen Nx586 or Cyrix 6x86). The Pentium Pro pipeline had extra decode stages to dynamically translate IA-32 instructions into buffered micro-operation sequences which could then be analysed, reordered, and renamed in order to detect parallelizable operations that may be issued to more than one execution unit at once. The Pentium Pro thus featured out of order execution, including speculative execution via register renaming. It also had a wider 36-bit address bus (usable by PAE).

200 MHz Pentium Pro with a 512 KiB L2 cache in PGA package

The Pentium Pro has an 8 KiB instruction cache, from which up to 16 bytes are fetched on each cycle and sent to the instruction decoders. There are three instruction decoders. The decoders are not equal in capability: only one can decode any x86 instruction, while the other two can only decode simple x86 instructions. This restricts the Pentium Pro's ability to decode multiple instructions simultaneously, limiting superscalar execution. x86 instructions are decoded into 118-bit micro-operations (micro-ops). The micro-ops are RISC-like; that is, they encode an operation, two sources, and a destination. The general decoder can generate up to four micro-ops per cycle, whereas the simple decoders can generate one micro-op each per cycle. Thus, x86 instructions that operate on the memory (e.g., add this register to this location in the memory) can only be processed by the general decoder, as this operation requires at a minimum of three micro-ops. Likewise, the simple decoders are limited to instructions that can be translated into one micro-op.

200 MHz Pentium Pro with a 1 MiB L2 cache in PPGA package

Uncapped Pentium Pro 256 KiB

Instructions that require more micro-ops than four are translated with the assistance of a sequencer, which generates the required micro-ops over multiple clock cycles.

Micro-ops exit the ROB and enter a reserve station, where they await dispatch to the execution units. In each clock cycle, up to five micro-ops can be dispatched to five execution units. The Pentium Pro has two integer units and one floating-point unit (FPU). One of the integer units shares the same ports as the FPU, and therefore the Pentium Pro can only dispatch two integer micro-ops and one floating-point micro-op per a cycle. Of the two integer units, only one has the full complement of functions such as a barrel shifter, multiplier and divider. The second integer unit, which shares paths with the FPU, does not have these facilities and is limited to simple operations such as add, subtract, and the calculation of branch target addresses.

Pentium II Overdrive with heatsink removed. Flip-chip Deschutes core is on the left. 512 KiB cache is on the right.

The FPU executes floating-point operations. Addition and multiplication are pipelined and have a latency of three and five cycles, respectively. Division and square-root are not pipelined and are executed in separate units that share the FPU's ports. Division and square root have a latency of 18 to 36 and 29 to 69 cycles, respectively. The smallest number is for single precision (32-bit) floating-point numbers and the largest for extended precision (80-bit) numbers. Division and square root can operate simultaneously with adds and multiplies, preventing them from executing only when the result has to be stored in the ROB.

After the microprocessor was released, a bug was discovered in the floating point unit, commonly called the "Pentium Pro and Pentium II FPU bug" and by Intel as the "flag erratum". The bug occurs under some circumstances during floating point-to-integer conversion when the floating point number won't fit into the smaller integer format, causing the FPU to deviate from its documented behaviour. The bug is considered to be minor and occurs under such special circumstances that very few, if any, software programs are affected.

The Pentium Pro P6 microarchitecture was used in one form or another by Intel for more than a decade. The pipeline would scale from its initial 150 MHz start, all the way up to 1.4 GHz with the "Tualatin" Pentium III. The design's various traits would continue after that in the derivative core called "Banias" in Pentium M and Intel Core (Yonah), which itself would evolve into the Core microarchitecture (Core 2 processor) in 2006 and onward.

Performance

Performance with 32-bit code was excellent and well ahead of the older Pentiums at the time, usually by 25-35%. However, Pentium Pro's 16-bit performance was the same as the original Pentium. It was this, along with the Pentium Pro's high price, that caused the rather lackluster reception among PC enthusiasts, given the dominance at the time of the 16-bit MS-DOS, 16/32-bit Windows 3.1x, and

32/16-bit Windows 95 (parts of Windows 95, such as USER.exe, were still mostly 16-bit). To gain the full advantages of Pentium Pro's P6 microarchitecture, one needed to run a fully 32-bit OS such as Windows NT 3.51, Unix, or OS/2.

Compared to RISC microprocessors, the Pentium Pro, when introduced, slightly outperformed the fastest RISC microprocessors on integer performance when running the SPECint95 benchmark. Floating-point performance was significantly lower, half of some RISC microprocessors. The Pentium Pro's integer performance lead disappeared rapidly, first overtaken by the MIPS Technologies R10000 in January 1996, and then by Digital Equipment Corporation's EV56 variant of the Alpha 21164.

An innovation in cache

Likely Pentium Pro's most noticeable addition was its on-package L2 cache, which ranged from 256 KiB at introduction to 1 MiB in 1997. At the time, manufacturing technology did not feasibly allow a large L2 cache to be integrated into the processor core. Intel instead placed the L2 die(s) separately in the package which still allowed it to run at the same clock speed as the CPU core. Additionally, unlike most motherboard-based cache schemes that shared the main system bus with the CPU, the Pentium Pro's cache had its own back-side bus (called *dual independent bus* by Intel). Because of this, the CPU could read main memory and cache concurrently, greatly reducing a traditional bottleneck. The cache was also "non-blocking", meaning that the processor could issue more than one cache request at a time (up to 4), reducing cache-miss penalties. (This is an example of MLP, Memory Level Parallelism.) These properties combined to produce an L2 cache that was immensely faster than the motherboard-based caches of older processors. This cache alone gave the CPU an advantage in input/output performance over older x86 CPUs. In multiprocessor configurations, Pentium Pro's integrated cache skyrocketed performance in comparison to architectures which had each CPU sharing a central cache.

However, this far faster L2 cache did come with some complications. The Pentium Pro's "on-package cache" arrangement was unique. The processor and the cache were on separate dies in the same package and connected closely by a full-speed bus. The two or three dies had to be bonded together early in the production process, before testing was possible. This meant that a single, tiny flaw in either die made it necessary to discard the entire assembly, which was one of the reasons for the Pentium Pro's relatively low production yield and high cost. All versions of the chip were expensive, those with 1024 KiB being particularly so, since it required two 512 KiB cache dies as well as the processor die.

Available models

Pentium Pro clock speeds were 150, 166, 180 or 200 MHz with a 60 or 66 MHz external bus clock. Some users chose to overclock their Pentium Pro chips, with the 200 MHz version often being run at 233 MHz, and the 150 MHz version often being run at 166 MHz. The chip was popular in symmetric multiprocessing configurations, with dual and quad SMP server and workstation setups being commonplace.

In Intel's "Family/Model/Stepping" scheme, the Pentium Pro is family 6, model 1, and its Intel Product code is 80521.

Evolution in fabrication

As time progressed, the process used to fabricate the Pentium Pro processor die and its separate cache memory die changed, leading to a combination of processes used in the same package:

- The 133 MHz Pentium Pro prototype processor die was fabricated in a 0.6 μm BiCMOS process.
- The 150 MHz Pentium Pro processor die was fabricated in a 0.50 μm BiCMOS process.
- The 166, 180, and 200 MHz Pentium Pro processor die was fabricated in a 0.35 μm BiCMOS process.
- The 256 KiB L2 cache die was fabricated in a 0.50 μm BiCMOS process.
- The 512 and 1024 KiB L2 cache die was fabricated in a 0.35 μm BiCMOS process.

Packaging

The Pentium Pro is packaged in a ceramic multi-chip module (MCM). The MCM contains two underside cavities in which the microprocessor die and its companion cache die reside. The dies are bonded to a heat slug, whose exposed top helps enables the heat from the dies to be transferred more directly to cooling apparatus such as a heat sink. The dies are connected to the package using conventional wire bonding. The cavities are capped with a ceramic plate. The Pentium Pro with 1 MiB of cache uses a plastic MCM. Instead of two cavities, there is only one, in which the three dies reside, bonded to the package instead of a heat slug. The cavities are filled in with epoxy.

The MCM has 387 pins, of which approximately half are arranged in a pin grid array (PGA) and half in an interstitial pin grid array (IPGA). The packaging was designed for Socket 8.

Upgrade paths

In 1998, the 300/333 MHz Pentium II Overdrive processor for Socket 8 was released. Featuring 512 KiB of full-speed cache, it was produced by Intel as a drop-in upgrade option for owners of Pentium Pro systems. However, it only supported two-way glueless multiprocessing, not four-way or higher, which did not make it a usable upgrade for quad-processor systems.

As Slot 1 motherboards became prevalent, several manufacturers released slocket adapters, such as the Tyan M2020, Asus C-P6S1, Tekram P6SL1, and the Abit KP6. The slockets allowed Pentium Pro processors to be used with Slot 1 motherboards. The Intel 440FX chipset explicitly supported both Pentium Pro and Pentium II processors, but the Intel 440BX and later Slot 1 chipsets did not explicitly support the Pentium Pro, so the Socket 8 slockets did not see wide use. Slockets, in the form of Socket 370 to Slot 1 adapters, saw renewed popularity when Intel introduced Socket 370 Celeron and Pentium III processors.

Core specifications

Pentium Pro

- L1 cache: 8, 8 KiB (data, instructions)
- L2 cache: 256, 512 KiB (one die) or 1024 KiB (two 512 KiB dies) in a multi-chip module clocked at CPU-speed
- Socket: Socket 8
- Front side bus: 60 and 66 MHz
- VCore: 3.1–3.3 V
- Fabrication: 0.50 μm or 0.35 BiCMOS
- Clockrate: 150, 166, 180, 200 MHz
- First release: November 1995

Pentium II Overdrive

- L1 cache: 16, 16 KiB (data + instructions)
- L2 cache: 512 KiB external chip on CPU module clocked at CPU-speed
- Socket: Socket 8
- Multiplier: Locked at 5×
- Front side bus: 60 and 66 MHz
- VCore: 3.1–3.3 V (has on-board voltage regulator)
- Fabrication: 0.25 μm
- Based on the Deschutes-generation Pentium II
- First release: 1997
- Supports MMX technology

Pentium Pro/6th generation competitors

- AMD K5 and K6
- Cyrix 6x86 and MII
- IDT WinChip
- Intel P5 Pentium (co-existed with Pentium Pro for several years)

See also

- List of Intel Pentium II microprocessors
- List of Intel Pentium Pro microprocessors

External links

- Backside Bus [1], searchstorage.techtarget.com
- Intel Pentium Pro images and descriptions [2], cpu-collection.de
- CPU-INFO: Intel Pentium Pro, indepth processor history [3], web.archive.org

Sega Nomad

Sega Nomad

Manufacturer	Sega
Type	Handheld game console
Generation	Fifth generation era
Retail availability	October 13, 1995
Units sold	1 million (as of July 30, 2007)
Media	Cartridge
CPU	Motorola 68000

The **Sega Nomad** (also called **Sega Genesis Nomad** or just **Nomad**) was a handheld game console sold for the North American consumer market which played Mega Drive/Genesis game cartridges. The system was similar to the Japanese Sega Mega Jet, but featured a built-in color screen; the Mega Jet needed a separate monitor. The Nomad was never officially released in PAL territories such as Europe and Australia, though the unit retained its PAL/NTSC switch on the internal board. It was released in Japan after a delay as the Mega Jet was already being sold in Japanese retail stores. The Nomad is one of the few Sega systems that can play most games regardless of region without an adapter. Its codename during development was **Project Venus**, as per Sega's policy at the time of codenaming their systems after planets.

Release and features

Sega released the Nomad in October 1995 for US$180. Marketed as a portable Genesis, the Nomad was primarily an evolution of the Japanese market Mega Jet. Whereas the Mega Jet was screenless and required an AC adapter, the Nomad featured a 3.25 inch color LCD screen and an external detachable battery pack was available that had room for six AA batteries, making it completely portable as opposed to simply being a small (travel-size) Genesis system. In addition to its other improvements over the Mega Jet, an A/V Out plug was added at the top of the unit, letting owners play games on a television screen with a separate A/V cable. One particularly interesting feature of the Nomad was its ability to allow one player to play using a connected TV, while another watched on the Nomad. The directional pad on the unit controlled all one-player games, and a port on the bottom allowed a second controller pad to be plugged in for two-player games. This meant that the Nomad could be a fully functional home system as well as a hand-held solution with a preexisting library of games.

Issues

While the Nomad won praise for its screen resolution and features, there were compatibility problems with the sister system's add-ons: the Sega 32X, the Sega CD, and the Power Base Converter. While they did work technologically, forcing compatibility involved modifying the add-on units' shapes or using 3rd party expanders. The Nomad had impressive technical specifications for the time including a full color backlit display, and supported an estimated 600 titles already on the shelves in addition to being a functional home system.

However, the Nomad was bulky and was not power efficient, offering limited battery life compared to contemporary handhelds (specifically Nintendo's Game Boy system). Rechargeable AA batteries were not recommended due to voltage problems (as Ni-Cds provide 1.2V instead of the 1.5V that alkaline batteries output, and Ni-MH AA batteries were neither widely available nor affordable at the time), though a rechargeable battery pack was available separately for $79.

Even after a $100 price drop, the handheld did not garner enough support to continue. By the time it was released, the Mega Drive was at the end of its lifespan – already being replaced by the Sega Saturn, PlayStation and upcoming Nintendo 64, and general indifference towards 16-bit era titles hastened the unit's demise.

The game X-Men requires the player to reset the game at one point to progress. It is impossible to continue the game on the Sega Nomad due to the lack of a reset button.

Technical specifications

See also: Sega Mega Drive technical specifications

Processor:	Motorola 68000 16 bit processor running at 7.67 MHz
Co-processor (Sound Controller):	Zilog Z80 8-bit at 3.58 MHz
Memory:	156KB total - 64 KB Main RAM, 64KB VRAM, 8KB Sound RAM. 20 Kb ROM
Display Palette:	512
Onscreen colors:	64
Maximum onscreen sprites:	80
Resolution:	320 × 224
Sound:	Yamaha YM2612 6 channel FM, additional 4 channel PSG. Stereo sound. Also Texas Instruments SN76489 PSG (Programmable Sound Generator)
Display:	Integrated CSTN LCD at 320 x 224
Power Rating:	9V 850mA (same as Genesis/Mega Drive model 2)

References

- Retro Gamer magazine, issue 69. Retroinspection: Sega Nomad, pages 46-53

External links

- Game Boy Competitors: Part 2 [1]
- Console Database [2]

IS-95

IS-95

Interim Standard 95 (IS-95) is the first CDMA-based digital cellular standard by Qualcomm. The brand name for IS-95 is **cdmaOne**. IS-95 is also known as TIA-EIA-95.

It is a 2G Mobile Telecommunications Standard that uses CDMA, a multiple access scheme for digital radio, to send voice, data and signaling data (such as a dialed telephone number) between mobile telephones and cell sites.

CDMA or "code division multiple access" is a digital radio system that transmits streams of bits (PN codes). CDMA permits several radios to share the same frequencies. Unlike TDMA "time division multiple access", a competing system used in 2G GSM, all radios can be active all the time, because network capacity does not directly limit the number of active radios. Since larger numbers of phones can be served by smaller numbers of cell-sites, CDMA-based standards have a significant economic advantage over TDMA-based standards, or the oldest cellular standards that used frequency-division multiplexing.

In North America, the technology competed with Digital AMPS (IS-136, a TDMA technology). It is now being supplanted by IS-2000 (CDMA2000), a later CDMA-based standard.

Protocol revisions

cdmaOne's technical history is reflective of both its birth as a Qualcomm internal project, and the world of then-unproven competing digital cellular standards under which it was developed. The **term IS-95** generically applies to the earlier set of protocol revisions, namely P_REV's one through five.

P_REV=1 was developed under an ANSI standards process with documentation reference *J-STD-008*. J-STD-008, published in 1995, was only defined for the then-new North American PCS band (Band Class 1, 1900 MHz). The term *IS-95* properly refers to P_REV=1, developed under the Telecommunications Industry Association (TIA) standards process, for the North American cellular band (Band Class 0, 800 MHz) under roughly the same time frame. IS-95 offered interoperation (including handoff) with the analog cellular network. For digital operation, IS-95 and J-STD-008 have most technical details in common. The immature style and structure of both documents are highly reflective of the "standardizing" of Qualcomm's internal project.

P_REV=2 is termed *Interim Standard 95A (IS-95A)*. IS-95A was developed for Band Class 0 only, as in incremental improvement over IS-95 in the TIA standards process.

P_REV=3 is termed *Technical Services Bulletin 74 (TSB-74)*. TSB-74 was the next incremental improvement over IS-95A in the TIA standards process.

P_REV=4 is termed *Interim Standard 95B (IS-95B) Phase I*, and P_REV=5 is termed *Interim Standard 95B (IS-95B) Phase II*. The IS-95B standards track provided for a merging of the TIA and ANSI standards tracks under the TIA, and was the first document that provided for interoperation of IS-95 mobile handsets in both band classes (dual-band operation). PREV=4 was by far the most popular variant of IS-95, with P_REV=5 only seeing minimal uptake in South Korea.

P_REV=6 and beyond fall under the CDMA2000 umbrella. Besides technical improvements, the IS-2000 documents are much more mature in terms of layout and content. They also provide backwards-compatibility to IS-95.

Protocol details

The IS-95 standards describe an *air interface*, a set of protocols used between mobile units and the network. IS-95 is widely described as a three-layer stack, where L1 corresponds to the physical (PHY) layer, L2 refers to the Media Access Control (MAC) and Link-Access Control (LAC) sublayers, and L3 to the call-processing state machine.

Physical layer

IS-95 defines the transmission of signals in both the *forward* (network-to-mobile) and *reverse* (mobile-to-network) directions.

In the forward direction, radio signals are transmitted by base stations (BTS's). Every BTS is synchronized with a GPS receiver so transmissions are tightly controlled in time. All forward transmissions are QPSK with a chip rate of 1,228,800 per second. Each signal is spread with a Walsh code of length 64 and a pseudo-random noise code (PN code) of length , yielding a PN roll-over period of ms.

For the reverse direction, radio signals are transmitted by the mobile. Reverse link transmissions are OQPSK in order to operate in the optimal range of the mobile's power amplifier. Like the forward link, the chip rate is 1,228,800 per second and signals are spread with Walsh codes and the pseudo-random noise code, which is also known as a Short Code.

Forward broadcast channels

Every BTS dedicates a significant amount of output power to a *pilot channel*, which is an unmodulated PN sequence (in other words, spread with Walsh code 0). Each BTS sector in the network is assigned a PN offset in steps of 64 chips. There is no data carried on the forward pilot. With its strong autocorrelation function, the forward pilot allows mobiles to determine system timing and distinguish different BTS's for handoff.

When a mobile is "searching", it is attempting to find pilot signals on the network by tuning to particular radio frequencies, and performing a cross-correlation across all possible PN phases. A strong correlation peak result indicates the proximity of a BTS.

Other forward channels, selected by their Walsh code, carry data from the network to the mobiles. Data consists of network signaling and user traffic. Generally, data to be transmitted is divided into frames of bits. A frame of bits is passed through a convolutional encoder, adding forward error correction redundancy, generating a frame of symbols. These symbols are then spread with the Walsh and PN sequences and transmitted.

BTSs transmit a *sync channel* spread with Walsh code 32. The sync channel frame is ms long, and its frame boundary is aligned to the pilot. The sync channel continually transmits a single message, the *Sync Channel Message*, which has a length and content dependent on the P_REV. The message is transmitted 32 bits per frame, encoded to 128 symbols, yielding a rate of 1200 bit/s. The Sync Channel Message contains information about the network, including the PN offset used by the BTS sector.

Once a mobile has found a strong pilot channel, it listens to the sync channel and decodes a Sync Channel Message to develop a highly-accurate synchronization to system time. At this point the mobile knows whether it is roaming, and that it is "in service".

BTSs transmit at least one, and as many as seven, *paging channel*s starting with Walsh code 1. The paging channel frame time is 20 ms, and is time aligned to the IS-95 system (ie. GPS) 2-second roll-over. There are two possible rates used on the paging channel: 4800 bit/s or 9600 bit/s. Both rates are encoded to 19200 symbols per second.

The paging channel contains signaling messages transmitted from the network to all idle mobiles. A set of messages communicate detailed network overhead to the mobiles, circulating this information while the paging channel is free. The paging channel also carries higher-priority messages dedicated to setting up calls to and from the mobiles.

When a mobile is idle, it is mostly listening to a paging channel. Once a mobile has parsed all the network overhead information, it *registers* with the network, then optionally enters *slotted-mode*. Both of these processes are described in more detail below.

Forward traffic channels

The Walsh space not dedicated to broadcast channels on the BTS sector is available for *traffic channel*s. These channels carry the individual voice and data calls supported by IS-95. Like the paging channel, traffic channels have a frame time of 20ms.

Since voice and user data are intermittent, the traffic channels support variable-rate operation. Every 20 ms frame may be transmitted at a different rate, as determined by the service in use (voice or data). P_REV=1 and P_REV=2 supported *rate set 1*, providing a rate of 1200, 2400, 4800, or 9600 bit/s. P_REV=3 and beyond also provided *rate set 2*, yielding rates of 1800, 3600, 7200, or 14400 bit/s.

For voice calls, the traffic channel carries frames of *vocoder* data. A number of different vocoders are defined under IS-95, the earlier of which were limited to rate set 1, and were responsible for some user complaints of poor voice quality. More sophisticated vocoders, taking advantage of modern DSPs and rate set 2, remedied the voice quality situation and are still in wide use in 2005.

The mobile receiving a variable-rate traffic frame does not know the rate at which the frame was transmitted. Typically, the frame is decoded at each possible rate, and using the quality metrics of the Viterbi decoder, the correct result is chosen.

Traffic channels may also carry circuit-switch data calls in IS-95. The variable-rate traffic frames are generated using the IS-95 *Radio Link Protocol (RLP)*. RLP provides a mechanism to improve the performance of the wireless link for data. Where voice calls might tolerate the dropping of occasional 20 ms frames, a data call would have unacceptable performance without RLP.

Under IS-95B PREV=5, it was possible for a user to use up to seven supplemental "code" (traffic) channels simultaneously to increase the throughput of a data call. Very few mobiles or networks ever provided this feature, which could in theory offer 115200 bit/s to a user.

Block Interleaver

After convolution coding and repetition, symbols are sent to a 20 ms block interleaver, which is a 24 by 16 array.

Capacity

IS-95 and its use of CDMA techniques, like any other communications system, have their throughput limited according to Shannon's theorem. Accordingly, capacity improves with SNR and bandwidth. IS-95 has a fixed bandwidth, but fares well in the digital world because it takes active steps to improve SNR.

With CDMA, signals that are not correlated with the channel of interest (such as other PN offsets from adjacent cellular base stations) appear as noise, and signals carried on other Walsh codes (that are properly time aligned) are essentially removed in the de-spreading process. The variable-rate nature of traffic channels provide lower-rate frames to be transmitted at lower power causing less noise for other signals still to be correctly received. These factors provide an inherent lower noise level than other cellular technologies allowing the IS-95 network to squeeze more users into the same radio spectrum.

Active (slow) power control is also used on the forward traffic channels, where during a call, the mobile sends signaling messages to the network indicating the quality of the signal. The network will control the transmitted power of the traffic channel to keep the signal quality just good enough, thereby keeping the noise level seen by all other users to a minimum.

The receiver also uses the techniques of the rake receiver to improve SNR as well as perform soft handoff.

Layer 2

Once a call is established, a mobile is restricted to using the traffic channel. A frame format is defined in the MAC for the traffic channel that allows the regular voice (vocoder) or data (RLP) bits to be multiplexed with signaling message fragments. The signaling message fragments are pieced together in the LAC, where complete signaling messages are passed on to Layer 3.

See also

* PN code
* Comparison of mobile phone standards
* CDMA Spectral Efficiency

Microsoft Agent

Microsoft Agent

Microsoft Agent is a technology developed by Microsoft which employs animated characters, text-to-speech engines, and speech recognition software to enhance interaction with computer users. Thus it is an example of an embodied agent. It comes preinstalled as part of Microsoft Windows 2000 through Windows Vista (it is not part of Windows 7). Microsoft Agent functionality is exposed as an ActiveX control that can be used by web pages.

The theory behind this software came from work on social interfaces by Clifford Nass and Byron Reeves at Stanford's Center for the Study of Language and Information.

Version History

Interactive character technology was first introduced in Microsoft Bob, which used an early version of Agent technology internally referred to as "Microsoft Actor." It was the code used in initial version of the Office Assistant in Office 97. Microsoft Agent was subsequently created by Tandy Trower in an attempt to offer technology that was more flexible and available to third-party developers to include in their applications and web pages. The software release also included four interactive characters as well as a utility that enables developers to assemble their own characters and interactions.

Microsoft Agent replaced the original Microsoft Bob code in Office 2000, although this use did not include Agent's much-touted speech synthesis or recognition capabilities or any of the four Microsoft Agent characters. Instead the Office team created their own characters include one dubbed "Clippit" or "Clippy". However, Bob Actors or Office 97 assistants are incompatible with Office 2000 and later versions, and vice-versa. The current version of Microsoft Agent was quietly released on MSDN in 1998. Microsoft recently announced that "Microsoft has decided to discontinue development of Microsoft Agent technologies. Beginning with Windows 7, Microsoft Agent will not be included or supported in future versions of the Microsoft Windows operating system. We encourage Microsoft Agent application developers and redistributors to evaluate their activities in light of this decision." Microsoft is no longer offering licenses and no longer distributes the SDK.

Technology

Microsoft Agent characters are stored in files of the .ACS extension, and can be stored in a number of compressed .ACF files for better World Wide Web distribution. Microsoft Office 97 and Microsoft Bob Actor characters are stored in files of the .ACT extension.

The speech engine itself is driven by the Microsoft Speech API (SAPI), version 4 and above. Microsoft SAPI provides a control panel for easily installing and switching between various available Text to Speech and Speech to Text engines, as well as voice training and scoring systems to improve the quality and accuracy of both engines.

Microsoft provides four agent characters for free, which can be downloaded from the Microsoft Agent website. These are called Peedy, Merlin, Genie, and Robby. Some characters also shipped with Microsoft Office up to version 2003 as the Office Assistants and with Windows XP as search assistants. New Agent characters can also be created using Microsoft's development tools, including the Agent Character Editor. Agents can be embedded in software with Visual Basic for Applications and in web pages with VBScript, and automated tools for the purpose of simplifying this exist. However, web page agents are only compatible with Internet Explorer, since alternative browsers like Opera or Mozilla Firefox do not support ActiveX. Additionally, users of Windows Me, Windows 2000, Windows XP, and above or owners of Microsoft Office 2000 and up are the only ones who have Agent software pre-loaded on their computers; others have to download the software and install it manually.

Unsupported in newer Windows versions

In Windows Vista, Microsoft Agent uses the Speech API (SAPI) version 5.3, which is also in-built in Windows Vista, as a primary Text-To-Speech provider. Previous versions of Microsoft Agent used the Speech API (SAPI) v4 which is not supported in Windows Vista and later. Multilingual features of Microsoft Agent under a particular language version of the OS are not supported beginning with Vista, that is, Agent will function in other languages only under a localized Windows version of the same language.

The Microsoft Agent runtime is not pre-installed with Windows 7, although SAPI v5.3 compatible speech engines continue to work. Due to customer feedback, Microsoft has decided to provide an installation package of the Microsoft Agent core components for use on Windows 7 [1]. This package includes the required components to enable applications to work with MS Agent. In addition it contains the character "Merlin" which was also shipped in Windows Vista.

Microsoft has announced in April 2009 that Microsoft Agent support will be discontinued after Windows 7.

See also

- Embodied agent
- Office Assistant
- Microsoft Voice Command

External links

- Microsoft Agent Official Homepage at Microsoft.com [2]
- Guile 3D Studio Photo-Realistic MSAgents [3]
- Deven Seven virtual newscaster and website guide uses Microsoft Agent [4]
- MS Agent Scripting Software [5]
- Double Agent is an Open Source alternative to Microsoft™ Agent that allows Agent applications to work on Windows 7. [6]
- MS Agent being used in Urdu Language software called Mutakallim [7]
- MS Agent Brazil [8]
- MS Agent youtube [9]
- Narod Russian (E-Clips Collection) [10]

Frappuccino

Frappuccino

A Venti Peppermint Java Chip Frappuccino

Type	Cold Beverage
Manufacturer	Starbucks
Country of origin	USA
Color	Light or dark Brown in the Coffee Versions, but the color can vary from green, chocolate, orange, and pink in the cream version of this drink.

Frappuccino is trademarked line of blended ice beverages sold by Starbucks. Frappuccinos also sold in the form of a bottled coffee beverage in stores across the US, UK, Canada, Mexico, South Korea, and also Singapore.

History

Frappuccino is a portmanteau of *frappe* and *cappuccino*, an espresso coffee with frothed milk. It is unclear whether *frappe* is taken from *frappé*, a Greek iced coffee, or from the Boston area term for a thick milkshake *frappe* (pronounced "frap"), both of which come from the French word *frappé*. The original *Frappuccino* beverage was developed, named, trademarked and sold by George Howell's Eastern Massachusetts coffee shop chain, The Coffee Connection. When Starbucks purchased The Coffee Connection in 1994, they also gained the rights to use, make, market, and sell the Frappuccino beverage , and soon after began to sell the beverage chain wide.

Varieties

"Light"

In 2004, Starbucks created a "Light" version which according to the company has 54% of the calories, 15% of the fat (0.5g vs 3g), and 52% of the carbohydrates of the original.

Decaffeinated

Decaffeinated Frappuccinos were discontinued in 2008 and made available again in 2010.

Crème

Alternatively, a coffee-free "cream" base was created to make a beverage called a Frappuccino Blended Crème. Examples of these beverages include the Green Tea Frappuccino and the popular Strawberries and Cream Frappuccino.

Vegan

Starting in May 2010, Frappuccinos using soy milk have become available in stores in the United States and Canada.

Available versions

The following is a list of the typical versions available of each type of Frappuccino.

Blended coffee

- Coffee (as a flavor) - Basic version of the blended ingredients with no added flavorings.
- Espresso - Coffee Frappuccino with one added shot of Espresso, which provides a stronger coffee taste (the amount of Frappuccino base is lessened to make room for the shot) as well as more caffeine. Served without whipped cream.
- Caramel - Blended coffee base, whole milk, caramel syrup, and ice. With Whipped Cream + Caramel Drizzle.
- Extra Coffee Caramel - More Blended coffee base, whole milk, caramel syrup, and ice. With Whipped Cream + Caramel Drizzle.
- [Syrup Flavor] Frappuccino - Blended coffee base, whole milk, any syrup, and ice. Without any toppings. Sugar-free must be requested, as normal syrup is used by standard.
- Mocha - Blended coffee base, whole milk, mocha sauce, blended with ice. With Whipped Cream.
- White Chocolate Mocha - Blended coffee base, whole milk, white chocolate syrup, and ice. With Whipped Cream.

- Java Chip - Coffee base, whole milk, cookie/chocolate chips and mocha sauce blended with ice. With Whipped Cream + Mocha Drizzle.
- Café Vanilla - Blended coffee base, whole milk, vanilla bean powder, and ice. With Whipped Cream.

Frappuccinos can be made with any type of Starbucks syrup, and any type of milk. Core flavors include Vanilla, SF Vanilla, Cinnamon Dolce, SF Cinnamon Dolce, Hazelnut, SF Hazelnut, Toffee Nut, Peppermint, Raspberry.. These are simply called as a "[Syrup Flavor] Coffee Frappuccino", and are served without whipped cream unless otherwise specified. Seasonal Frappuccinos, such as Pumpkin Spice, Gingersnap, and Peppermint Mocha are also popular, and often contain special toppings, such as Pumpkin Spice powder or peppermint sugar sprinkles over peppermint whipped cream.

Blended crème

- Vanilla Bean - Crème base and whole milk with vanilla bean powder added, blended with ice. Topped with whipped cream.
- Double Chocolaty Chip - Crème base and whole milk with mocha sauce and java chips. Topped with mocha drizzle and whipped cream and occasionally chocolate powder upon request.
- Strawberries & Crème - Crème base and whole milk, classic syrup, strawberry puree, and blended with ice.
- Chai - Crème base, whole milk, and chai tea concentrate with cinnamon sprinkled on top.
- Green Tea - Crème base, whole milk, classic syrup, sweetened matcha green tea powder blended with ice. (Note: Melon syrup was the previous standard, but this syrup is discontinued.)
- Syrup Crème - Crème base and whole milk with any kind of available syrup. Typically served with whipped cream unless otherwise specified.

Juice Blend

In the summer of 2006, Starbucks introduced the *Frappuccino Juice Blend*, which is described as being "real fruit juices combined with Tazo Tea, blended with ice." This version seems to be different from the Tazoberry "blended tea" versions of several years ago since it uses more "real juice" and "freshly brewed" ice teas to the drink instead of a bottled, premixed concentrate. Juice Blends were discontinued in 2007/2008, with the Pomegranate the first to go. The Tangerine Juice Blend was discontinued shortly thereafter. The drinks in this category included:

- Pomegranate (raspberry & blackcurrant in UK & Ireland) - Pomegranate, peach and "other fruit juices" [1] combined with 'Zen' Iced Tea. Pomegranate Frappuccino Juice Blend has been discontinued in the US.
- Tangerine (mango passionfruit in UK & Ireland)- Tangerine and "other fruit juices" [2]. combined with Passion Iced Tea. Tangerine Frappuccino Juice Blend has been discontinued in the US.
- Blended Strawberry Lemonade - A combination of Strawberry Sauce and Lemonade.

- Lemonade Blended Beverage - Fresh lemonade flavor with real lemon zest, blended with ice. Introduced in the US in the Summer of 2008. A "Lemon" version of the chilled beverage was introduced to UK stores in June 2010, following a minor menu change and price increases across the majority of the ranges sold.

The Lemonade Blended Beverage was made with a proprietary Blended Lemonade base, that consisted of real lemon zest and was thicker than the Lemonade that is currently used for Ice Tea Lemonades. This Blended Lemonade Base was discontinued in the Fall of 2008. A Blended Lemonade can still be bought at Starbucks, however it will be made with the "old" Lemonade, and thus be a different taste and consistency.

Vivanno Nourishing Blends

In Summer 2008, Starbucks introduced Vivanno Nourishing Blends. This drink comes in three flavors: Chocolate Smoothie (CS), Orange Mango Smoothie (OMS), and introduced in Summer 2009, Strawberry Smoothie (SS). Each of the drinks have 2% milk as a standard (though any type of dairy or soy may be requested), ice, whey protein/fiber powder, and one whole banana. The CS has three pumps of mocha syrup, while the OMS is made with a Starbucks brand orange and mango juice concentrate. The SS is made with the new *real strawberry* fruit juice that is used for the Strawberries and Creme Frappuccino as well. Customers are encouraged to add Matcha Powder to the Orange Mango Banana Smoothie or an Espresso Shot to the Banana Chocolate Smoothie for an extra charge. These drinks are marketed as a healthier alternative to the Frappuccino.

The name "Vivanno" comes from the Italian word for "live".

Special versions

Starbucks introduces special, Limited Time Offerings every quarter. Based on feedback from customers, these are occasionally added to the permanent menu. The following are some of the popular drinks that have been available:

- *Peppermint Mocha Blended Coffee/Peppermint Double Chocolate Chip Blended Crème* - This was originally introduced in the coffee flavor only at Christmas and was no longer available by Valentine's Day. Peppermint flavor is added to the Mocha/DCC drinks. After positive customer feedback, Starbucks replaced the Crème de Menthe syrup with the Peppermint flavor so it would be available year round to anyone who requested it.
- *Toffee Nut Blended Coffee/Toffee Nut Blended Crème* - Starbucks introduced this flavor for a fall promotion with rave reviews by many customers. It consisted of adding toffee nut syrup to the coffee mix or creme mix, with whipped cream and toffee nut sprinkles on top. It was brought back the following fall, and the flavor was added to the permanent core offerings.
- *Pumpkin Spice Blended Coffee/Pumpkin Spice Blended Crème* - This drink was introduced in the fall of 2005. This drink consisted of a pumpkin spice syrup (pumpkin, cinnamon, and nutmeg

flavors) added to the coffee mix or creme mix. Even though the demand for such a flavor seemed high, actual sales of the product was said to have been moderately low. The drink continues to be a seasonal beverage returning to some areas each year.

- Cinnamon Dolce Blended Coffee/Blended Crème - This drink was introduced in January 2006. Originally a seasonal syrup, Cinnamon Dolce has been added as a semi-permanent flavor due to high demand during the Winter 2 season. The syrup tastes like sweet cinnamon buns, with an aftertaste reminiscent of butter.
- Maple Blended Coffee/Blended Crème - This drink was introduced in the fall of 2006 and uses a syrup made with maple syrup and topped with whipped cream and maple drizzle.
- Gingerbread Blended Coffee/Blended Crème - This drink was introduced during the holiday season of 2000 and has a strong gingerbread cookie taste.
- *Mint Mocha* (Bottled) - This was a bottled version of a Starbucks Frappuccino that had similar consistency to other bottled frappuccinos and had a peppermint flavoring to it. Before it even hit stores in mid-2005, it was announced it would be a limited edition item, but it sold very well. It lived up to the limited edition name, and Starbucks dropped it in January 2006. Starbucks began selling the bottled drink again for the 2006/2007 Holiday season. There is no other bottled frappuccino on the market with this flavor or any similarity to this flavor.
- *Dulce De Leche* - This new drink was introduced in April 2005. It has a sweet caramel flavor and is often drizzled with caramel on top of the whipped cream. It is also available in latte form. It was introduced in Peruvian Starbucks' stores named "Manjar Blanco" and it has been expanded around Latin America.
- Maple White Chocolate Crème - A seasonal drink that is a standard white chocolate creme based frappuccino but with added maple syrup. Serves with whipped cream and maple topping or white chocolate sauce.

Modifications

As the varieties of drinks listed above show, many drinks include additional ingredients, which can include espresso shots, flavored syrups, brownie chips, and flavored powders. Frappuccinos can also be double blended, or made with more or less ice. If ordered in a Starbucks retail location, whipped cream is no longer added by default on all Frappuccinos. In addition, mocha drizzle is added to the Java Chip and Double Chocolaty Chip by standard, and caramel drizzle is added to the Caramel. Any drink can have an additional syrup/espresso or many other flavorings added at request for an additional charge.

Yet another modification, though less popular, is to order the Frappuccino *"affogato style"*. The Italian word "affogato" translates to "drowned" in English. An affogato Frappuccino has a shot of espresso on top rather than blended into the rest of the drink. The most common versions of this variation are known as "caramel affogato" and "mocha affogato" style, in which the espresso shot is poured on top of a crosshatch pattern of either caramel or mocha sauce in place of whipped cream.

International varieties

There are also different versions available only in certain countries, such as *Banana Java Chip* and *Mango*, *Azuki* in the Philippines and *azuki* (red bean) in Japan. Also, the Blackberry Green Tea is currently available in the Philippines and Australia. The Coffee Jelly Frappuccino before was a seasonal offering in the Philippines but later it was included in the Philippine permanent menu for Starbucks. There is also a Coconut Mocha Frappuccino available only in Hawaii, in Argentina as a Frappuccino *Dulce de Leche,"* and all across Geneva, Switzerland.

Bottled version

A bottled beverage, also called *Frappuccino*, is sold in retail stores and vending machines. The 9.5-ounce bottled version is manufactured by PepsiCo, the maker of Pepsi. This product uses a different recipe from that of the blended drink of the same name.

A mocha flavored bottled Frappuccino.

The following flavors are available:

- Caramel - the most popular flavor made with a hint of caramel flavoring
- Mocha - made with chocolate
- Mocha Lite - made with chocolate and special creme to make it less fattening
- Vanilla - a hint of vanilla flavoring
- Coffee - similar to iced coffee
- Strawberries & Crème - crème based and coffee-free
- Mint Mocha (Limited Edition) - Since its addition in July, 2005, it has appeared during the holiday seasons.
- Dark Chocolate Peppermint Mocha (Limited Edition) - Just like mint mocha but with extra chocolate and mint flavor. New for the 2007 holiday season and re-released for the 2008 holiday season.
- Dark Chocolate Mocha (Limited Edition)- Just like Mocha with extra chocolate. Released February 2008.
- Dark Mocha Raspberry (Limited Edition)- Dark chocolate with a hint of raspberry. Released August 2008.

External links

- Starbucks Official Website [3]

Apple Bandai Pippin

Apple Bandai Pippin

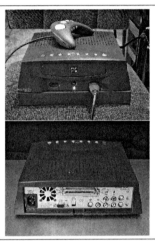

Manufacturer	Bandai, engineered by Apple Computer, Inc. (now Apple Inc.)
Type	multimedia player
Generation	Fifth generation era
Release date	/ [🇨🇦] September 1, 1996 (@World Player) Limited December 1995, full March 28, 1996 (Atmark Player)
Retail availability	1995/1997
Units sold	42,000
Media	CD-ROM
CPU	PowerPC 603 RISC (66 MHz)
Storage capacity	5 MB combined system and video memory,128kb Flash RAM
Graphics	"taos" (VGA/16-bit)
Controller input	"Applejack": control pad with embedded trackball
Connectivity	14.4, 28.8, 33.6 kbit/s modems
Online services	PSINet/@World

The **Pippin**, known in Japan as Pippin Atmark (ピ ピ ン ア ッ ト マ ー ク *Pipin Attomāku*), and marketed as **Pipp!n**, was a multimedia platform designed by Apple Inc. (then Apple Computer Inc.) and produced by Bandai in 1995. It was based on a 66 MHz PowerPC 603 processor, a 14.4 kbit/s modem and ran a stripped version of the System 7.5.2 operating system.

The goal was to create an inexpensive computer aimed mostly at playing CD-based multimedia titles, especially games, but also functioning as a network computer. It featured a 4x CD-ROM drive and a video output that could connect to a standard television display.

The platform was named for the Newtown Pippin, an apple cultivar, a smaller and more tart relative of the McIntosh apple (which is the namesake of the Macintosh).

History

Apple never intended to release Pippin on its own. Instead it intended to license the technology to third parties; Bandai was looking at entering the console video game market, and chose the Pippin as its platform. Much later Katz Media also entered production, planning to use the platform as a low cost PC with web ability.

By the time the Apple Bandai Pippin was released (1995 in Japan; 1996 in the United States), the market was dominated by the Sega Saturn, PlayStation, Nintendo 64 and PC. In addition there was little ready-to-use software for Pippin, the only major publisher being Bandai itself. It cost US$599 on launch, and while touted as a cheap computer, the system, in reality, was a video game console. As such, its price was considered too expensive in comparison to its contemporaries.

Bandai manufactured fewer than 100,000 Pippins (reported sales were 42,000) before discontinuing the system; production was so limited that there were more keyboard and modem accessories produced than actual systems.

Katz Media Productions produced 5,000 units in Ireland for Europe, labeled it the KMP 2000; it is the rarest of the Pippin models. The images here are of the KMP developer unit, which include the 50-pin SCSI connector for external devices used for developing new software.

In May 2006, the Pippin placed 22nd in PC World Magazine's list of the "25 Worst Tech Products of all Time", and in 2009, ScrewAttack.com ranked it #10 on their Top 10 Biggest Busts.

Technical specifications

Hardware

- 66 MHz PowerPC 603 RISC microprocessor
    - Superscalar, three instructions per clock cycle
    - 8 KB data and 8 KB instruction caches
    - IEEE standard single and double precision Floating Point Unit (FPU)
- 5 MB combined system and video memory, advanced architecture
    - Easy memory expansion cards in 2, 4, 8, and 16 MB increments.
- 128 K Flash memory accessible storage space.
- 4 x CD-ROM drive
- Two high-speed serial ports, one of which is GeoPort ready, the other is LocalTalk
- PCI-compatible expansion slot
- Two "AppleJack" ruggedized ADB inputs
    - Supports up to four simultaneous players over Apple Desktop Bus (ADB)
    - Supports standard ADB keyboards and mice with mechanical adapters

Video

- 8-bit and 16-bit video support
- Dual frame buffers for superior frame-to-frame animation
- Support for NTSC and PAL composite, S-Video and VGA (640x480) monitors
- Horizontal and vertical video convolution

Audio

- Stereo 16-bit 44 kHz sampled output
- Stereo 16-bit 44 kHz sampled input
- Headphone output jack with individual volume control
- Audio CD player compatibility

System software

- 3 MB ROM version 7.7.D (version number on ROM boards is development 1.1, 1.2; production 1.3).
- Runtime environment derived from System 7, System 7.5.2 (if used, Enabler 1.1).
- PowerPC native version of QuickDraw.
- Reduced system memory footprint (most computer extensions features removed).

The Pippin firmware board.

- Disk-resident System Software stamped on CD-ROM with title.
- System boots off of CD-ROM by default (but can boot off any SCSI device).
- Pippin System Software upgrades released through CD-ROM stamping operations.
- 68k emulator.
- Macintosh Toolbox intact.

Software

In every way, the Pippin is a Macintosh. Most of the Pippin software will run on Classic Mac OS (few will work with Mac OS 9). A third party created a Pippin bootable CD with Netscape that had the Macintosh GUI (Enabler 1.1), but was stripped of many of the extensions and control panels found on regular Macs. At least one Japanese title (*Ultraman*) existed that could run on Pippin, Mac, and Windows.

Pippin CDs were created on a Macintosh or a Pippin with a SCSI connected external CD drive (for functionality testing). Once the final version of the software was ready, a checksum of the CD was sent to Apple and signed with Apple's private key. The signed checksum was applied to the gold master CD that was to be pressed and released to the public. The Pippin, during its boot process, would generate a checksum of the CD and compare it to the one signed with Apple's private key. Only if the checksums compared successfully would the boot process continue.

Software titles: Japan

Very few titles were produced for the Japanese version on release in early 1995. While some promised titles may not have been released, the number that was released is less than 80 titles.

Software titles: USA

When Bandai released the U.S. version, it had only 18 titles sold separately, and six CDs came with the Pippin itself. Upgrades to the Pippin Browser were released as a new CD over time, and so was an update to *TV Works* (a text and drawing program).

Software titles: other

As mentioned before, a third party made a custom Pippin bootable CD with the Macintosh GUI on it. There were also a few demo CDs made by Bandai and Katz Media. Others may exist that have not circulated.

Accessories

- AppleJack controller
- AppleJack Wireless (IR) controller
- Pippin keyboard with drawing tablet
- Pippin Modems (14.4, 28.8, 33.6 kbit/s)
- Pippin memory (2, 4, 8, 16 MB)
- Pippin Floppy Dock
- Pippin MO 256 MB optical disk
- Pippin ADB adapter (for connecting Macintosh devices to Pippin)
- AppleJack to Macintosh (ADB) adapter (for connecting Pippin devices to Macintosh)

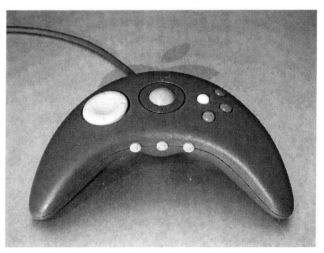

An AppleJack controller

Printers

Pippin can use the Apple Color StyleWriter 2400 and 2500 series through its serial port.

External links

- Pictures of Pippin Hardware and Games [1]
- Apple's original Pippin site [2]
- Katz Media mission statement on the Pippin [3]
- Bandai Pippin Museum & Archive, including PDF Technical Notes [4]
- Overview [5]
- Pippin screenshots [6]
- The Computer Chronicles' coverage of CES 1996, including Apple's demonstration of the Pippin [7]

Initial D

Initial D

Initial D franchise Logo	
頭文字D (*Inisharu Dī*)	
Genre	Action, Racing, Drama
Manga	
Written by	Shuichi Shigeno
Published by	Kodansha
English publisher	Tokyopop Madman Entertainment
Demographic	*Seinen*
Magazine	*Weekly Young Magazine*
Original run	1995 – ongoing
Volumes	41
TV anime	
Directed by	Noboru Mitsusawa
Studio	Pastel, Studio Gallop
Licensed by	Funimation Entertainment Madman Entertainment
Network	Fuji TV, Animax
Original run	April 18, 1998 – November 28, 1998
Episodes	26
TV anime	
Initial D Second Stage	
Directed by	Shin-ichi Masaki
Studio	Pastel, OB Planning
Network	Fuji TV, Animax

Original run	October 14, 1999 – January 6, 2000
Episodes	13
Original video animation	
Initial D Extra Stage 1.0 & 1.5	
Directed by	Shishi Yamaguchi
Studio	Pastel, OB Planning
Released	February 22, 2000 – February 29, 2000
Runtime	25 minutes (each)
Episodes	4 (total), 2 (1.0), 2 (1.5)
Anime film	
Initial D Third Stage	
Directed by	Noboru Mitsusawa
Studio	Pastel, OB Planning
Released	January 13, 2001
Runtime	105 minutes
Original video animation	
Initial D Battle Stage 1	
Directed by	Shishi Yamaguchi
Studio	Pastel, OB Planning
Released	May 15, 2002
Runtime	45 minutes
TV anime	
Initial D Fourth Stage	
Directed by	Tsuneo Tominaga
Studio	Frontline, Gainax
Network	Animax, Sky PTV
Original run	April 17, 2004 – February 18, 2006
Episodes	24
Original video animation	
Initial D Battle Stage 2	
Directed by	Tsuneo Tominaga

Studio	Frontline, OB Planning
Released	May 30, 2007
Runtime	45 minutes
Original video animation	
Initial D Extra Stage 2	
Directed by	Tsuneo Tominaga
Studio	A.C.G.T, OB Planning
Released	October 3, 2008
Runtime	55 minutes

Initial D (頭文字D *Inisharu Dī*) is a manga by Shuichi Shigeno which has been serialized in Kodansha's *Young Magazine* since 1995. It has been adapted into a long-running anime series by Pastel, Studio Gallop, OB Planning, Frontline, Gainax and A.C.G.T which premiered in Japan on Fuji TV and Animax, and a live action film by Avex and Media Asia. Both the manga and anime series were licensed for distribution in North America by Tokyopop (2002-2009), licence to anime then went to Funimation Entertainment, while manga is no longer available in english.

The story focus on the world of illegal Japanese street racing, where all the action is concentrated in the mountain passes and rarely in cities nor urban areas, and the drift racing style is emphasized in particular. Keiichi Tsuchiya helps with editorial supervision. The story is centered on the Japanese prefecture of Gunma, (mostly Shibukawa where Takumi's home is) more specifically on several mountains in the Kantō region and in their surrounding cities and towns. Although some of the names of the locations the characters race in have been fictionalized, all of the locations in the series are based on actual locations in Japan.

American licensing and alterations

The manga was also subject to the same name editing as the anime; the street slang was toned down and Tokyopop has been leaning toward the Japanese names in later volumes.

The first edition also had some translation errors. One example was the technical term "Waste Gate" (which is a mechanisim used to regulate the boost pressure generated by a turbocharger) that was translated as "West Gate". Another was a inaccurate explanation of how an engines displacement is calculated. (The explanation given is how a ships displacement is calculated, which is totally different).

In 2006, Funimation Entertainment announced that it would be distributing the DVDs of the series (since Tokyopop's original distributor went bankrupt). At the New York Anime Festival 2009, Funimation Entertainment announced that it will be re-releasing and re-dubbing Initial D: First Stage, Second Stage, Extra Stage, Third Stage, and Fourth Stage. They will not be using the original

Tokyopop dubbing in the re-release. It will include a brand new English Dubbing and it will retain the original music from the Japanese series in uncut format, but they are starting with the release of the Third Stage and going up, before rereleasing the earlier stages.

Synopsis and Stages

See also: List of Initial D chapters

Set in the late 1990s in Japan's Gunma Prefecture, the series follows the adventures of Takumi Fujiwara, an eighteen year old who helps his father run a tofu store by making deliveries every morning to a hotel on Akina with his father's Toyota Sprinter Trueno GT-APEX (AE86). It is revealed that Takumi has been driving on Mt. Akina every morning to deliver Tofu to the summit five years before he even had his license. As a result his skills in mountain racing were honed, and is able to drive under adverse weather conditions.

First Stage

The story begins when street racers called the Red Suns, a team from Mt. Akagi, come to challenge Mt. Akina's local Speed Stars team to a "friendly" race. After seeing how skilled the Red Suns are, the Speed Stars treat it as a race for pride, determined not to be humiliated on their home turf. However, the Speed Stars are left in a bind when their team leader and primary downhill driver Iketani has an accident during a practice run. They were desperate for a replacement, until Iketani learns from Yuuichi, the manager of the petroleum station he is working in, that the fastest car in Akina's downhill was a panda-colored AE86 owned by a Tofu store owner, and traces the car back to a local Tofu store. He discovers that the store's owner, Bunta Fujiwara, was a street racer of great repute in his younger days known as the "Ghost of Akina" . Iketani appeals to the older man to take his place in the race against the Red Suns. Iketani is confident that Bunta will come to save the day. But when the race day comes, his son Takumi appears with his Trueno instead. Although at first reluctant to let Takumi race, Ikatani relents after it is revealed that he is actually the "Ghost of Akina," the one who outran Keisuke while on one of his delivery runs. Takumi proceeds to defeat Keisuke Takahashi and his Mazda RX-7 (FD3S), causing considerable astonishment in the local racing community and putting an end to the Red Suns winning streak.

Despite being originally apathetic about the notion of racing, Takumi begins to grow more interested as he receives other challenges, and begins to understand the concept of a street racer's pride. He then proceeds to defeat drivers in more advanced and more powerful cars, such as the Honda Civic (EG6) hatchback, the Nissan Sileighty, and the Nissan Skyline GT-R (R32). He defeats them in all sorts of conditions, mostly for the first time (Duct Tape Deathmatch, wet weather race, first race in a course other than Mount Akina), culminating in the battle between him and Ryosuke Takahashi, the so-called "White Comet of Akagi." Takumi handed Ryosuke his first defeat.

Second Stage

A group of street racers called Team Emperor, all using Mitsubishi Lancer Evolutions, appear in the Gunma area, defeating anyone in their path, until their No. 2 racer, Seiji Iwaki, was defeated by Takumi, breaking their winning streak. Their leader, a professionally-trained driver named Kyouichi Sudo, challenged Takumi to a race to "teach him some things" and as a sort of cover event for his race with Ryosuke, his primary target. This race saw Takumi's AE86 blow its engine. While it may have been a defeat for Takumi, Kyouichi did not consider it a race instead considering it more as a seminar to show Takumi how much he needs a better car as he believes the 86 is far too old to match Takumi's skill level. Kyouichi, believing in his street racing philosophy that professional circuit techniques were adequate to conquer the mountains passes, races Ryosuke who had the opposing philosophy that somehow, the fastest street racing required more than just what the circuit could teach. Ryosuke proceeds to defeat Kyouichi after noticing and exploiting Kyouichi's inability to tackle some right-hand corners with full confidence. When Kyouichi confronted Ryosuke about the loss, Ryosuke explains that their techniques and abilities are actually quite close but that Kyouichi's weakness were right-hand corners which, on Japan's right-handed roads, had the possibility of encountering head-on collisions. He goes on to cite how Kyouichi was unable to conquer this fear due to the fact that circuits don't have the danger of head-on collisions and that his home-course, Irohazaka pass, was a one-way road. This proved once and for all to Kyouichi that street-racing had its own special requirements just as Ryosuke had believed.

Meanwhile, Bunta knew that the engine in the 86 was about to give out. In fact, one of Bunta's "secret" tasks for Takumi was "to lose." In anticipation, he had already bought a new engine [1]- a high revving, race bred variation of the standard Toyota 4A-GE 20 valve twin cam engine, which is used for Group A Division 2 Touring Class races in the Japanese Touring Car Championship. This is extremely unusual, because this type of engine is supplied to race teams only, and is not street legal. The source of the engine was unknown. It should be noted that in addition to being a high-revving engine, the 4AGE in Takumi's car is missing the pulley cover and runs Individual Throttle Bodies (ITB). Bunta installs the engine without a new tachometer to teach Takumi the importance of learning mechanical knowledge and understanding why the car behaves as it does, though he has an instrument set ready for installation once Takumi knows of it. A fellow AE86 driver named Wataru Akiyama, who was surprised with Takumi's lack of mechanical knowledge, told him that he needs a new tachometer.

Once Takumi unsealed the power of his new engine, Wataru challenges him to a race anywhere of Takumi's choosing. Choosing Wataru's home course, the treacherous Shomaru pass, Takumi went on to race Wataru despite the risks. Wataru, who knew the course well, was absolutely sure that Shomaru pass was a test of endurance and that it was not a course where overtaking was possible. Despite this, Takumi, upon noticing that in the process of four back-to-back runs through the course that the landslide which covered one half of the road at a certain part of the course had flattened out leaving enough space for another car, took advantage of Wataru not noticing the change in the course and went side-by-side with Takumi eventually overtaking the clearly shocked Levin driver and winning the battle.

Extra Stage 1.0 & 1.5

Capitalizing on the popularity of the all-female street racing team known as Impact Blue which appeared in First Stage, this OVA focuses on Impact Blue's dynamic duo of Mako and Sayuki rather than Takumi and the usual main cast.

As Extra Stage begins, Mako is battling emotional wounds from what she thinks was a rejection by Iketani, while Sayuki's childhood friend Shingo (of the Myogi Night Kids) and his teammate Nakazato arrive to warn them about Team Emperor, which defeated the Night Kids on their home course just as they have so many other street racing teams from around the region. Mako's driving has been adversely affected by her preoccupations, and she worries about her ability to measure up to the Emperor's challenge in her current emotional state. Finally, a pair of Emperor affiliated Evos show up in Usui. The challenger, an arrogant blonde driving an Evo 4, belittled the female racers and felt confident enough to win easily. Later on in the race, the Evo 4 could barely keep up with the Sil-80, until the battle was finally decided in a extended corner, called C-121 (also called "The Terror of Usui"). where the Evo 4 hit the guardrail and lost control. Shingo and Nakazato were late and didn't get to see the race. Thinking the girls also lost, they consoled them saying they lost in their home course as well, but Sayuki unexpectedly told them they won. The Night Kids leaders were startled, thinking they raced against the top Emperor drivers whereas they only defeated an off-beat member.

Though Mako decides she does not need a man in her life for a while, she gradually develops a relationship with a friend of Shingo's named Miyahara after Shingo and Sayuki discreetly play matchmaker. Miyahara is a street racer himself, not a good one though, and he intends to give it up because he believes he has reached the highest level he possibly can, with no chance of progressing further. He has lost interest and intends to move on. He drives a red Toyota MR2 and plans to switch to an SUV in pursuit of settling down after racing. Mako feels differently, knowing there are many drivers better than her whose level she wishes to attain. As Mako and Miyahara grow closer, Miyahara reveals that he wishes Mako would quit racing also for her safety's sake, because if she was his girlfriend he would be consumed with worry for her each time she raced.

However, after Mako takes him on a drive on an unknown pass, that was home to the mountain snow resort they were vacationing at, he finally understands why she will not give up racing and realizes that she is in love with another man, Iketani.

Third Stage

By this time Ryosuke approaches Takumi with an offer. Ryosuke has been putting together a racing team featuring the best racers of the Gunma prefecture, and would like Takumi to join. Takumi doesn't want to decide whether or not to accept the proposal until he settles his score with Team Emperor leader Sudou Kyouichi, who had looked down on the AE86 because of the car's age and had seriously damaged Takumi's confidence in the AE86 after being defeated by him. Takumi proceeds to Irohazaka pass to challenge Kyouichi. Kyouichi had chosen to let Takumi lead; if Takumi prevents Kyouichi from passing him, he wins, if Kyouichi passes him, he loses. Takumi notes how the match is unfair, but this is quickly dismissed by Kyouichi. In the end, Takumi is able to prevent Kyouichi from passing. Kyouichi, who takes great pride in his knowledge and ability to race on his home course, concedes defeat and also gave praise to the new AE86, although Takumi still believes it was more of a tie and was more concerned about Kyouichi finally acknowledging the abilities of the AE86.

Kogashiwa Kai, the son of Bunta's old rival, driving a Toyota MR2 (SW20) later challenges Takumi upon knowing he beat his original target, Kyouichi. He and his father planned to beat Takumi by using a line strategy his father had devised and used against Bunta: the In-Air hairpin jump on the 33rd, 36th, 37th, 38th, and 39th hairpins of Irohazaka. Bunta, knowing how Kogashiwa has used the special line factor before, predicted to Takumi that Kai would surely be in front by the later half of the race and proceeds to give Takumi some obscure advice on how to beat Kai. Kyouichi, who had been with Iwaki Seiji , Keisuke, and Takahashi Ryouske, had predicted as well that Kai would use the technique and explains how he himself could not come to use the strategy due to his pride in his skills alone without need for strategy. Kai, upon realizing that he cannot win in a straight-forward clash of skill, uses the line strategy to overtake and further distance himself from Takumi. Takumi then finds it in himself to try this technique and masters it at the first try, finding himself catching up to Kai. At the last moment before they reach the finish Takumi realizes the meaning behind the advice given earlier by Bunta when he notices dead leaves piling up on one side of the road. Takumi proceeds puts his car past the shrubs and into the gutter to sling shot side-by-side forcing Kai to the side of the road where Takumi guesses the leaves would pile up on. Bunta, while talking to Yuuichi, has predicted that Takumi had a 50% chance of passing Kai. As they pass the bridge side-by-side airborne, the 50% chance presents itself as Kai had landed on the side of the road where the leaves had piled up where he lost control and spun out right before the goal.

This stage also saw the appearance of Miki, a former student at the same high school Takumi attended who Takumi once punched over Miki's bragging about his sexual exploits with Natsuki (seen in a flashback from 1st Stage). It was Christmas season, and Natsuki surprises Takumi at his house, and celebrates Christmas with him and Bunta. On New Year's Day, Miki takes Natsuki under duress, even attempting to rape her near Lake Akina. But Takumi, after hearing a few words of a call from Natsuki which was cut short, came to the rescue.

As spring comes, Takumi tells Ryosuke that he wants to request another battle with him, this time on Mt. Akagi, before making his decision regarding the team. It is unclear who actually wins the race, but during the race Keisuke reveals to the other members of the Red Suns that the race is not really about who wins or loses. As they approach the finish, side by side, Takumi decides that it is his desire to remain with Ryosuke and join the team.

Battle Stage

Initial D Battle Stage (special) summarizes the major street races from the two TV series. Rather than simply using clips from the TV series, the new special entirely re-animated all of the original CG car and background footage with new computer graphics rendering. The special also features a battle between the yellow FD3S of Keisuke against the white Evo 4 of Seiji, but no such race took place in the anime (although it does take place in the manga). Music is from an entirely new Super Eurobeat songs and guest commentary from legendary "Drift King" Keiichi Tsuchiya.

Fourth Stage

This series focuses on the exploits of the new team founded by Ryosuke, Project.D, which is composed of Ryosuke (leader and strategist), downhill specialist Takumi, uphill specialist Keisuke, and a staff consisting primarily of members of the Akagi Red Suns. The team travels the region, challenging other teams and posting the results of the battles on their website. Each race is intended by Ryosuke to develop a specific area of his drivers' skills. By this time, Takumi matures slowly into a more confident and knowledgeable street racer, while Keisuke improves on his technical driving skills. Takumi instinctively develops many new techniques through his own ingenuity after some prompting by Ryosuke, such as passing with his headlights off so that his opponent is unable to see him coming and block him, and using weight shifting to execute maneuvers similar to the gutter-hook technique on Akina. Ryosuke also formed the team because in a few months he is headed for medical school, and this is his last chance in a long time to indulge in street racing. Takumi, on the other hand, contends with the "Four-Wheel Drive Complex" when he was overtaken by a Subaru Impreza WRX STI, a 4WD car, on one of his delivery runs. It is later revealed that his father was driving the car. Bunta then allowed Takumi to deliver Tofu, as well as practice, in the Impreza (alternating with the Trueno) to improve his skills as a driver and to get a feel of what modern cars can do.

Project.D's opponents grew tougher and tougher, as well as more deceitful and threatening. They defeated local racing teams (like the Seven Star Leaf), students of the Todo-juku racing school (including a professional driver who is a graduate of the school), the combined forces of the Northern Saitama Alliance (who even used a Suzuki Cappuccino kei-car), thugs in Lan Evos, and the "Godfoot" and "Godhand" tandem of Team Purple Shadow. In the shadows, Wataru Akiyama watches Takumi from a distance and looks for weaknesses, but it ceased when Project.D conquered Saitama, so he began giving Takumi a few pointers, especially with the 4WD problem. There are also glimmers of romance, like Kyoko Iwase, Keisuke's fellow Mazda RX-7 FD driver and uphill ace racing for the Northern Saitama Alliance, falling in love with him, even lending her precious car to Keisuke—but, although he likes her, he rejected her, deciding to focus more on driving.

Takumi also learned a lot, including the theory of infinite lines and Joushima (the "Godhand" of Team Purple Shadow) teaching him the theory of one handed driving. Though he doubted that Takumi would start driving with one hand, he did believe he would master using the infinite lines to his advantage in future races. Hoshino, the "Godfoot" of Purple Shadow, offered his racing connections to Keisuke, who refused, saying he has still got a lot to do in street racing.

This seems to be the conclusion of Initial D. The audience was left with the unanswered question as to what the D in Project D stood for and who was the better driver between Takumi and Keisuke.

Battle Stage 2

Initial D Battle Stage 2 summarizes the major street races from the recent Fourth Stage TV series. While the first *Battle Stage* had every battle re-animated from scratch, the only episodes altered in the second version were the early races in stage 4, to match with the visual style of the latter portion of Stage 4. Additionally, two races that were previously seen only in the manga were animated specially for the feature. The first race is Takahashi Keisuke vs. Atsuro Kawai's Nissan Skyline 25GT Turbo (ER34), and the other is Keisuke vs. Smiley Sakai's Honda Integra DC2. Both races are noticeably shorter than the other races in the feature.

Battle Stage 2 was released on DVD on May 30, 2007. The official soundtrack to Battle Stage 2, featuring 24 Eurobeat songs that played during the feature, was released on September 5, 2007.

Extra Stage 2

Extra Stage 2 provides a closure on the relationship between Iketani and Mako. This story took place during the time Project D battled the Toudo school. Iketani finally met up with Mako Sato and apologized for not being able to meet her 6 months ago. Mako told Iketani she had something to tell him and asked him to meet her again. Iketani was excited that Mako gave him a second chance, he arrived 2 hours early this time. However, an old man was lost and asked Iketani for directions. Being a good person, Iketani agreed to help the old man back but on his way back. The only problem was, the old man's destination would take almost 2 hours roundtrip. While making his way back, Iketani hit the tire's shoulder on a jagged rock and got a flat tire, but he ran and was lucky to find a public phone and called Mako to take him to where they first met. This time, however, Mako tells him that she is leaving for Tokyo for a one-year professional racing season sponsored by a publishing company and the experience will be published on a magazine. With Iketani's blessing and his goal of making her happy, Mako pursues her dreams. Mako also discussed her situation with her teammate Sayuki, whom she also gave Mako her blessing, disbanding Team Impact Blue in the process. Iketani then goes back to Akina and tries to forget about her for now while replenishing his driving skills with Kenji, while Mako and

Sayuki are gearing up for their final race in Usui as Team Impact Blue... In the end, they never knew that Iketani and Mako would never see each other again directly and admit their true feelings for each other.

Announced in chapter 530 of the Initial D manga, Extra Stage 2 aired on pay-per-view on October 3, 2008 and is available on DVD from December 5, 2008.

Characters

Main article: List of Initial D characters and teams

Initial D contains a myriad of characters, many of whom appear in a very small number of episodes, usually to race one of the main characters or as a teammate of another racer. The most frequently recurring characters are the protagonist Takumi Fujiwara, his love interest Natsuki Mogi, his father Bunta, the members of the *Akina Speed Stars*, and the members of the *Akagi Redsuns* (later *Project D*).

List of releases

Manga

- Initial D Manga Japanese Release - 41 Volumes (1995 - ongoing, Vol. 41 released on August 6, 2010)
- Initial D Manga Tokyopop Release - 33 Volumes (2002–2009, ended due to expired license)

Anime

Avex has released the anime in several parts called **Stages**. One noticeable feature is that it uses Eurobeat music as background music in race scenes.

- Initial D (referred to retroactively by fans as "First Stage") - 26 episodes (1998)
- Initial D Second Stage - 13 episodes (1999)
- Initial D Extra Stage - 2 episode OVA side-story focusing on Impact Blue (2000)
- Initial D Third Stage - a 2 hour movie (2001)
- Initial D Battle Stage - a 50 minute movie (2002)
- Initial D Fourth Stage - 24 episodes (2004—2006)
- Initial D Battle Stage 2 - a 1 hour movie (2007)
- Initial D Extra Stage 2 - a 50 minute OVA side-story focusing on Mako and Iketani (2008)

Games

Main article: Initial D Arcade Stage

Numerous arcade and other platforms video games have been released (note: The U.S. versions of the arcade titles are called simply "Initial D").

- Initial D Arcade Stage Version 1 (Arcade)
- Initial D Arcade Stage Version 2 (Arcade)
- Initial D Arcade Stage Version 3 (Arcade)
- Initial D Arcade Stage Version 4 (Arcade)
- Initial D Arcade Stage Version 5 (Arcade)
- Initial D (Sega Saturn)
- Initial D (PS1)
- Initial D: Special Stage (PS2)
- Initial D Mountain Vengeance (PC)
- Initial D: Street Stage (PSP)
- Initial D Gaiden (Game Boy)
- Initial D Another Stage (GBA)
- Initial D Collectible Card Game (Collectible Card Game)
- Initial D Extreme Stage (PS3)
- Initial D RPG (Sony Ericsson mobile phone)

Feature film

Main article: Initial D (film)

A live-action movie based on Initial D was released on June 23, 2005 in Asia. The movie was jointly produced by Japan's Avex Inc. and Hong Kong's Media Asia Group. It was directed by Andrew Lau and Alan Mak, whose credits include the 2002 Hong Kong Blockbuster *Infernal Affairs* and 1999's *The Legend of Speed*, a previous street racing melodrama directed by Lau. The movie featured Taiwanese star Jay Chou as Takumi Fujiwara and Hong Kong stars Edison Chen as Ryosuke Takahashi and Shawn Yue as Takeshi Nakazato.

Reception

Some fans of *Initial D* reacted negatively to the English dub of the anime series and the editing of character names in the English language version of the manga. Tokyopop said that it was trying to Americanize the series so it could be aired on television, while at the same time keeping the Japanese spirit of the series.

See also

- List of Initial D episodes
- List of Initial D chapters
- List of Initial D characters and teams
- Initial D Arcade Stage
- Initial D: Street Stage
- Initial D: Extreme Stage

External links

- Avex webpage for Initial D [2] (Japanese)
- North America Premier of the Live Action Initial D [3]
- Initial D Arcade Stage Version 3.0 [4]
- Initial D Games Official Website [5] - *Sega*
- Initial D Games Official Website [6] - *Sega* (Japanese)

Dan Hibiki

Dan Hibiki

Dan Hibiki

Dan in *Street Fighter Alpha 3*, drawn by Bengus.	
Series	*Street Fighter* series
Voiced by (English)	Ted Sroka (*Street Fighter IV*)
Voiced by (Japanese)	Osamu Hosoi (all but SFIV) Kazuyuki Ishikawa (*Street Fighter Alpha: The Animation*) Toshiyuki Kusuda (*Street Fighter IV*)
Fictional information	
Fighting style	Saikyo style Karate (サイキョウ流空手 *Saikyō Ryū Karate*)

Dan Hibiki (火引 弾 *Hibiki Dan*) is a character from Capcom's Street Fighter series of fighting games. Dan is consistently portrayed as an arrogant, overconfident, yet utterly feeble character in many of the games he is featured in.

Concept and creation

Shortly after the release of *Street Fighter II*, rival video game company SNK finished development on, and subsequently released, their own fighting game, *Art of Fighting*. The principal character of this series, Ryo Sakazaki, bore a resemblance in appearance and name to Ryu, as well as other aesthetic similarities to Ken, wearing an orange gi and sporting blonde hair.

In humorous retaliation, *Street Fighter II* co-designer Akiman drew an artwork of Sagat holding a defeated opponent by the head during the release of *Street Fighter II' - Champion Edition*. The defeated opponent wore an attire similar to Ryo's: an orange karate gi with a torn black shirt underneath and geta sandals; but had long dark hair tied to a ponytail like Robert Garcia, another character from the *Art of Fighting* series. This character design would become the basis of Dan, who was introduced as a secret character in *Street Fighter Alpha* until finally becoming a selectable character on the game's sequel, *Street Fighter Alpha 2*. His fireball is telling: instead of using both hands to unleash his *Gadōken*, as Ryu and Ken do for the *Hadōken*, he propels it with one hand, like Ryo, Robert and Yuri do for the

Kooh-ken (though Dan's Gadōken has pitifully short range and does mediocre damage.It only gains a bit longer range when you use the super version of the move, the *Shinkū Gadōken*). Dan can also taunt infinitely like the *Art of Fighting* games, unlike his fellow *Street Fighter Alpha* characters who can only taunt once per round in the Alpha series.

When developing *Street Fighter IV*, executive producer Yoshinori Ono emphasized Dan as a character he strongly wanted to have appear in the game, stating that while the character's personality and actions earned him the label of a joke character, he felt Dan was a very technical fighting game character that could be used well and bring something unique to the game. In a later interview, he emphasized his desire to have Dan in the game again, citing the then-unveiled inclusion of Sakura Kasugano in home versions as added incentive.

As a parody

In *Street Fighter Alpha 2*, Dan is Ken's secret challenger (reached by finishing several fights in a row with super combos) and they exchange dialog, one line of which is Ken asking Dan if he knows the "art of fighting". This is a reference to the *Art of Fighting* series by SNK.

In Dan's ending in *Marvel Super Heroes vs. Street Fighter*, Dan's sister appears to prevent him finishing off Cyber-Akuma saying "Don't you know who he is? He's our..." parodying the ending of the original *Art of Fighting* where Ryo was about to kill Mr. Karate before being told he is their father by Yuri (Dan's sister even looks like her). Also, Dan is the only character in the game to have a super taunt as one of his super combos.

One of Dan's win quotes in *Street Fighter Alpha 3* is "I hate the art of fighting, but I wanna be the king of fighters!" This is a direct reference to the *Art of Fighting* and *King of Fighters* series by SNK.

Also Dan's fighting style, the Saikyō-ryū, is a parody of Kyokugen-ryū, the fighting style used by Ryo and Robert. To further the parody, Saikyō-ryū means "Strongest style" while Kyokugen-ryū means "Extreme style". Not only that, but he's a Japanese immigrant who came to Hong Kong to change his nationality for reasons unknown.

In the *SNK vs. Capcom* series (more specifically in *SNK vs. Capcom: SVC Chaos*), there is a running gag where Dan is often mistaken for Ryo or Robert, even by himself in a mirror match (Kasumi Todoh is one example: even after Dan tells her he is not Robert, she still does not believe him). In these games, Dan parodies even more of Ryo's attacks. He also mistook Mr. Karate for his father's ghost (though, in his ending in Neo Geo Pocket's *SNK vs. Capcom: The Match of the Millennium*, he seems to acknowledge that Takuma and Go are different people). In Ryo's ending for *Capcom vs. SNK 2*, it is hinted that Dan came to the Sakazaki's Kyokugen-ryū Karate school to sign up. In *Super Gem Fighter Mini Mix*, Dan can call on the ghost of his father, whose face resembles the same tengu mask as Mr. Karate. This is mirrored in Capcom's official artwork for *Street Fighter Alpha*; earlier works featured Dan's father as wearing a tengu mask, while later ones show that the long nose was indeed a feature of Go Hibiki. All other instances of Go Hibiki's face are obscured.

His status as a parody is further increased by Dan's new Ultra move in Super Street Fighter IV, where he focuses his Gadouken into a gigantic orb and thrusts it out with his two arms, a motion resembling the Haoh Sho Kou Ken made popular by the Kyokugen-ryu masters in King of Fighters. When the fireball makes contact, its power sends Dan spiraling back to the other side of the screen. The name of this move is *Haoh Gadouken*.

Character design

Dan has a similar outfit to Ryu and Ken, wearing a traditional Karategi. Dan also wears a black undershirt like Ryo. His head and face closely resembles Robert from *Art of Fighting*, while his outfit is bright pink, reminiscent of Ryo's orange outfit in *Art of Fighting*.

Though his fighting stance is similar to Ken and Ryu's, it is more "loose" and animated. Many of his mannerisms directly mirror those of Yuri Sakazaki. In Street Fighter IV Dan's stance more closely resembles Ryo Sakazaki's fighting stance, rather than Ryu and Ken's.

In *Street Fighter IV*, he can be seen with the kanji 最強流 (Saikyō-ryū) on his lapel. During some moves, the kanji 父 (father) or 弾 (bullet, pronounced 'Dan') appears on his back, similar to Akuma.

Appearances

In the *Street Fighter* series

Dan's father, Gou Hibiki, was a rival of Sagat. Gou gouged out Sagat's eye and Sagat beat him to death in retaliation. Because of this, Dan sought revenge on Sagat, training to become a fighter, but was expelled from Gouken's dojo when his motivations were learned. Dan thus developed his own fighting style called *Saikyō-ryū*, "The Strongest Style", despite the considerable lack of power in his techniques.

After the events of *Street Fighter Alpha* and *Street Fighter Alpha 2*, Dan believed he had achieved his revenge by defeating Sagat (who had actually thrown the fight), and his motivation switched to promoting and expanding his Saikyo-style school, even to the point of offering exercise videos and correspondence courses. He has seemingly had some limited success promoting Saikyo-style.

In *Alpha 3*, he was Sakura Kasugano's supposed sensei, who followed him around in order to meet Ryu. He's also good friends with Blanka too, since Blanka saved Dan during the events of *Sakura Ganbaru!* manga.

Dan also appears in *Street Fighter IV*, entering the tournament and just barely qualifying (as seen in Seth's intro movie) in an effort to make his Saikyo-style more popular. He mentions offhand he was not allowed in the last tournament, (*Street Fighter II*) although Blanka mentions he tried to call him about the tournament, only to find that Dan hadn't paid his phone bill. He also appears as Sakura's mentor and fights her as a rival in the penultimate fight of his Arcade mode. In Super Street Fighter IV, he continues fighting to promote and gain membership into his Saikyo Dojo (which currently has no members). Dan is used as the dummy opponent for the Challenge Mode in the home versions.

In other games

In the parody game *Pocket Fighter*, Dan's story begins with himself looking to expand his Saikyo-ryuu school, and subsequently chooses Sakura as his student. Upon meeting Sakura, he offers to teach her his style, and she accepts after Dan defeats her in a fight. Sakura masters the entire Saikyo-ryuu style, and chooses to forget the entire style three days after mastering it, humiliating Dan.

His stance as a "weak" character is emphasized in the puzzle game *Super Puzzle Fighter II*, in which Dan is a hidden character who drops only red counter gems, making him extremely easy to beat.

Dan appears as a playable character in some Capcom crossover projects including: *Marvel Super Heroes vs. Street Fighter*, *Marvel vs. Capcom 2*, *Capcom vs. SNK* and its sequel, and *SNK vs. Capcom: SVC Chaos*.

During the debut trailer for the crossover fighting game *Street Fighter X Tekken*, Dan is beaten through a door following an unfortunate encounter with *Tekken* fighter Kazuya Mishima.

References in other games

- Chairperson from the fighting game series *Rival Schools* learned to fight from a Saikyou-Ryuu correspondence course.
- Ran Hibiki from the same series, has been speculated to be Dan's younger sister, as Yuri Sakazaki is to Ryo, but it hasn't been confirmed. Although Dan mentions he has a sister in the NeoGeo Pocket Color title, SNK vs. Capcom: Match of the Millennium, while ironically discussing similarities between himself and Ryo.
- Sean from the *Street Fighter III* series, a student of Ken who has a very limited mastery of the fighting style, has the win quotes, "Don't call me Dan!" and "Rule #1: Never give up! Rule #2: Don't fight me! Rule #3: Don't be like Dan!"
- He appears in Blanka's ending in *Street Fighter IV* helping Samantha (Blanka's mother) search for him. Only his back is shown and the character identified by the game as a "passerby". However, the kanji for his name is written on the back of his gi.

Promotion and reception

IGN ranked Dan at number twelve in their "Top 25 Street Fighter Characters" article, noting his role as a "fan favourite" despite his status as a joke character. GameDaily listed Dan at number eighteen in their "Top 20 Street Fighter Characters of All Time" article and at number two in their "Top 25 Most Bizarre Fighting Characters" article, stating that despite the character's handicaps "...Dan is fun". In the January 30, 1997 issue of *Gamest* magazine in Japan, Dan ranked at the top from the poll Top 50 Characters of 1996. GamesRadar listed Dan's uselessness as the number one in-game in-joke, stating that the character has become a fan favourite for overconfident players who want to show their skills.

External links

- Dan's Street Fighter Alpha [1], Marvel vs. Capcom [2], and Street Fighter IV [3] entries at StrategyWiki.org [4]
- Dan's Super Dojo [5]
- Saikyo Crusher [6]

SmartMedia

SmartMedia

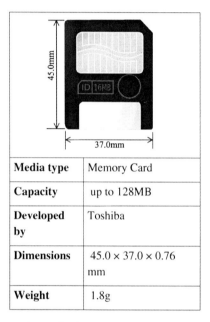

Media type	Memory Card
Capacity	up to 128MB
Developed by	Toshiba
Dimensions	45.0 × 37.0 × 0.76 mm
Weight	1.8g

SmartMedia is a flash memory card standard owned by Toshiba, with capacities ranging from 2 MB to 128 MB. SmartMedia memory cards are no longer manufactured.

History

A SmartMedia card consists of a single NAND flash chip embedded in a thin plastic card, although some higher capacity cards contain multiple, linked chips. It was one of the smallest and thinnest of the early memory cards, only 0.76mm thick, and managed to maintain a favorable cost ratio as compared to the others. SmartMedia cards lack a built-in controller chip, which kept the cost down. This feature later caused problems, since some older devices would require firmware updates to handle larger capacity cards. The lack of built-in controller also made it impossible for the card to perform automatic wear levelling, a process which prevents premature wearout of a sector by mapping the writes to various other sectors in the card.

SmartMedia cards can be used in a standard 3.5" floppy drive by means of a FlashPath adapter. This is possibly the only way of obtaining flash memory functionality with very old hardware, and it remains one of SmartMedia's most distinctive features. This method's big drawback is that it is very slow. Read/write is limited to floppy disk speeds, meaning that copying 64 megabytes of data by this method is a very tedious process, although usually preferable to not copying it at all.

Typically, SmartMedia cards were used as storage for portable devices, in a form that could easily be removed for access by a PC. For example, pictures taken with a digital camera would be stored as image files on a SmartMedia card. A user could copy the images to a computer with a SmartMedia reader. A reader was typically a small box connected via USB or some other serial connection. Modern computers, both laptops and desktops, will occasionally have SmartMedia slots built in. While availability of dedicated SmartMedia readers has dropped off, readers that read multiple card types (such as 4-in-1, 10-in-1) continue to include the format, but even these have decreased in quantity, with many dropping SmartMedia in favour of MicroSD and/or Memory Stick Micro.

A 32MB SmartMedia flash memory card (on keyboard for scale). The position of the notch indicates that this is a 3.3 volt card.

SmartMedia cards came in two formats, 5 V and the more modern 3.3 V (sometimes marked 3 V), named for their main supply voltages. The packaging was nearly identical, except for the reversed placement of the notched corner. Many older SmartMedia devices only support 5V SmartMedia cards, whereas many newer devices only support 3.3V cards. In order to protect 3.3V cards from being damaged in 5V-only devices, the card reader should have some mechanical provision (such as detecting the type of notch) to disallow insertion of an

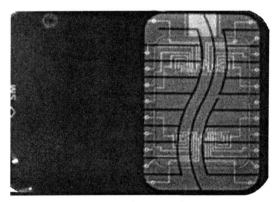

A radiograph of SmartMedia card.

unsupported type of card. Some low-cost, 5V-only card readers do not operate this way, and inserting a 3.3V card into such a 5V-only reader will result in permanent damage to the card. Dual-voltage card readers are highly recommended.

There is an oversized xD-to-SmartMedia adapter that allows xD cards to use a SmartMedia port, but it does not fit entirely inside a SmartMedia slot. There is a limit on the capacity of the xD card when used in such adapters (sometimes 128 MB or 256 MB), and the device is subject to the restrictions of the SmartMedia reader as well.

SmartMedia memory cards are no longer manufactured. There have been no new devices designed for SmartMedia for quite a long time now. Old stocks of new 128MB cards can be obtained from specialist suppliers while their supplies last.

Copy protection

Many SmartMedia cards include a little-known copy protection feature known as "ID". This is why many cards are marked with "ID" beside the capacity. This gave every card a unique identification number for use with copy protection systems. The only known use of this primitive DRM system was the Korean company Game Park, which used it to protect commercial titles for the GP32 handheld gaming system.

Format errors & data loss

Specifications

- Weight: 2 g
- Size: $45.0 \times 37.0 \times 0.76$ mm
- Capacities: 2, 4, 8, 16, 32, 64, 128 MB
- Uses 16-Mbit, 32-Mbit, and 64-Mbit Toshiba TC58-compatible NAND-type flash memory chips
- Flat electrode terminal with 22 pins — (32M & 64M compatible)
- 8-bit I/O Interface (16-bit in some cases)
- Data transfer rate: 2MB/s
- 1,000,000 read/write cycles
- ten year storage time without power
- metallic write-protect sticker
- Compatible with PCMCIA with an adapter
- Compatible with CompactFlash Type II with an adapter
- Compatible with 3.5" Floppy drive using FlashPath adapter

See also

- Comparison of memory cards
- Memory card
- Flash memory
- Circuits

External links

- [1] SSFDC News Site with PDF document listing news of the 256 MB SmartMedia card technical specifications being released in SmartMedia NEWS 2002.1 NO.1
- Olympus Emporium page on xD/SM to PCMCIA adapter [2]
- SmartMedia format introduction (software considerations) [3]

[[

System Management Bus

System Management Bus

The **System Management Bus** (abbreviated to **SMBus** or **SMB**) is a single-ended simple two-wire bus for the purpose of lightweight communication. Most commonly it is found in computer motherboards for communication with the power source for ON/OFF instructions.

It is derived from I²C for communication with low-bandwidth devices on a motherboard, especially power related chips such as a laptop's rechargeable battery subsystem (see Smart Battery Data). Other devices might include temperature, fan or voltage sensors, lid switches and clock chips. PCI add-in cards may connect to a SMBus segment.

A device can provide manufacturer information, indicate its model/part number, save its state for a suspend event, report different types of error, accept control parameters and return status. The SMBus is generally not user configurable or accessible. Although SMBus devices usually can't identify their functionality, a new PMBus coalition has extended SMBus to include conventions allowing that.

The SMBus was defined by Intel in 1995. It carries clock, data, and instructions and is based on Philips' I²C serial bus protocol. Its clock frequency range is 10 kHz to 100 kHz. (PMBus extends this to 400 kHz.) Its voltage levels and timings are more strictly defined than those of I²C, but devices belonging to the two systems are often successfully mixed on the same bus.

SMBus/I²C Interoperability

While SMBus is derived from I²C, there are several major differences between the specifications of the two busses in the areas of electricals, timing, protocols and operating modes.

Electrical

Input Voltage (V_{IL} and V_{IH})

When mixing devices, the I²C specification defines the V_{DD} to be 5.0 V ±10% and the fixed input levels to be 1.5 and 3.0 V. Instead of relating the bus input levels to V_{DD}, SMBus defines them to be fixed at 0.8 and 2.1 V. This SMBus specification allows for bus implementations with V_{DD} ranging from 3 to 5 V.

Sink Current (I_{OL})

SMBus has a 'High Power' version 2.0 that includes a 4 mA sink current that cannot be driven by I²C chips unless the pull-up resistor is sized to I²C-bus levels.

NXP devices have a higher power set of electrical characteristics than SMBus 1.0. The main difference is the current sink capability with $V_{OL} = 0.4$ V.

- SMBus low power = 350 µA
- SMBus high power = 4 mA
- I²C-bus = 3 mA

SMBus 'high power' devices and I²C-bus devices will work together if the pull-up resistor is sized for 3 mA.

Frequency (F_{MAX} and F_{MIN})

The SMBus clock is defined from 10–100 kHz while I²C can be 0–100 kHz, 0–400 kHz, 0–1 MHz and 0–3.4 MHz, depending on the mode. This means that an I²C bus running at less than 10 kHz will not be SMBus compliant since the SMBus devices may time out. Many SMBus devices will however support lower frequencies.

Timing

- SMBus defines a clock low time-out, TTIMEOUT of 35 ms. I²C does not specify any timeout limit.
- SMBus specifies TLOW: SEXT as the cumulative clock low extend time for a slave device. I²C does not have a similar specification.
- SMBus specifies TLOW: MEXT as the cumulative clock low extend time for a master device. Again I²C does not have a similar specification.
- SMBus defines both rise and fall time of bus signals. I²C does not.
- The SMBus time-out specifications do not preclude I²C devices co-operating reliably on the SMBus. It is the responsibility of the designer to ensure that I²C devices are not going to violate these bus timing parameters.

Protocols

ACK and NACK usage

There are the following differences in the use of the NACK bus signaling: In I²C, a slave receiver is allowed to not acknowledge the slave address, if for example it's unable to receive because it's performing some real time task. SMBus requires devices to acknowledge their own address always, as a mechanism to detect a removable device's presence on the bus (battery, docking station, etc.) I²C specifies that a slave device, although it may acknowledge its own address, may decide, some time later in the transfer, that it cannot receive any more data bytes. I²C specifies that the device may indicate this by generating the not acknowledge on the first byte to follow. Other than to indicate a slave's device-busy condition, SMBus also uses the NACK mechanism to indicate the reception of an invalid command or data. Since such a condition may occur on the last byte of the transfer, it is required that SMBus devices have the ability to generate the not acknowledge after the transfer of each byte and before the completion of the transaction. This is important because SMBus does not provide any other resend signaling. This difference in the use of the NACK signaling has implications on the specific implementation of the SMBus port, especially in devices that handle critical system data such as the SMBus host and the SBS components.

SMBus protocols

Each message transaction on SMBus follows the format of one of the defined SMBus protocols. The SMBus protocols are a subset of the data transfer formats defined in the I²C specifications. I²C devices that can be accessed through one of the SMBus protocols are compatible with the SMBus specifications. I²C devices that do not adhere to these protocols cannot be accessed by standard methods as defined in the SMBus and ACPI specifications.

Address Resolution Protocol

The SMBus uses I²C hardware and I²C hardware addressing, but adds second-level software for building special systems. In particular its specifications include an Address Resolution Protocol that can make dynamic address allocations. Dynamic reconfiguration of the hardware and software allow bus devices to be 'hot-plugged' and used immediately, without restarting the system. The devices are recognized automatically and assigned unique addresses. This advantage results in a plug-and-play user interface. In both those protocols there is a very useful distinction made between a System Host and all the other devices in the system that can have the names and functions of masters or slaves.

Time-out feature

SMBus has a time-out feature which resets devices if a communication takes too long. This explains the minimum clock frequency of 10 kHz to prevent locking up the bus. I²C can be a 'DC' bus, meaning that a slave device stretches the master clock when performing some routine while the master is accessing it. This will notify to the master that the slave is busy but does not want to lose the communication. The slave device will allow continuation after its task is complete. There is no limit in the I²C-bus protocol as to how long this delay can be, whereas for an SMBus system, it would be limited to 35 ms. SMBus protocol just assumes that if something takes too long, then it means that there is a problem on the bus and that all devices must reset in order to clear this mode. Slave devices are not then allowed to hold the clock LOW too long.

Packet Error Checking

SMBus 2.0 and 1.1 allow enabling **Packet Error Checking** (**PEC**). In that mode, a PEC (packet error code) byte is appended at the end of each transaction. The byte is calculated as CRC-8 checksum, calculated over the entire message including the address and read/write bit. The polynomial used is x^8+x^2+x+1 (the CRC-8-ATM HEC algorithm, initialized to zero).

SMBALERT#

The SMBus has an extra optional shared interrupt signal called SMBALERT#, which can be used by slaves to tell the host to ask its slaves about events of interest. SMBus also defines a less common "Host Notify Protocol", providing similar notifications but passing more data and building on the I²C multi-master mode.

SMBus Support

SMBus devices are supported by FreeBSD, OpenBSD, NetBSD, DragonFly BSD, Linux, Windows 2000 and newer server editions, and Windows XP and newer desktop editions.

See also

*   I²C (I2C)
*   Power Management Bus (PMBus)
*   Advanced Configuration and Power Interface (ACPI)
*   List of network buses

External links

*   SMBus website [1]
*   SBS forum [2]
*   SMBus at tech-faq.com [3]

3D Movie Maker

3D Movie Maker

Developer(s)	Microsoft Kids
Operating system	Windows
Type	3D computer graphics software
License	Proprietary

3D Movie Maker (often abbreviated as *3DMM*) is a program created by Microsoft's "Microsoft Kids" subsidiary in 1995. Using this program, directors are able to place 3D characters into pre-made environments, add actions, sound effects, music, text, speech, and special effects then show these movies off to friends, family, and the world. These are saved in the 3D Movie formats: ".3mm" and ".vmm".

A Japanese expansion pack for 3DMM was released with characters from the popular children's manga and anime series *Doraemon*.

The last release of 3D Movie Maker was *Nickelodeon 3D Movie Maker*, a spin-off using actors and scenes from *Rocko's Modern Life*, *Ren & Stimpy* and *AAAHH!!! Real Monsters*.

The program features two helper characters to guide users through the various features of the program. The character *McZee* provides help throughout the studio while his assistant Melanie provides various tutorials. In Nickelodeon 3D Movie Maker, the user is guided by Stick Stickly.

3D Movie Maker is built on the BRender, a 3D graphics engine created by Argonaut Software. The models and prerendered backgrounds were created by Illumin8 Digital Pictures, a now defunct graphics studio, using Softimage modelling software. The cinematic introduction and help sequences were created by Productions Jarnigoine, a now inactive production company directed by Jean-Jacques Tremblay.

System requirements

The system requirements for 3D Movie Maker are:

- Windows 95 (or Microsoft Windows NT, version 3.51 or later)
- 256 color or better
- 486 SX/ 50 MHz or better
- 12 MB of available hard disk space
- 8 MB of memory (RAM)
- 16-bit sound card, plus headphones or speakers (microphone also recommended)

Making movies

Creating animation in 3D Movie Maker is a straightforward process, allowing younger users to create movies with ease. By default, 40 actors/actresses are available, each with 4 different costumes and a number of actions, as well as 20 different props. Eleven different scenes are available to the user, each containing several different camera angles. Many sample voice and MIDI music clips are included, but extra voices can be recorded using a microphone, and external wav and MIDI files can be imported.

The way movies are made in 3D Movie Maker is not like that of, for example, a video camera. A video camera works by recording images (frames) in quick succession. 3D Movie Maker stores the positions of the characters and objects for each frame. It moves at about 6 to 8 frames per second, which makes the movies choppier than expected.

The finished movie, however, can only be viewed inside 3D Movie Maker using the virtual auditorium or the studio, unless converted to a video file format with a third-party utility.

Expansions and utilities

3D Movie Maker has been discontinued for several years. Regardless, several user-made expansions and animation tools exist.

- 3DMM Animation Pro: (2002) Binds mouse movements to the keyboard, allowing directors to create more fluid movements on screen.
- Doraemon Expansion Pack: This pack, based on the Japanese character, was only released in Japan.
- 3DMM Expansion Pack: (2003) A user-created software patch, that introduced the first new textures, actors, and objects to the software since release.
- Virtual 3D Movie Maker (V3DMM): (2004) An expansion management program allowing users to include their own customized expansions in their movies and allow them to be freely distributed.
- 7gen: (2005) A GUI for creating V3DMM expansions.
- 3DMM Pencil++ 2: A program for editing 3D Movie Maker datafiles, allowing users to edit expansions.

- Nickelodeon Expansion pack: An unofficial expansion pack adds all the actors, props, textures, scenes, and sounds from Nickelodeon 3D Movie Maker. Download Demo [1]

See also

- Hollywood High
- Kahootz
- The Movies
- Theatrix's Hollywood
- Windows Movie Maker

External links

- 3dmm Community [2] - The main hub for discussing 3dmm, asking questions, releasing modifications, releasing films, and building hype for future films.
- Microsoft Nickelodeon 3D Movie Maker Trial download [1]
- Microsoft 3D Movie Maker Trial download [3]
- 3dmm Studio [4] - Movie archive and utilities for 3D Movie Maker.

Rapi:t

Rapi:t

rapi:t
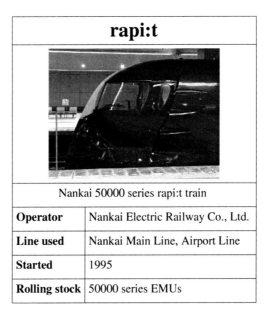
Nankai 50000 series rapi:t train

Operator	Nankai Electric Railway Co., Ltd.
Line used	Nankai Main Line, Airport Line
Started	1995
Rolling stock	50000 series EMUs

rapi:t (ラピート *rapiito*) is a rapid train service between Kansai International Airport and Namba Station in Osaka, Japan. It is operated by Nankai Electric Railway, and the train service uses on the Nankai Main Line and the Airport Line. The name comes from the German word *rapid*, pronounced German pronunciation: [ʁaˈpiːt].

The futuristic six-car *rapi:t* trainsets, officially designated as the Nankai 50000 series, were designed by architect Wakabayashi Hiroyuki and won the Blue Ribbon Prize after entering service in 1995.

Station Stops

There are two classes of *rapi:t* service. *rapi:t* β takes 34 minutes from Namba to Kansai Airport, stopping at Shin-Imamiya, Tengachaya, Sakai, Kishiwada, Izumisano, and Rinkū Town. *rapi:t* α takes 29 minutes, stopping at Shin-Imamiya, Tengachaya, Izumisano, and Rinku Town. Both trains cost ¥1,390 for a one-way ticket, ¥500 more than the normal rapid service train.

β trains operate every day, with a β train per hour from 7 a.m. until 10 a.m. and 2 β trains per hour from 10 a.m. until the last train on weekdays. There are only three α trains in the morning on weekdays (departing Namba for Kansai Airport at 7 o'clock a.m., 8 o'clock a.m. and 9 o'clock a.m.). On Saturdays and holidays, there are only 2 β trains per hour. All seats are reserved.

- rapi:t α: Namba Station - Shin-Imamiya Station - Tengachaya Station - Izumisano Station - Rinkū Town Station - Kansai Airport Station
- rapi:t β: Namba Station - Shin-Imamiya Station - Tengachaya Station - Sakai Station - Kishiwada Station - Izumisano Station - Rinkū Town Station - Kansai Airport Station

See also

- Haruka, limited-express service operated by JR West to Kansai Airport

External links

- Nankai official website [1]

Cheese-eating surrender monkeys

Cheese-eating surrender monkeys

"**Cheese-eating surrender monkeys**," sometimes shortened to "**surrender monkeys**," is a derogatory description of French people that was coined in 1995 by the writers of *The Simpsons*. It gained notoriety in the United States, particularly in the run-up to the Iraq War.

Origin

The phrase first appeared in an episode of *The Simpsons* entitled "'Round Springfield" (first aired on April 30, 1995). Groundskeeper Willie, the school janitor, is teaching French due to budget cuts, dressed in a striped shirt and a beret. In a heavy Scottish accent, he greets the class with "Bonjourrr, yah cheese-eatin' surrender monkeys!" According to the DVD commentary for the episode, the line was "most likely" written by Ken Keeler.

The "surrender" element of the phrase refers to the Anglo-American perception of the Battle of France as being virtually a "surrender" to Nazi Germany. This was again referenced in the episode "The Blunder Years", when Lenny (while scared) said, "I'm shaking like a French soldier!" It was also referenced in "The Trouble with Trillions", in which the aid plan to Europe is given "to our allies, who fought so poorly and surrendered so readily." The "cheese eating" element relates to the well known cheese production and consumption in France.

In the European French-language version of that *Simpsons* episode, Willie's line was dubbed as *"singes mangeurs de fromage"* (cheese-eating monkeys) without any mention of "surrender". The line does not translate easily because "surrender" forms part of an English compound noun. The rules of French syntax do not allow such ready formation of nouns by noun stem compounding.

Iraq War

The line was first picked up and used predominantly by Republican American politicians and publications. They were led, according to the British national newspaper *The Guardian*, by Jonah Goldberg, a columnist for the U.S. bi-weekly *National Review* and editor of their website National Review Online. Goldberg's online-only column, the G-File, is written in a more casual, personal manner and in the late 1990s often contained *Simpsons* (and other pop-cultural) references. Goldberg's repeated aggressive use of the phrase "cheese-eating surrender monkeys" led to its more widespread use amongst his readers, although Goldberg had stopped using it by the time the phrase was gaining mainstream popularity post-9/11.

The *New York Post* resurrected the phrase "Surrender Monkeys" as the headline for its December 7, 2006, front page, referring to the Iraq Study Group and its recommendation that U.S. combat brigades be withdrawn from Iraq by early 2008.

Correspondent Ed Helms from the Daily Show also used this expression when interviewing a US Congressman; when told this was not the most constructive way of critiquing the French, Helms offered the expression "truffle-shaving, fondue-dipping, bidet slurpers" as a possible substitute.

Use outside the United States

On another British TV show, *QI*, Graeme Garden turned the phrase around, referring to Americans as "Burger-eating invasion monkeys". The phrase "haggis-eating suspender monkey" was also used by Garden, as his character, Dougal, on an episode of radio programme *You'll Have Had Your Tea* to describe his friend Hamish, who is Scottish and was wearing ladies' clothing at the time. Also on QI Series F Episode 11 Emma Thompson called the French "cheese-eating surrender monkeys" when she found out that the French had called the British "lazy".

British TV show presenter Jeremy Clarkson described the Renault Clio V6 as a "surrender monkey" in terms of handling at its limits on BBC 2's *Top Gear*, and the Renault A610 Turbo as a "cheese-eating surrender monkey" on his DVD *Supercar Showdown*. Again, in series 10 of Top Gear, he described a panel of judges including Jay Leno, Carroll Shelby, and Jean-Michel Cousteau by "imitating" Shelby telling Cousteau "shut up Frenchie you cheese-eating surrender monkey." In his review of the Citroën C6, Clarkson questioned whether the car had become too sensible and German, and whether the cheese-eating surrender monkeys had bottled it.

See also

*   Tim Schultz
*   Anti-French sentiment in the United States
*   Freedom fries
*   Axis of weasels
*   Francophobia

References

*   "'Round Springfield" episode review and partial transcript [1] – *The Simpsons* Archive
*   References to France on *The Simpsons* [2] – *The Simpsons* Archive

Iori Yagami

Iori Yagami

Iori Yagami

Official *The King of Fighters XI* artwork for Iori Yagami	
Series	*The King of Fighters* series *SNK vs. Capcom* series
First game	*The King of Fighters '95* (1995)
Voiced by (English)	Eric Summerer (*Maximum Impact* series)
Voiced by (Japanese)	Kunihiko Yasui
Live action actor(s)	Will Yun Lee
Fictional information	
Birthplace	Japan
Fighting style	Yagami style of ancient martial arts

Iori Yagami (八神 庵 *Yagami Iori*) is a character from the SNK Playmore's *The King of Fighters* video game series that first appeared in *The King of Fighters '95* as the leader of the Rivals Team. He is an iconic character of the series, and regularly appears on publicity material and merchandise. Iori is a central character to the series' plot, and the initial enemy and eventual rival of Kyo Kusanagi. He was created specifically to become Kyo's rival as his name and abilities were designed to relate him with the *Yamata no Orochi* legend. The designers ended up liking him so much that they take care how his character is developed along the series.

Iori is the heir of the Yagami clan, who wield pyrokinetic powers and sealed the Orochi demon along with the Kusanagi and Yata clans. However, after betraying the Kusanagi clan, the Yagami are cursed by Orochi giving them powers that cause all members to die young. The character harbors hatred against the other clans, but later becomes obsessed to kill their heir Kyo. Due to that, Iori sometimes helps him in order to have the opportunity to have a final fight against him. Aside from the main series, Iori appears in several other media series such as spin-offs and crossover video games, and comic adaptations of the series.

Video games reviewers have praised the character as one of the most powerful characters from the series. Reviewers also noted Iori as one of the best characters from the games, labeling him as a veteran character and praising his appearance as one of the best creations of SNK. Within Gamest's 1997 Heroes Collection, Iori was voted as the staff's first favorite character. A variety of collectibles based on Iori's likeness have been created, including key chains and figurines.

Conception and creation

A main objective planned for *The King of Fighters '95* was to properly introduce Iori as Kyo's rival. Creators have stated Iori's personality and other aspects to his character "broke the mold for characters in fighting games at that time" commenting on his phrases and moves as unique. Like Kyo, several aspects of Iori, including his surname and abilities, were designed to relate him with the *Yamata no Orochi* legend, which was the inspiration for the plot. After observing initial location testing for *King of Fighters '95*, several staff members predicted that Iori would be popular on his release. Iori is a berserker due to the Orochi demon blood within him. This version of him, officially named "Orochi Iori", is hinted to exist before its debut in *The King of Fighters '97* as one of the game's mid bosses. This form of Iori was specifically designed to easily over power other characters. Series' flagship director, Toyohisa Tanabe, states that the staff was initially reluctant to add this version of Iori to the series' roster—worried about fans' reactions—but did so to add more impact to the Orochi saga's climax. He was particularly pleased to see surprised reactions from female fans to this form during KOF '97's location testing. Another minor development to his character was his change of "most valued possession/valued treasure" information. A girlfriend was also listed more than once, specifically in '95, '99, and 2000. However, starting in *KOF 2001* and every entry onwards, the space is listed as "None". The SNK staff commented that it is curious how he does not have a girlfriend anymore.

During the early development stages of *The King of Fighters '99*, SNK planned to exclude Iori and Kyo to the game, as the story's focus was meant to center on the new protagonist, K'. However, they retracted this decision because of the popularity of the characters. Iori's repeated appearances in the series is due to the marketers and main planners' insistence to add him, Kyo, and other SNK regulars in every game—making it a challenge to decide the story for each title. Because of his popularity amongst fans, some of the main designers for the series have stated that he is "difficult to draw for". Illustrator Shinkiro thought Iori as one of the series' most wild characters because of his hairstyle with similar sentiments being made by *Last Blade* illustrator, Tonko. Additionally, *KOF: Maximum Impact* producer, Falcoon, stated that attempting to change an "untouchable" design such as Iori's put him under severe pressure. He stated that designing Iori's alternate design that appears in the *Maximum Impact* series almost felt "unforgivable", as he felt unsure of fans' reaction to the change.

Attributes

Iori is a violent and sadistic person who suffers from trauma due to the past of his clan. In ancient times, the Yagami clan was known as the Yasakani. With the help of the Yata and Kusanagi clans, they sealed the demon Orochi. As time passed, the Yasakani, tired of living in the shadow of the Kusanagi, made a blood pact with Orochi. This gave them greater powers, but in return, they and their descendants were forever cursed. They renamed their clan the Yagami and set out to destroy the Kusanagi with their new powers. In response, the Kusanagi declared war on the Yagami, which led to many clan members on both sides being killed.

As a side-effect of the Orochi's curse, the flames of the Yagami have a bluish tint. The curse also causes each heir to die young and each mother to die in childbirth. Iori suffers from an additional curse named "The Riot of the Blood" (血の暴走 *Chi no Bōso*) in which he becomes more powerful, wilder, and tends to indiscriminately attack anybody near him. In this state Iori is commonly named "Wild Iori" or "Orochi Iori" (ツキノヨルオロチノチニクルフイオリ *Tsuki no Yoru Orochi no Chi ni Kurufu Iori*). Due to this curse, Iori hates the Kusanagi clan, but later becomes obsessed to kill their heir Kyo, disregarding their clans' past. This sometimes results in Iori helping him to defeat his enemies to finish their battle. In order to find him, he sometimes enters the *The King of Fighters* tournaments and uses his teammates as tools in order to get to him. Iori appears in most of the games from the series, and is voiced by Kunihiko Yasui.

Appearances

In video games

First appearing in *The King of Fighters '95*, Iori enters the annual tournament as the leader of the Rival Team (composed of he, Billy Kane and Eiji Kisaragi) as he learns that the heir of the Kusanagi clan, Kyo, is expected to be there. However, the team fails to defeat the Kyo's team and Iori betrays his teammates. In the next video game, Iori teams up with two women, Vice and Mature, servants of the Orochi demon. The same team would be repeated in *KOF '98*, *KOF 2002*, and *Neowave, games which do not feature a storyline. During the '96 competition, Iori meets Chizuru Kagura, heir of the Yata clan, who wants to gather Kyo and Iori in her team to seal Orochi. Together they defeat the Orochi follower Goenitz but neither Iori and Kyo agree with the idea. When Iori leaves with his teammates, he is unable to control this surge of Orochi power, resulting in their deaths. Iori continued to suffer from multiple outbreaks and during* The King of Fighters '97, *attacks other team members. As such, Iori appears as a sub-boss character on the game depending on the characters that the player use. Immediately after entering his cursed form again, Iori finds himself along with Chizuru and Kyo confronted by the three last servants of Orochi, who are meant to revive him. When they are defeated, Orochi awakes in the body of one of his followers, but he is defeated and sealed by Iori's group.*

In *The King of Fighters '99* Iori is a secret character in most versions of the game. Iori can be faced as a bonus fight in the end of the game if the player manages to get a high score. In the story, Iori discovers the creation of clones of Kyo and enters the annual tournament where he finds those responsible, an organization named Nests. Iori follows the battles in secret and fights against the Nests agents to continue his fight against Kyo. An assistant version of his character (named Striker) also appears for Iori in *The King of Fighters 2000* but with an outfit based on his illustrations from artbooks. In *The King of Fighters 2001*, an agent named Seth invites Iori to join his team for the next *King of Fighters* tournament, under the presumption that he would get his shot against Kyo. In *The King of Fighters 2003*, Chizuru appears to both Kyo and Iori, requesting that they form a team and investigate suspicious activities concerning the Orochi seal. During the investigation, the team is ambushed by the fighter Ash Crimson who plans to get the power the descendants of the clans who sealed Orochi and steals the ones from Chizuru. In the following video game, Iori and Kyo form a team once again with Kyo's student Shingo Yabuki to fill Chizuru's spot to stop Ash. At the end of the tournament, the strengthening presence of Orochi causes Iori to enter the Riot of Blood state, in which he attacks Kyo and Shingo. Ash Crimson appears afterward and defeats Iori, stealing his powers. Iori is a playable character in *The King of Fighters XII*. Iori is featured with a different outfit and with a new moveset that does not use purple flames. Like each character, he does not have a team. Iori's appearance in *The King of Fighters XIII* sees him teamed with his former team members from the 1996 tournament, Mature and Vice, who return as spirits.

In *The King of Fighters: Kyo*, a role-playing game situated before *KOF '97*, Iori appears as an antagonist to Kyo in his journey around the world. Iori appears in the spin-off video games *Maximum Impact* series. In the North American editions of *Maximum Impact*, Iori is voiced by Eric Summerer. Iori also appears as a sub-boss during *The King of Fighters Ex: Neo Blood*, which is situated after his fight against Orochi. Although Iori enters the tournament to fight Kyo, Geese Howard, the organizer of the tournament, tries to make him awake his Riot of the Blood to absorb his powers, but Iori avoids doing it. In *The King of Fighters EX2: Howling Blood*, Iori enters another tournament, and is joined by Miu Kuroaaki and Jun Kagami, two women who want to find Miu's brother, who is being controlled by the Orochi power. He will also be playable in the upcoming shooter game *KOF: Sky Stage*.

Iori also appears in SNK's hand-held game, *SNK Gals' Fighters*, as a comical interpretation called Miss X (ミス X *Misu Ekusu*). The character insists he is a female to participate in the game's *Queen of Fighters* tournament, though several female fighters easily see through his disguise. In the crossover video games *NeoGeo Battle Coliseum* and *SNK vs. Capcom* series, Iori appears as a playable character; the latter includes his Riot of the Blood state. His character is also a boss character (along with Geese) in the GameBoy version from *Real Bout Fatal Fury Special*.

In other media

Aside from the *King of Fighters* series, the character is featured in his own drama CD and character image album. In the anime *The King of Fighters: Another Day*, Iori is seen searching for Ash to regain his powers. Iori appears in the spin-off manga story based on his adventure in *The King of Fighters '96* entitled, *The King of Fighters: Kyo*. The character appears in the manhua adaptation of *The King of Fighters: Zillion* created by Andy Seto. The manhua retells Iori's story from his fight against Orochi until he attacks NESTS to destroy Kyo's clones. He also stars in further manhua for the games, starting in *The King of Fighters 2001* through *2003* along with the *Maximum Impact* series. In the upcoming *The King of Fighters* movie Iori will be played by Will Yun Lee.

Reception

Iori's character mostly receives good reception from several video game publications and other media. IGN considered him as the one of the most useful characters from the games and one of the best ones for the "veteran players". In another review, they praised Iori's appearance in *KOF: Maximum Impact* as one of the best designs from the game, but complained his lack of bloody scenes considering his action in previous games. The character's ending in *The King of Fighters '97* has been considered by 1UP.com as one of the strangest parts of the story. However, they considered his winning quotes and appearance as one of the bests creations of SNK. Eurogamer praised Iori, along with Kyo, as having one of the most unpredictable appearances in the series, and considered him a veteran character. In the top ten fighting games from Gametrailers, Iori has been noted to be one of the main innovators figures from the series, having liked his introduction in *The King of Fighters '95* and his development through the following games. His new design from *The King of Fighters XII* has not been well received by 1UP.com writer Richard Li; Li complained about the lack from Iori's signature moves such as his fireballs and while some of them remained, Li noted that they now require a different input from the one they normally require.

In an interview with Iori's Japanese voice actor, Kunihiko Yasui comments that he feels responsible as a voice actor for his performances as Iori, taking care to sound different in each installment as a means of developing and "protecting" his character's humanity. Iori has been highly popular within video gamers. In Gamest's 1996 Heroes Collection, Iori was at no. 2 in the poll "Best Character from 1996." In the issue from 1997, Iori was voted as the staff's favorite character, claiming first place out of fifty other characters. He also received the same rank on Neo Geo Freak's website with a total of 3,792 votes. In a 2005 poll made by SNK-Playmore USA, he was voted as the eighth fan favorite character with 145 votes. Merchandising based on Iori has also been released including figurines, key-chains and puzzles.

See also

- List of *The King of Fighters* video games

External links

- The King of Fighters 10th Anniversary Official Website [1]

Josta

Josta

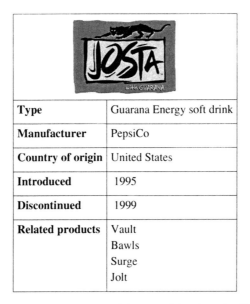

Type	Guarana Energy soft drink
Manufacturer	PepsiCo
Country of origin	United States
Introduced	1995
Discontinued	1999
Related products	Vault Bawls Surge Jolt

Josta was a soft drink brand that was produced by PepsiCo. Josta's flavor has been described as predominately fruity, with a hint of spice and a touch of the key ingredient guaraná. It was marketed as a "high-energy drink" with guaraná and caffeine.

Josta was introduced in 1995, but PepsiCo pulled the drink from its lineup due to a change in corporate strategy in 1999. Shortly before the beverage was discontinued, an "Association for Josta Saving" was started. A "Save Josta" campaign was also launched by fans of the drink; their website "www.savejosta.com" is now defunct.

The introduction of this soft drink in Brazilian market has been a complete failure; Max Gehringer , responsible for developing the brand in the country, said that this is due to the association of the word Josta with Bosta, a portuguese translation for Shit.

Ryuji Yamazaki

Ryuji Yamazaki

Ryuji Yamazaki

Ryuji Yamazaki in *The King of Fighters 2003*	
Series	*Fatal Fury* series *The King of Fighters* series *SNK vs. Capcom* series
First game	*Fatal Fury 3: Road to the Final Victory* (1995)
Voiced by	Kōji Ishii
Fictional information	
Birthplace	Okinawa, Japan
Blood type	A
Fighting style	Deadly Brawling Arts

Ryuji Yamazaki (リュージ・ヤマザキ 山崎 竜二 *Yamazaki Ryūji*) is a video game character appearing in *Fatal Fury* series and *The King of Fighters* developed by SNK Playmore (formerly known as SNK). Yamazaki is first introduced as the sub-boss character of *Fatal Fury 3: Road to the Final Victory*, where he is a criminal known as "Dark Broker". In the game Yamazaki hired by the Jin brothers into recovering their sacred scrolls able to give immortality to its user. In following titles from the series Yamazaki does not work for anybody, normally making crimes just to entertain himself. He has also become a character from *The King of Fighters*, in which participates in the annual tournaments from some games being hired by the Southtown crime lord Geese Howard.

Yamazaki's introduction in *The King of Fighters* series was made as a result of three popularity polls developed by three video games journals in which players voted which character they wanted to see in *The King of Fighters '97*, the upcoming game from the series at that time. Yamazaki has also appeared in the crossover games *Capcom vs. SNK: Millennium Fight 2000* and *Capcom vs. SNK 2* as a playable character. Video games publications have commented on Yamazaki's character, with some praising his introduction in *Fatal Fury 3* and development in titles from *The King of Fighters*. However, other reviewers criticized how hard defeating him is in the *Fatal Fury* games and how strong he is in

Capcom vs. SNK: Millennium Fight 2000 in comparison to other popular characters.

Character design

Yamazaki has black hair, but above his forehead it is blonde. He has a total of two outfits, both with black clothes. Before fighting and in cutscenes, Yamazaki sports a white fur coat which covers almost all his body. In *Fatal Fury 3: Road to the Final Victory*, Yamazaki wears a black t-shirt with short sleeves and black pants. He also sports gloves which do not cover his finger and shoes, both of the same color. He also appears with this outfit in all the games from the *Fatal Fury* series, the *SNK vs. Capcom* series and *The King of Fighters 2003*. *The King of Fighters '97* and all the other games from the same series except *KOF 2003* show Yamazaki with a black shirt which also covers his neck. He also sports a black sleeveless jacket which covers his shirt.

Attributes

Yamazaki was raised in Okinawa after and which he developed while growing up on the streets alone fighting against sailors during his teenage years, then as an enforcer for a criminal mob. In contrast with most of the other fighters in combat video games, Yamazaki does not use any particular martial art - he is a self-taught brawler, and uses a wide variety of attacks in his fighting, including unfair and dishonest moves such as kicking sand in his opponent's eyes, and his ever-present knife. He also rarely takes his right hand out of his pocket unless he is using his knife. In order to adapt him to *KOF*, the game planner had to provide new moves to Yamazaki. The new moves were initially noted to be failures, but designers later thought of them as successful. Yamazaki is a very sadistic person who enjoys violence as well as injuring people and making them bleed. However, he normally hides this madness with a calmer and more confident personality which he has when he is not fighting. As a criminal, Yamazaki started a rivalry with the Hong Kong detective Hon Fu, who becomes determinted to arrest Yamazaki, while Yamazaki does not want to be arrested by him.

Appearances

Starring in *Fatal Fury 3: Road to the Final Victory*, Yamazaki is hired by the Jin brothers to help them search for the Secret Scrolls of the Jin in order to obtain immortality. He appears after as a mid-boss character to have one round after the player fights four fights. After six fights, Yamazaki will have a full battle against the player as a sub-boss or final boss depending on the grade average from the player. In the following game, *Real Bout Fatal Fury*, he competes in the tournament King of Fighters in order to obtain the Jin scrolls for himself. Although a regularly selectable playable character, Yamazaki is one of three final opponents the players face against the CPU. He also appears in *Real Bout Fatal Fury Special* and *Real Bout Fatal Fury 2: The Newcomers* as a regular character. Despite not being featured in the first *Fatal Fury* game, Yamazaki was added to the 3D game *Fatal Fury: Wild Ambition*, which retells the events from such game, with Yamazaki being against the boss Geese Howard.

Yamazaki would appear in *The King of Fighters* series as a member of the '97 Special Team in *The King of Fighters '97*, along Blue Mary and Billy Kane. In the backstory of the game, the three fighters are arranged into the same team due to the manipulations of Geese Howard. The game also establishes Yamazaki as one Eight Heralds of the Orochi Clan. However, Yamazaki has no interest in serving Orochi, engaging the other Heralds in combat. In order to have all of the eight servants from Orochi confirmed by this game, Yamazaki was chosen to be the new member as the staff noted him to be a good villain and liked that he was similar to a snake (as the ancient Orochi was a giant snake). Although the '97 Special Team was disbanded in the storyline at end of *KOF '97*, the team would be featured in later "Dream Match" (games without storylines) installments in the series such as *The King of Fighters '98*, *The King of Fighters 2002* and *The King of Fighters Neowave*. Ryuji and Billy would also return in *The King of Fighters 2003*, only this time they team up with Gato (from *Garou: Mark of the Wolves*) and forms the "Outlaw Team" in order to conquer Southtown. Although he is not playable in other games from the series, Yamazaki appears as an assistant character (dubbed as "Striker") in *The King of Fighters '99: Evolution* and *The King of Fighters 2000*. While in the former he appears as a Striker for every character, in the latter he is the "Another Striker" for Blue Mary. He is also a recurring opponent in the spin-off *The King of Fighters: Kyo*, normally allying with the Orochi servant Yashiro Nanakase into attacking the lead character Kyo Kusanagi although Yamazaki is only interested in fighting. His character was also added to the crossover game *Capcom vs. SNK: Millennium Fight 2000* and its sequel, *Capcom vs. SNK 2*, developed by Capcom.

Yamazaki is also featured in the volume 7 from the soundtracks series *SNK Character Sounds Collection* released by Pony Canyon. The CD features several songs based on his character such as monologues and soundstracks from the games in which he appeared. He also appears in *The King of Fighters 2003* manwhua adaptation authored by Wing Yan, fighting against Ash Crimson prior to the 2003 tournament, but he is interrupted by Geese. In the tournament, however, the Outlaw Team is defeated by Ash's team.

Reception

The character of Yamazaki has been well-received by gamers from the games in which he appears, having ranked high in popularity polls from various journals. In Gamest's 1997 Heroes Collection, Yamazaki was voted as the staff's fifteenth favorite character. He shared the spot with *Samurai Shodown* character, Galford, and *Street Fighter* character, Ken. In order to decide who would become the members of the '97 Special Team from *The King of Fighters '97*, three polls were conducted by the videogames journals Famitsu, Gamest and Neo Geo freak, in which readers voted who was the character they wanted to see in the team. Yamazaki was Famitsu's winner. Additionally, the three journal created a team, which players can view an image of them after beating the game in the Japanese port. The Famitsu created a team composed of Chang Koehan, Choi Bounge and Yamazaki. Shane

Bettenhausen, Ignition Entertainment's Director of Business Development, commented that Yamazaki is one of his favourites characters from *The King of Fighters* series, and would have liked he appeared in the latest game, *The King of Fighters XII*.

His character has also received mixed reviews from video game publications. Kurt Kalata from Armchairempire.com praised Yamazaki's introduction in *Fatal Fury 3* as one of the best ones from the game. He also liked his character and considered him as a good replacement for the ones who were removed from that game. William Usher from Cinemablend.com found Yamazaki to be his favourite character out of *The King of Fighters* series. He also liked Yamazaki's development in *The King of Fighters*, additionally noting him to be one of the most popular new characters in *Fatal Fury 3*. Gamezone reviewer Eduardo Zacarias noted Yamazaki to be one of the "powerhouses" from the *Fatal Fury* series due to how difficult is to defeat him in a similar way to the other boss Geese Howard. In contrast to this Jeremy Dunham from IGN noted that Yamazaki's ratio of three over four (a rank given to character at the time of playing with various of them) in *Capcom vs. SNK: Millennium Fight 2000* was "absurd" as other characters who have good movesets in the game like Benimaru Nikaido or Blanka from *Street Fighter II* had only one ratio.

External links

- Fatal Fury 15th Anniversary Official Website [1] (Japanese)
- The King of Fighters 10th Anniversary Official Website [1]

French Toast Crunch

French Toast Crunch

French Toast Crunch is a breakfast cereal launched in 1995 artificially flavoured to taste like French toast, by the General Mills company.

The cereal pieces originally looked like mini slices of French toast, but General Mills changed the cereal to a style similar in appearance to Cinnamon Toast Crunch; a thin, wavy square sprinkled with flavoring.

In 2006, General Mills discontinued French Toast Crunch in the United States. French Toast Crunch is still produced and marketed in Canada as "French Toast Crunch" and "Croque pain doré." Canadian French Toast Crunch is made in the original recipe and form (mini slices)

External links

- General Mills Website [1]
- General Mills Introduces French Toast Crunch [2]

.ci

.ci

Introduced	1995
TLD type	Country code top-level domain
Status	Active
Registry	Network Information Center - Côte d'Ivoire
Sponsor	Institut National Polytechnique Felix Houphouet Boigny
Intended use	Entities connected with ▌ ▌ Côte d'Ivoire
Actual use	Gets some use in Cote d'Ivoire
Registration restrictions	Name must match official name of company, organization, or trademark
Structure	Registrations are made directly at the second level, or at third level beneath some second-level labels
Documents	Charte de nommage [1]
Website	nic.ci [2]

.ci is the Internet country code top-level domain (ccTLD) for Côte d'Ivoire.

External links

- IANA .ci whois information [3]
- .ci domain registration website [2]

krc:.ci

Dippin' Dots

Dippin' Dots

Type	Private
Industry	Retail
Founded	Lexington, Kentucky (1995)
Headquarters	Paducah, Kentucky, U.S.
Website	www.dippindots.com [1]

Dippin' Dots is an ice cream snack, invented by Southern Illinois University graduate Curt Jones in 1987. The confection is created by flash freezing ice cream mix in liquid nitrogen; consequently, Dippin' Dots contain less air than conventional ice cream. The resulting small spheres of ice cream are stored at temperatures ranging from -70 to -20 °F (from -57 °C to -29 °C). The marketing slogan is **"Ice Cream of the Future"**. The snack is made by Dippin' Dots, Inc., headquartered in Paducah, Kentucky.

The company, headquartered in Paducah, Ky, United States, only recently began selling its product in stores such as supermarkets in the United States. On its official website, the company notes that its product requires storage at temperatures below -20 °F (about -29 °C), which is considerably colder than standard home freezers. Dippin' Dots are sold in individual servings at franchised outlets, many in stadiums, shopping malls, and in vending machines. Many theme parks such as Schlitterbahn, Six Flags, Cedar Point, PARC Management, Kennywood, SeaWorld, stadiums and arenas also sell Dippin' Dots. The ice cream is also sold over the Internet for delivery to homes and businesses.

Dippin' Dots Flavored Ice Cream

Several competing beaded ice-cream lines have been introduced in recent years. Some of these competing brands are similar to Dippin' Dots in shape or size, yet differ in that they use dairy stabilizers and artificial sweeteners, in an effort to keep the beads from adhering to one another. Dippin' Dots, made from conventional ice cream ingredients, are held at sub-zero temperatures to keep the beads separate and free-flowing.

The company has a line of novelties called Dot Delicacies made by combining the Dippin' Dots ice cream with other snack foods. A **dotwich** is an ice cream sandwich made by combining Dippin' Dots and fudge and placing between two cookies. Milk shakes, sundaes and ice cream floats are also sold at many locations. The company also has a line of ice cream cakes sold only at its franchised retail stores.

Dippin' Dots Franchising, LLC is the franchise division of the company. The company sells franchise rights to sell Dippin' Dots ice cream at retail stores in the U.S.

Dippin' Dots Global, Inc. represents the company in select markets outside the U.S. and its territories. Dippin' Dots are produced in Seoul, South Korea, for distribution throughout the Pacific Rim. The company maintains a distribution center in Melbourne, Australia as well.

Dippin' Dots were patented, but the patent was ruled invalid in February 2007. The jury found for the

Amusement park stand, Valleyfair amusement park, Shakopee, Minnesota.

Dippin' Dots Amusement Park Stand in Cedar Point of Sandusky, Ohio.

defendants more on the validity of the original patent than on the actual infringement accusations. The jury's decision was primarily based on a finer point of patent law. The defense alleged that Jones attempted patent fraud by not disclosing that he sold the ice cream more than a year before applying for the patent, despite IRS instruction that Jones' sales were done for research purposes only. The litigation continues to be in the appeals process.

Dippin' Dots, as the originators of the beaded ice cream concept, are featured quite often in the media. The ice cream has been featured on the Oprah Winfrey show, Food TV, and The Travel Channel. It was featured on *Gene Simmons Family Jewels* on A&E Network. Dippin' Dots was recently the title sponsor for the "Celebrity Grand Slam Paddle Jam" celebrity ping pong tournament in Hollywood. Proceeds went to benefit St. Jude Children's Research Hospital in Memphis, Tennessee. The company is also a contributor to the charity Give Kids the World Village in Kissimmee, Florida. The show "Modern Marvels" recently included Dippin' Dots in their segment on the history and future of ice cream. Dippin' Dots most recently collaborated with the newest adaptation of Journey to the Center of the Earth, awarding the winner a trip to Iceland, the location of the film.

On December 19, 2008, the company made an announcement that it is exploring the option of combining resources with another, unknown company. The spokesperson for the company stated "Dippin' Dots will continue to take orders and ship product as we have for the past twenty years". The Dippin' Dots Franchising, Inc. brand earned rank 112 on the Entrepreneur "Franchise 500" in 2008.

External links

- Official Website [2]

NV1

NV1

Nvidia NV1 / STG2000	
Codename(s)	NV1
Release date	1995
Direct3D and shader version	none

Nvidia NV1, manufactured by SGS-THOMSON Microelectronics under the model name STG2000, was a multimedia PCI card released in 1995 and sold to retail as the Diamond Edge 3D. It featured a complete 2D/3D graphics core based upon quadratic texture mapping, VRAM or FPM DRAM memory, an integrated 32-channel 350 MIPS playback-only sound card, and a Sega Saturn compatible joypad port. As such, it was intended to replace the 2D graphics card, Sound Blaster-compatible audio solutions, and 15-pin joystick ports, then prevalent on IBM PC compatibles.

Several Saturn games were converted to NV1 on the PC such as Panzer Dragoon and Virtua Fighter Remix. However, the NV1 struggled in a market place full of several competing proprietary standards, and was marginalised by emerging polygon-based 2D/3D accelerators such as the low-cost S3 Graphics ViRGE, Matrox Mystique, ATI Rage, and Rendition Vérité V1000 among other early entrants.

NV1's biggest initial problem was its cost and overall quality. Although it offered credible 3D performance, its use of quadratic surfaces was anything but popular, and was quite different than typical polygon rendering. The audio portion of the card was of questionable quality, receiving ratings of merely acceptable quality in reviews, with the General MIDI quality receiving lukewarm responses at best (a critical component at the time). The Sega Saturn console was a market failure compared to Sony's PlayStation, and so the unique and somewhat limiting support of these gamepads was

Diamond EDGE 3D 3400

of limited benefit. Nvidia, by integrating all of these usually separate components, raised their costs considerably above what they would have been if the card had been designed solely for 3D acceleration.

During the NV1's release timeframe, the transition from VLB/ISA (486s) to PCI (Pentiums) was taking place, and games often used MIDI for music because PCs were still generally incapable of large-scale digital audio playback due to storage and processing power limitations. Reaching for the best music and sound quality, and flexibility with MS-DOS audio standards, often required 2 sound cards be used, or a sound card with a MIDI daughtercard connector. Additionally, NV1's 2D speed and quality were not competitive with many of the high-end solutions available at the time, especially the then-critical-for-games DOS graphics speed. Many consumers were simply not interested in replacing their often-elaborate system setups with an expensive all-in-one board and so the heavy integration of NV1 hurt sales simply through inconvenience.

Market interest in the product quickly ended when Microsoft announced the DirectX specifications, based upon polygon rendering. This release by Microsoft of a major industry-backed API that was generally incompatible with NV1 ended Nvidia's hopes of market leadership immediately. While demos of quadratic rendered round spheres looked good, experience had proved working with quadratic texture maps was extremely difficult. Even calculating simple routines such as collision detection was problematic. Nvidia

Diamond EDGE 3D 2120

did manage to put together limited Direct3D support, but it was slow and buggy (software-based), and no match for the native polygon hardware on the market.

Subsequent NV1 quadratic-related development continued internally as the NV2.

3D games that supported NV1

- Nascar Racing
- Panzer Dragoon
- Virtua Fighter Remix
- Virtua Cop

Retail products

- Aztech
  - 3D Galaxy
- Diamond Multimedia
  - EDGE 3D 2120
  - EDGE 3D 2200
  - EDGE 3D 3240
  - EDGE 3D 3400
- Genoa Systems
  - Stratos 3D

- Jazz Multimedia
  - 3D Magic
- Leadtek
  - WinFast Proview 3D GD400
  - WinFast Proview 3D GD500
- Videoforte
  - VF64-3DG-01
  - VF64-3DG-02
- YUAN
  - JRS-3DS100

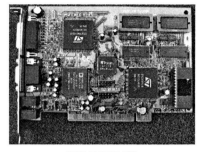

YUAN 3DS-100

See also

- Comparison of Nvidia graphics processing units

References

- "EDGE 3D 3000 Series" [1]. Diamond Multimedia. Archived from the original [2] on 1996-12-19.
- Thomas Monk (December 26, 2006). "7 Years of Graphics" [3]. accelenation.com. Retrieved 2008-06-15.
- Alan Dang (February 16, 2001). "NVIDIA NV2 Report—1995: The launch of the NV1" [4]. FiringSquad. Retrieved 2008-06-15.

Alec Trevelyan

Alec Trevelyan

'006' redirects here. For other uses, see 006 (disambiguation).

Alec Trevelyan (Janus)	
Character from the *James Bond* franchise	
Occupation	Head of Janus (Former MI6 operative)
Affiliation	Janus
Portrayed by	Sean Bean

Alexander "Alec" Trevelyan (**006**), also known as **Janus**, is a fictional character and the main antagonist in the 1995 James Bond film *GoldenEye*, portrayed by actor Sean Bean. The likeness of Bean as Alec Trevelyan was also used for the 1997 video game, *GoldenEye 007*.

Film Biography

Character Information

Once known as **Agent 006** under the employment of Her Majesty's Secret Service, Trevelyan betrays MI6 during a mission to blow up the Arkhangelsk chemical weapons facility in the Soviet Union while working with his close friend, James Bond (Pierce Brosnan). During the operation, Trevelyan is caught and apparently executed by the base's commander, Colonel Arkady Ourumov (Gottfried John). Presuming Trevelyan dead, Bond continues the mission and escapes aboard a supply plane.

Nine years later, Bond's pursuit of a stolen helicopter and investigation of an explosion at Severnaya leads him to Saint Petersburg, where he learns from Valentin Zukovsky (Robbie Coltrane) that "Janus", the head of the crime syndicate responsible for the theft, is a Lienz Cossack. Later, when he finally meets Janus, Bond is shocked to discover Trevelyan, who staged his execution at Archangelsk and now employs Ourumov, now a General in The Russian Army. Trevelyan's face is scarred from the explosion at the weapons factory, a direct result of Bond changing the sequence detonation timers.

Trevelyan reveals that his motive for his betrayal is a personal one. His parents were Lienz Cossacks who had collaborated with the Nazis but attempted to defect to the British at the end of World War II. When The British instead sent them back to the USSR, many were executed by Stalin's execution squads. Though Alec's parents survived, his father, ashamed to have lived, killed his wife and himself. At the time, Alec was only six years old. He was then transported to the United Kingdom and was taken in by MI6, who issued him the new surname Trevelyan, chosen because it had origins in the British Isles (specifically Cornwall) but bore coincidental phonetic similarities to Armenian and other southeastern European surnames. MI6 continued to sponsor his training and education throughout his childhood, and he began formal work for the British government upon attaining his majority, in order to set revenge against the British government for his family's demise.

Scheme

Trevelyan's scheme begins with the theft of the experimental Tiger helicopter from the French frigate *La Fayette* docked in Monte Carlo, using his two primary operatives, Ourumov and Xenia Onatopp (Famke Janssen). With the helicopter, the two fly to the GoldenEye satellite facility in Severnaya, where they murder the staff and steal the access disk and keys for the GoldenEye satellite and program the satellite to target the facility. The GoldenEye satellite, actually two disposable satellites named *Petya* and *Mischa*, are capable of emitting targeted electromagnetic pulses capable of destroying any machinery with an electronic signal. As *Petya* destroys the Severnaya facility, Ourumov and Onatopp escape aboard the Tiger helicopter, which is insulated against electromagnetic radiation.

Mischa would then be used to aid Trevelyan in stealing hundreds of millions of pounds via computer from the Bank of England in London, and erasing all evidence of the transaction. *Mischa* would destroy the city, crippling the British economy and government, triggering a catastrophic currency crisis, and causing global stock market and economic chaos. Trevelyan, having obtained the only valuable currency of pounds sterling, could have economic supremacy over the British and the world in an era of terrorism for decades. Before doing so he states "England is about to learn the cost of betrayal. Inflation adjusted for 1945."

Bond stops this scheme with the help of former Severnaya technician Natalya Simonova (Izabella Scorupco) and CIA agent Jack Wade (Joe Don Baker), Wade helping Bond and Natalya track Trevelyan's headquarters and Natalya subsequently programming the GoldenEye satellite to crash after resetting the access codes. While Bond is running across the cradle to disable the GoldenEye antenna, Trevelyan starts chasing him. In the subsequent fight, Trevelyan finally gets the better of Bond- mockingly saying as he prepares to shoot his former ally "You know, James, I was always better"-, and is about to shoot him when Bond kicks a ladder releasing it, and carrying Bond to the bottom of a satellite antenna, suspended high above the dish. Trevelyan then climbs down to Bond, who slips and is just able to stay on the tiny platform. Bond eventually knocks Trevelyan off the antenna, but reflexively grabs him by the legs, the last vestige of their friendship. While hanging, Trevelyan smugly asks Bond, "For England, James?" to which Bond replies, "No, for me." Bond then lets go, and Trevelyan falls all the way down to the dish, but survives the fall, albeit badly wounded. The antenna array, due to Bond's sabotage, explodes and collapses in a fiery wreck onto a screaming Trevelyan, crushing him to death.

Production facts

Trevelyan is the only 00 agent (other than Bond himself) to have a main character role in a Bond movie which includes a sizeable screen and speaking time. The only other 00 agent to have any amount of screentime is 009 in *Octopussy*, portrayed by stuntman Andy Bradford. Besides seeing the back of their heads or before they are shortly killed and/or dead already (*Thunderball*, *The Living Daylights*, and *A View to a Kill*, respectively), other 00 agents are rarely seen and only spoken of. Bean auditioned, and was considered for the role of Bond (*see List of actors considered for the James Bond character*).

Max Cunningham

Max Cunningham

Max Cunningham	
Hollyoaks character	
Portrayed by	Ben Sheriff (1995–96) Matt Littler (1996–2008)
Created by	Phil Redmond
Duration	1995–2008
First appearance	6 November 1995
Last appearance	11 July 2008
Classification	Former; regular
Profile	
Date of birth	20 March 1982
Occupation	Co-owner of MOBS

	Family
Wife	Clare Devine (2006–07) Steph Dean (2008)
Father	Gordon Cunningham
Mother	Angela Cunningham
Sisters	Dawn Cunningham Cindy Cunningham Jude Cunningham
Half brothers	Tom Cunningham
Nieces	Bethany Cunningham Holly Cunningham
Other relatives	Benny Cunningham

Max Cunningham is a fictional character from the British Channel 4 soap opera *Hollyoaks*, played by Matt Littler. From 1995 to 1996, Max was portrayed by Ben Sheriff before Littler took over. In 2008, Max, along with Tony Hutchinson (Nick Pickard), was the longest running character in *Hollyoaks*. In May 2008, it was announced that Littler had decided to leave the show and would depart in August 2008.

Character creation

The character of Max first appeared in 1995 as one of the original *Hollyoaks* characters. At this time, he was played by actor, Ben Sheriff. In 1996, after only a year on the show, *Hollyoaks* producer Phil Redmond decided to recast the character, where he found Matt Littler. Littler spoke of playing an already established character stating: "I didn't really watch it much, so it didn't really affect me" and also revealed he had met with Sheriff and his career was fine post filming. Littler followed the role for almost twelve years until his decision to leave the show in 2008.

Development

Family deaths

Max found himself surrounded by death, with older sister Dawn died of leukaemia. His stepbrother Lewis committed suicide in 2001. His death made Max look at life in a different way, deciding to spend less time with OB and open a new business, a burger van. Max also began dating Jodie Nash, however it was soon over. In 2004, Max saw more misery when his father Gordon and stepmother

Helen were killed in a car crash. Max took it upon himself to raise younger half brother Tom. In 2006, another death hit the family, this time Max's step niece Grace Hutchinson, who died to suspected Sudden Infant Death Syndrome. With the four deaths, Max decided to live his life to the full rather than not get to live in at all. Max then met and fell in love with Clare Devine.

Marriage to Clare

Max found himself engaged to Clare Devine, who he had previously hired as an event organiser for The Loft. OB saw through gold-digging Clare and tried to tell Max. Max and OB ended up falling out over Clare. After Max suffered a heart attack, Clare took it upon herself to make sure he never recovered. She started tampering with his pills. During Christmas in a secluded cottage, Max found out that Clare had tampered with his pills and realised OB was right about her. Clare had put Tom's jacket in an icy lake outside, which made Max jump in. Clare the revealed Tom was in no danger as he was not in the lake. Luckily, OB turned up and rescued Max.

Clare called the social services and told them Max was hurting Tom, and also told Tom that he was the cause of his parents and Grace's deaths and if he spoke to Max, Max would die. Clare, who had built up many enemies in Hollyoaks, was pushed over a balcony at The Loft and was left for dead. Max and OB were two of the suspects, however Max's name was soon cleared. Max made a visit to a recovering Clare at her home and threatened her, telling her if she did not tell the social services she made Max's abuse of Tom up, he would kill her. Clare then agreed. Clare was forced out of Hollyoaks, however kidnapped Katy Fox. Max, Warren Fox and Justin Burton followed Clare to save her. A high speed car chase led to Clare and Katy plummeting over a quarry into water below. Warren and Justin jumped in to save Katy. Max then leapt in to save Clare, even though she had repeatedly tried to kill him. Under the water, Max tried to save Clare who was pulled away by the current and apparently drowned. Back in Hollyoaks, Max had a heart to heart with Steph Dean, who told Max it was not his fault Clare had died.

Second love

Max and Steph grew closer and eventually found themselves in love. The pair found themselves breaking up on several occasions. Steph then embarked on a relationship with Niall Rafferty, however, realising she loved Max, ended it and got back with Max. Max and Steph then announced their engagement. Matt Littler made the decision to leave the show after eleven years. Speaking of his decision to leave, Littler stated, "I feel that I have grown up on *Hollyoaks* over the past eleven years and I'm not only leaving behind friends but also family. I wouldn't change a second of my time at *Hollyoaks* and working with Darren Jon Jefferies has been amazing – every second of it! I'd just like to thank everyone who has made my life at *Hollyoaks* a very happy one." It was also announced that Max's departure would involve his wedding to Steph. *Hollyoaks* producer Bryan Kirkwood commented on what the future holds for Littler, stating, "Matt, together with Darren Jon Jefferies have created a partnership in Max and O.B. that has been at the heart of Hollyoaks success for the last eleven years. Matt is a talented directed as well as a successful actor and although Max's exit marks the end of an era on screen, Matt's not going too far as he will be directing a few episodes of Hollyoaks in the not too distant future."

On their wedding day, Niall, still angry and upset over his break-up with Steph, raced off in his car, unknowingly towards Tom. Max saw this and pushed Tom out of the way, however Niall ended up running him over. Max died in OB's arms with Steph and Tom also present. Max's final appearance was the month following his death. While OB was leaving for a new life in America, he turned around and saw Max standing outside Drive 'n' Buy.

Storylines

1995–2008

Max first appears as part of the Cunningham family in 1995. He becomes the only child left when his sister Dawn dies from leukaemia and other sisters Jude and Cindy flee the country. Max and OB make up money-making schemes, and create their own single. The CD became a failure. Max starts working at Hollyoaks College. Another tragedy hits the family when stepbrother Lewis commits suicide. Max decides to make the most of his life, opening a burger van and going on a date with Jodie Nash. Max reveals his sensitive side in his affection for Anna Green, helping her during the difficult stages of her pregnancy. Max and Anna both admit their feelings to each other and they sleep together in Max's van. Anna tells boyfriend Alex Bell about the affair and she moves in with Max and her son Charlie. Max finds it difficult staying with Anna as he never really has much time for social life. Another tragedy hits Max whilst he, OB, Ben Davies, Kristian Hargreaves, Jamie Nash and Theo Sankofa go potholing. The trip results in a rock fall and leaves Theo and Jamie dead. After returning home, Max ends his relationship with Anna.

OB tells Max that his stepmother Helen Cunningham is having an affair with Tony Hutchinson. Max is angered by Helen and Tony's actions towards his father so he warns them if they continue, he will tell Gordon. Helen and Tony continue their affair so Max tells a devastated Gordon. Helen then leaves Gordon for Tony and prepare to leave. During a journey together, Gordon and Helen are involved in a car accident when he Gordon takes a heart attack at the wheel of the car. Luckily, Tom is uninjured. With Gordon already dead, Helen passes away in hospital, leaving Max as Tom's legal guardian. Max's stepsister Mandy supports Max, as does OB. After Tom burns down the house after playing with firecrackers, the social services arrive. Max tells Mandy he thinks Tom should be put into care, which Tom overhears. Tom then runs away from home and is found at his parents grave. Max, OB and Tom then move into the flat next to Mandy and new fiancé Tony. Yet another tragedy hits the family when Mandy and Tony's daughter Grace dies of SIDS.

Tony makes OB and Max managers of The Loft after the pair work hard to show him they are responsible. Tony eventually gives The Loft to them as a Christmas present. Max and OB's first major decision for the club is to hire an events organiser, Clare Devine. Both Max and OB immediately fall for Clare. After an ultimatum, Clare chooses Max. Max and Clare's relationship begins well and Max asks her to move in with him, OB and Tom. OB's girlfriend Mel Burton catches Clare having an affair with Sean Kennedy and tries to tell Max. Due to her alcoholism, no one believes Mel except OB, causing a drift between Max and OB. Max and Clare get engaged. OB tries to make Max see Clare's true self, however is unsuccessful. At their wedding, OB bursts in begging Max to rethink his engagement. Max hits him and vows never to speak to him again. After the wedding, Max tells her he wants to start a family. Clare fakes being pregnant and also a miscarriage and tells Max she cannot have children. After finding Clare and Warren Fox taking cocaine, Max decides to join them and takes some as well. This causes a heart attack which leads to Max having to go on medication. Clare begins to tamper with this medication in order to bring on a second heart attack. During a Christmas break at an isolated cottage, Max finds the tampered medication and realises the truth. On seeing Tom supposedly in an icy lake, Max jumps in after him, however Clare has tricked him and refuses to help. OB arrives, punches Clare, saves Max and struggles to revive him. Luckily, he does. Max apologises to OB over not believing him. After Clare threatens him, Max signs The Loft over to Clare. With their friendship back on track, Max and OB open a new business, a juice bar called MOBS.

Clare is pushed over the balcony of The Loft and Max becomes one of five named suspects for her attempted murder. Tony and Dom give Max their alibi for the night. Clare returns from hospital and tells social services Max is hurting Tom. Max breaks into Clare's flat and threatens to kill her if she does not tell them she made everything up, which she does. Clare signs The Loft over to Warren Fox and is forced out of Hollyoaks. She also discovers Justin Burton pushed her over The Loft balcony. In revenge, Clare kidnaps Katy Fox. Warren, Justin and Max set off to find her. After a dangerous car chase, Clare's car goes over a quarry into water below. Warren and Justin jump in after Katy while Max attempts to save Clare. Clare is dragged underwater by a current and apparently drowns, however is revealed to have survived. Max tells Steph Dean of his guilt over letting Clare die and have a heart to heart, in which they appear to grow close.

Steph begins helping Max look after Tom. The pair begin to fall for each other. After several failed attempts, Max finally tells Steph his true feelings and they begin a relationship. With Max spending more time with Steph, OB begins to feel left out. OB befriends Simon Crosby, who apparently turns out to be a paedophile. Max and Jake Dean attack Simon's home with other residents. Innocent Simon tries to commit suicide, however survives. After Max discovers Simon was innocent, he apologises to OB, who is disgusted, although they later made up. OB decides to leave for London with girlfriend Summer Shaw. Max and Tom bare OB a sad farewell as he leaves. Max decides to propose to Steph, which she accepts. Max and Steph's engagement is short-lived when they split up and she seeks comfort in Niall Rafferty. Niall falls in love with Steph, who then gets back together with Max. With the wedding back on, Max's mother Angela, sister Cindy, niece Holly, stepsister Mandy and also OB return for his wedding. After a perfect wedding, distraught Niall speeds off in his car. Max sees him driving unknowingly towards Tom and rushes, pushing him out of the way in time. Tragically, Max is hit. Max is held by OB and Tom as he bleeds. Steph rushes to his side as he passes away.

Reception

For his portrayal of Max, Matt Littler won the 'Outstanding Serial Drama Performance' at the 2008 National Television Awards. Subsequent to his National Television Awards nomination, the character has also won the award for 'Best On-screen Partnership' with Darren Jeffries (OB) at The 2008 British Soap Awards. The same year, Littler, along with Gemma Bissix (Clare), Jamie Lomas (Warren), Chris Fountain (Justin) and Hannah Tointon (Katy), won the award for 'Spectacular Scene of the Year' for Clare kidnapping Katy and driving the car over the edge of the cliff. In 2009, Littler's exit from the show got his nominated for 'Best Exit' and 'Best Single Episode' for Max and Steph's wedding day.

External links

- Max Cunningham [1] on the Channel 4 website [2]

Sun Ultra series

Sun Ultra series

The original **Sun Ultra series** was a series of UltraSPARC-based workstations and servers developed and sold by Sun Microsystems from 1995 to 2001. The Ultra series introduced the 64-bit UltraSPARC processor and in later versions, lower-cost PC-derived technology, such as the PCI and ATA buses (the initial Ultra 1 and 2 models retained the SBus of their predecessors).

Sun Ultra 1 workstation

The **Ultra** workstations and the **Ultra Enterprise** (later, simply **Enterprise**) servers replaced the earlier SPARCstation and SPARCcenter/SPARCserver series respectively. The Ultra/Enterprise series itself was later replaced by the Sun Blade (workstations) and Sun Fire (servers) ranges.

Sun Ultra 5 workstation

The Enterprise 220R is an Ultra 60 motherboard in a rackable server chassis with hot-swappable power supplies. Similarly, the Enterprise 420R is an Ultra 80 motherboard in a server chassis.

The Ultra brand was later revived in 2005 with the launch of the Ultra 20, Ultra 40 and Ultra 45 workstations and the Ultra 3 laptop. Confusingly, some of these "Ultra" workstations are *not* UltraSPARC-based systems, but are based on x86-64-architecture processors (where Sun uses the term "x64"). However, Sun discontinued the UltraSPARC-based systems on July 2008, effectively ending the production of workstations with an UltraSPARC processor.

Sun Ultra models

Ultra workstations (1995-2001)

Model	Code	Codename	Processor(s)	Processor MHz
Ultra 1	A11	Neutron	UltraSPARC I	143, 167
Ultra 1E	A12	Electron	UltraSPARC I	143, 167, 200
Ultra 2	A14	Pulsar	Up to two UltraSPARC I or II	143, 167, 200, 300, 400
Ultra 30	A16	Quark	UltraSPARC II	250, 300
Ultra 3000	A17	Duraflame	Up to six UltraSPARC I or II	167, 250, 336, 400
Ultra 4000	A18	Campfire	Up to 14 UltraSPARC I or II	167, 250, 336, 400
Ultra 450	A20	Tazmo	Up to four UltraSPARC II	400
Ultra 5	A21	Otter	UltraSPARC IIi	270, 333, 360, 400
Ultra 10	A22	Sea Lion	UltraSPARC IIi	300, 333, 360, 440
Ultra 60	A23	Deuterium	Up to two UltraSPARC II	300, 360 or 450 (400 works, but is unsupported)
Ultra 80	A27	Quasar	Up to four UltraSPARC II	450

Ultra Enterprise/Enterprise servers

See also: Sun Enterprise

Entry-level

Model	Code	Codename	Processor(s)	Processor MHz
UltraServer 1 Ultra Enterprise 1	A11	Neutron	UltraSPARC I	143 or 167
UltraServer 1E Ultra Enterprise 1E	A12	Electron	UltraSPARC I	143, 167, 200
UltraServer 2 Ultra Enterprise 2	A14	Pulsar	Up to two UltraSPARC I or II	143, 167, 200, 300
Ultra Enterprise 150	E150	Dublin	UltraSPARC I	167
Enterprise Ultra 5S	A21	Otter	UltraSPARC IIi	270, 333, 360, 400
Enterprise Ultra 10S	A22	Sea Lion	UltraSPARC IIi	300, 333, 360, 440
Enterprise 450	A25	Tazmax	Up to four UltraSPARC II	250, 300, 400, 480
Enterprise 250	A26	Javelin	Up to two UltraSPARC II	250, 300, 400
Enterprise 420R	A33	Quahog	Up to four UltraSPARC II	450
Enterprise 220R	A34	Razor	Up to two UltraSPARC II	360, 450

Mid-range and high-end

Model	Code	Codename	Processor(s)	Processor MHz
Ultra Enterprise 3000	E3000	Duraflame	Up to six UltraSPARC I or II	167, 250, 336, 400, 464*
Ultra Enterprise 4000	E4000	Campfire	Up to 14 UltraSPARC I or II	167, 250, 336, 400, 464*
Ultra Enterprise 5000	E5000	Campfire	Up to 14 UltraSPARC I or II	167, 250, 336, 400, 464*
Ultra Enterprise 6000	E6000	Sunfire	Up to 30 UltraSPARC I or II	167, 250, 336, 400, 464*
Enterprise 3500	E3500	Duraflame+	Up to eight UltraSPARC I or II	167, 250, 336, 400, 464
Enterprise 4500	E4500	Campfire+	Up to 14 UltraSPARC I or II	167, 250, 336, 400, 464
Enterprise 5500	E5500	Campfire+	Up to 14 UltraSPARC I or II	167, 250, 336, 400, 464
Enterprise 6500	E6500	Sunfire+	Up to 30 UltraSPARC I or II	167, 250, 336, 400, 464
Enterprise 10000	E10000	Starfire	four to 64 UltraSPARC II	250, 336, 400, 466

- • = available as upgrade option only

Ultra workstations (2005 on)

UltraSPARC

Model	Code	Codename	Processor(s)	Processor freq.
Ultra 3	A60/A61	?	UltraSPARC IIi or IIIi	550 MHz, 650 MHz, 1.28 GHz
Ultra 45	A70	Chicago	Up to two UltraSPARC IIIi	1.6 GHz
Ultra 25	A89	South Side	UltraSPARC IIIi	1.34 GHz

x86

Model	Code	Codename	Processor(s)	Processor freq.
Ultra 20	A63	Marrakesh	AMD Opteron Dual Core 144, 148 or 180	1.8, 2.2, 2.6, 3.0 GHz
Ultra 40	A71	Sirius	Up to two AMD Opteron Dual Core 246, 254 or 280	2.0, 2.4, 2.8 GHz
Ultra 40 M2	A83	Munich	AMD Opteron Dual Core 2000 Series	1.8, 2.2, 2.6, 2.8, 3.0 GHz
Ultra 20 M2	A88	Munich	AMD Opteron Dual Core 1200 series	1.8, 2.2, 2.6, 2.8, 3.0 GHz
Ultra 24	B21	Ursa	Intel Core 2 Duo/Quad/Quad Extreme	2.0, 2.2, 2.4, 2.66, 3.0, 3.16 GHz
Ultra 27	B27	Volo	Intel Xeon Quad Core 3500 series	2.66, 2.93, 3.20, 3.33 GHz

External links

- Sun System Handbook [1]
- Sun Field Engineer Handbook, 20th edition [2]
- Sun graphics cards [3]

Security Administrator Tool for Analyzing Networks

Security Administrator Tool for Analyzing Networks

The tool was developed by Dan Farmer and Wietse Venema. Neil Gaiman drew the artwork [1] for the SATAN documentation.

SATAN was designed to help systems administrators automate the process of testing their systems for known vulnerabilities that can be exploited via the network. This is particularly useful for networked systems with multiple hosts. Like most security tools, it is useful for good or bad purposes - it is also useful to would-be intruders looking for systems with security holes.

SATAN is written mostly in Perl and utilizes a web browser such as Netscape, Mosaic or Lynx to provide the user interface. This easy to use interface drives the scanning process and presents the results in summary format. As well as reporting the presence of vulnerabilities, SATAN also gathers large amounts of general network information, such as which hosts are connected to subnets, what types of machines they are and which services they offer.

SATAN was released in 1995 and is not being further developed. In 2006, SecTools.Org [2] conducted a security popularity poll and developed a list of 100 network security analysis tools in order of popularity based on the responses of 3,243 people. Results suggest that SATAN has been replaced by Nessus and to a lesser degree **SARA** [3] (Security Auditor's Research Assistant), and SAINT.

For those offended by the name, the package contains a program called *repent*, which changes everything named SATAN to SANTA.

See also

- Penetration test
- Nessus
- Nmap
- SAINT

External links

- SATAN [4] - Official SATAN home page
- [5] - History of SATAN

Blue Mary

Blue Mary

Blue Mary

Blue Mary in *The King of Fighters XI*	
Series	*Fatal Fury* series *The King of Fighters* series
First game	*Fatal Fury 3: Road to the Final Victory* (1995)
Voiced by	Harumi Ikoma
Fictional information	
Birthplace	USA
Blood type	AB
Fighting style	Combat Sambo

Blue Mary (ブルー・マリー *Burū Marī*), real name **Mary Ryan** (マリー・ライアン *Marī Raian*), is a video game character from both the *Fatal Fury* and *The King of Fighters* series of fighting games developed by SNK Playmore (formerly "SNK"). Blue Mary's first appearance was in the arcade and console game *Fatal Fury 3: Road to the Final Victory* which introduced her as an agent who investigates two criminals known as the Jin Brothers. During the series, Mary meets Terry Bogard, to whom she develops a strong attachment. She is also featured in *The King of Fighters* in which she enters several consecutive 'King of Fighters' tournaments, changing teams over time. Blue Mary has also appeared in the twenty-minute featurette *Memories of Stray Wolves* based on the *Fatal Fury* series.

Android 18, a character from the *Dragon Ball* manga was Blue Mary's model during development of the series. Her appearances in *The King of Fighters* owe to popularity polls developed by three video game journals: Mary being first in Gamest's poll allowed to her to become playable for *The King of Fighters '97* and subsequent installments. Video game publications have commented on Blue Mary's character, praising her introduction in *Fatal Fury 3* and her development through various games.

Character design

Blue Mary's original visual inspiration was Android #18, a character from the *Dragon Ball* manga by Akira Toriyama. Blue Mary is noted for having short blonde hair and blue eyes, and a fairly muscular body. In *Fatal Fury 3* and *Real Bout Fatal Fury*, Mary wears a small sleeveless red top and loose blue jeans with the sign of a star. She also wears a brown belt around the jeans (which is noted to become longer in following games), blue fingerless gloves and a green leather jacket that she takes off before fighting. In *Real Bout Fatal Fury Special* Mary now wears her green jacket in battles and now has her top replaced with a blue brassiere. In contrast to this, her "EX" form - as well as her character in the PlayStation port from this game - has the same appearance, but with the jacket red and a black brassiere. Although Blue Mary had this new look, for *KOF* her designer wanted to use the original *Fatal Fury 3* design as he liked it more. However, she appears in *KOF: Maximum Impact Regulation A* with her *Real Bout Fatal Fury Special* design. Although Mary does not appear in the final *Fatal Fury* game, *Garou: Mark of the Wolves* (situated ten years after *Real Bout Fatal Fury*), she appears in the short *Memories of Stray Wolves* from the same game. During the featurette, Mary now has long hair and wears a red and white jacket with the number "8" on her shoulder. She also sports a white blouse under the jacket and now has brown jeans.

Attributes

According to her background story in *Fatal Fury 3: Road to the Final Victory*, Mary is the granddaughter of Tatsumi Suoh (周防 辰巳 *Suō Tatsumi*), the Japanese Kobujutsu master who trained Geese Howard, and she has been trained in martial arts since childhood, with her specialty being Combat Sambo. On her 20th birthday, she was introduced to her father's Secret Service partner Butch, who gave her the leather jacket she wears as a birthday present. Mary and Butch began dating, and Butch began training her in Combat Sambo. However, Butch and Mary's father were one day assigned to guard the President during a parade. After the parade was over, a group of assassins tried to kill the President, and both men, Mary's father and Butch, lost their lives protecting him. After that Mary became a regular customer in a bar to take her mind out of her sorrow. The bartender of the place created an original blue cocktail named after her. Later she begins to travel the world, and, while on a case, meets Terry Bogard, with whom she develops a strong bond. She has a pet dog named Anton which normally accompanies her to wherever she has a fight. Blue Mary is very friendly towards everyone, but she knows that her job must come first before anything else. The fighting art she employs, Combat Sambo, uses striking and grappling techniques.

Appearances

In the *Fatal Fury* series, Blue Mary has different assignments as an agent which take her to confront criminals from the city of Southtown. She makes her first appearance in *Fatal Fury 3: Road to the Final Victory*, investigating the Secret Scrolls of the Jin Brothers, items able to give immortality to their users. *Real Bout Fatal Fury* shows Mary allying with Terry Bogard and his friends to fight the crime lord from Southtown Geese Howard. The two following games, *Real Bout Fatal Fury Special* and *Real Bout Fatal Fury 2: The Newcomers*, also feature Blue Mary as a playable character but neither of them presents a storyline. *Real Bout Fatal Fury Special* also features an "EX" version from Mary with her movesets from *Fatal Fury 3*. The PlayStation version of *Real Bout Fatal Fury Special* also contains a video clip featuring the song "Blue Mary's Blues" by Harumi Ikoma, Mary's voice actress.

Following her *Fatal Fury* inception, Blue Mary becomes a regular character with frequently changing team membership in *The King of Fighters* series, beginning as a member of the '97 Special Team in *The King of Fighters '97* along with Billy Kane and Ryuji Yamazaki. A mysterious benefactor (Geese Howard) requests her services to enter the King of Fighters tournament, along with Billy and Yamazaki, who starts to become insane due to the power from the demon Orochi. However, after discovering that Geese was her client, Mary leaves the team. The team is also featured in *The King of Fighters '98*, *The King of Fighters 2002*, and *The King of Fighters Neowave*, which do not contain a storyline. In *The King of Fighters '99*, she joins up with King, Li Xiangfei, and Kasumi Todoh as the new Women Fighters Team, but leaves and becomes the fourth member of the Fatal Fury Team (composed by Terry, Andy Bogard and Joe Higashi) in *The King of Fighters 2000* and *The King of Fighters 2001*. She would join forces with King again as member of the Women Fighters Team in *The King of Fighters 2003*, this time with Mai Shiranui as their third member. In *The King of Fighters XI*, she joins Vanessa and Ramon as a member of the Agents Team in order investigate the host from The King of Fighters tournaments, an organization named Those from the Past. She also appears in the 3D game *KOF: Maximum Impact Regulation A*, which does not feature official teams. In the spin-off game *The King of Fighters Kyo*, Blue Mary appears investigating the actions from Geese along with Kyo Kusanagi and King.

Blue Mary also makes an appearance in the *Memories of Stray Wolves* twenty-minute featurette that serves as a retrospective of the *Fatal Fury* series, with Terry narrating the events of the games ten years after *Real Bout Fatal Fury*. She also stars in manhua based on the games retelling her actions in the series.

Reception

Blue Mary has been well received by gamers, having appeared in several popularity polls from video game journals. In the character popularity poll on Neo Geo Freak's website, her character was voted as the fifteenth favorite with a total of 857 votes. To decide what character should appear in *The King of Fighters '97* as part of the Special team, three video game journals, Gamest, Famitsu and Neo Geo Freak also made popularity polls. Blue Mary was first in the poll from Gamest. For the special endings in *The King of Fighters '97*, the three journals had to create a team composed of three characters from the game so that they would be featured in an image after completion of the arcade mode; the Gamest employees created a team composed of Terry Bogard, Blue Mary and Joe. This special ending only appears in Japanese versions of the game. A sign of her popularity was the Blue Mary action figure released by SNK Playmore, depicted in her original outfit.

The character of Blue Mary has received praise and criticism from video game publications, regarding her fighting style and traits. Kurt Kalata from Armchairempire.com commented that Mary was one of the best new characters from *Fatal Fury 3*, noting her to be a good replacement for the characters who were removed from the game. Gamezone writer Eduardo Zacarias noted Mary to be similar to other female assasains from video games such as *Tekken*'s Nina Williams or Christie from *Dead or Alive*. Nick Valentino from the same website praised Mary's development in the *Real Bout Fatal Fury* games as her techniques became more straightforward, relying now more on strength. Harumi Ikoma, Blue Mary's voice actress, has been criticized for her role with Mary in the first game she appeared by Robert Workman from GameDaily who commented that "Blue Mary should take a few vocal lessons and work on that high-pitched squeak of hers".

External links

- Fatal Fury 15th Anniversary Official Website [1] (Japanese)
- The King of Fighters 10th Anniversary Official Website [1]

138

Cray T3E

Cray T3E

The **Cray T3E** was Cray Research's second-generation massively parallel supercomputer architecture, launched in late November 1995. The first T3E was installed at the Pittsburgh Supercomputing Center in 1996. Like the previous Cray T3D, it was a fully distributed memory machine using a 3D torus topology interconnection network. The T3E initially used the DEC Alpha 21164 (EV5) microprocessor and was designed to scale from 8 to 2,176 *Processing Elements* (PEs). Each PE had between 64 MB and 2 GB of DRAM and a 6-way interconnect router with a payload bandwidth of 480 MB/s in each direction. Unlike many other MPP systems, including the T3D, the T3E was fully self-hosted and ran the UNICOS/mk distributed operating system with a *GigaRing* I/O subsystem integrated into the torus for network, disk and tape I/O.

The original T3E (retrospectively known as the **T3E-600**) had a 300 MHz processor clock. Later variants, using the faster 21164A (EV56) processor, comprised the **T3E-900** (450 MHz), **T3E-1200** (600 MHz), **T3E-1200E** (with improved memory and interconnect performance) and **T3E-1350** (675 MHz). The T3E was available in both air-cooled (*AC*) and liquid-cooled (*LC*) configurations. AC systems were available with 16 to 128 user PEs, LC systems with 64 to 2048 user PEs.

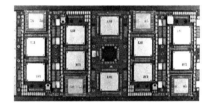
T3E-600 processor board

A 1480-processor T3E-1200 was the first supercomputer to achieve a performance of more than 1 teraflops running a computational science application, in 1998.

After Cray Research was acquired by Silicon Graphics in February 1996, development of new Alpha-based systems was stopped. While providing the -900, -1200 and -1200E upgrades to the T3E, in the long term Silicon Graphics intended Cray T3E users to migrate to the Origin 3000, a MIPS-based distributed shared memory computer, introduced in 2000. However, the T3E continued in production after SGI sold the Cray business the same year.

External links

- Top500 description of T3E [1]
- Inside Cray T3E-900 Serial Number 6702 [2]
- *Performance Analysis of the CRAY T3E-1200E*, Edward Anderson, Lockheed Martin Services Inc., 1999 [3]

Jack (mascot)

Jack (mascot)

Jack (full name: **Jack Box**) is the mascot of American restaurant chain Jack in the Box. In the advertisements, he is the founder, CEO, and ad spokesman for the chain. According to the company's web site, he has the appearance of a typical male, with the exception of his huge round white head, blue dot eyes, black pointy nose, and a linear red smile. He is most of the time seen wearing his yellow clown cap, and a business suit.

The company's "bio" of him claims the following facts:

* According to his California driver's license, Jack I. Box is 6'-8" tall and weighs 195 pounds. It also shows his birthday to be May 16.

* Jack was born on a cattle ranch in Colorado. He later moved to Southern California, where he met his blonde wife, Cricket. They now have a young son named Jack Jr. (who, like all males in the Box family tree, also has an oversized bald head). However, in May 2010, Jack appeared in a new commercial with a woman that did not resemble Cricket, who appeared with him in a commercial in 1997. The pair took in a movie where Jack complained and cried about the price of popcorn in relation to his low-priced menu.

* Jack is an alumnus of Ball State University

* Jack, fluent in English and Spanish, has starred in more than 300 television and radio commercials, including more than 100 Spanish-language ads. Jack's linguistic talents also include Mandarin, which he spoke in the 1999 television ad "Titans."

* A true man of the people, Jack ran for president in 1996 and beat out Bill Clinton, Bob Dole and Dogbert in a national independent Virtual Vote poll; no recounts required.

* During Super Bowl XXXV, Jack in the Box debuted a television commercial in which Jack announced his purchase of a professional American football team, the Carnivores. His team played against teams such as the Tofu Eaters and the Vegans.

* In late 2009, the company began to run a commercial in which Jack visited his cousin Jim, who was serving time in prison. Jim has a large white head that resembles a Ping-Pong ball squashed from both sides, with wispy gray hair and beard, along with a surly voice and facial expression. He does not wear a clown cap.

* Jack's smile can change to reflect his mood (puzzlement, fear, etc.). During one commercial, in which he was playing Texas hold 'em against several celebrities, he made his eyes and mouth

disappear completely. The announcer remarked, "Now *that's* a world-class poker face."

History

Prior to 1980, the chain used a huge clown head as its symbol, which sat atop the remote activated talking drive-thru menus (in the 1960s and early '70's the rotating clown head was also at the top of the large signs at each location). In 1980, the chain decided to establish a more "mature" image by introducing a wider variety of menu items and, most notably, discontinuing the use of Jack. A series of television commercials announced "We're blowing up clowns!" and showed the dramatic explosion of the notorious clown heads. These commercials led to many complaints by parents over the violence. Throughout the late 1980s to the 1990s, Jack in the Box tried to position itself as a premium fast food alternative, with varying results.

In 1993, a major food contamination crisis was linked to Jack in the Box restaurants and by 1994, a series of lawsuits and negative publicity took their tolls and pushed their corporate parent, Foodmaker Inc. to the verge of bankruptcy. In the short term, they decided to promote their initiatives on food safety and then approved a new guerilla advertising campaign created by Dick Sittig, of Secret Weapon marketing in Santa Monica which brought back their original mascot, Jack as a savvy, no-nonsense businessman.

A series of new commercials featured a new, more-serious Jack with a smaller head and wearing a business suit (according to him, "thanks to the miracle of plastic surgery"). In the very first of these new commercials, he blew up the board of directors as retribution for his supposed destruction in 1980. This image of destruction angered many, as it occurred at nearly the same time as several domestic bombings hitting the news in those days (see Oklahoma City bombing). But the ad agency and the corporation stuck by the new campaign. Their intent was to prove to a wary public that the company was no longer the same restaurant chain plagued by the food safety scandal, and because the commercials had a definite humorous element to them that undermined the alleged "retribution" that Jack was supposedly demonstrating in these commercials and overall, the public responded positively.

Car antenna ornaments shaped like Jack's head have been a mainstay of the restaurant chain's promotion for several years.

Dick Sittig, a marketing executive who started the Jack advertising campaign, is the voice of Jack. The man inside the suit is Jason Curtis from Phoenix, AZ.

On February 1, 2009, a new ad campaign began with a Super Bowl ad that showed Jack being struck by a bus outside his corporate office. The ad ends with Jack lying on the ground badly injured while the paramedics are being summoned. Viewers were then directed to visit the website hanginthererejack.com to check on his condition. The next ad showed Jack being checked into the hospital and being operated on as his heart stopped. The third ad showed Jack in a coma, and an employee of Jack in the Box volunteering to take his place at the company's head (despite Jack not being dead). The fourth ad showed the employee, Phil, taking Jack's place and declaring his intention to rename the restaurant "Phil in The Box," but Jack woke up and started to choke Phil. What Jack said was, "Phil in the Box?!! I don't think so!! Somebody get my pants, I've got work to do!" The words "Jack's back" were then shown on-screen.

Media

The Pilot Episode of American Dad! shows Stan Smith falsely blaming a student body candidate at his son's school for having a sexual relationship with Jack. When his son, Steve states that he thought that Jack was in the basement of the Smith house, it cuts to houseguest Roger Smith finding Jack in the basement, tied up and stripped down to presumably nothing.

The April 24, 2009 edition of the Adam Carolla Podcast featured Sittig, in character as Jack, involving a humorous discussion on other restaurant mascots (Ronald McDonald, The Burger King), the fast food business and general listener Q&A. In the podcast, Jack insinuates that The Burger King is bisexual, citing his attire (tights, felt shoes and a cape). Carolla jumps in with a tale of the King buying a drink for a male friend of his in Canada, though this claim cannot be verified.

External links

- Jack [1] at MySpace
- http://www.jackinthebox.com/pressroom/factssheet_jack.php

Tony Hutchinson

Tony Hutchinson

Tony Hutchinson	
Nick Pickard as Tony Hutchinson (2009)	
Hollyoaks **character**	
Portrayed by	Nick Pickard
Created by	Phil Redmond
Duration	1995—
First appearance	23 October 1995
Classification	Present; regular
Spin-off appearances	*Hollyoaks Later*
Profile	
Date of birth	30 October 1977
Home	1 Oakdale Drive
Occupation	Businessman/chef
Family	
Wife	Mandy Richardson (2005–2006) Cindy Cunningham (2009–2010)
Father	Brian Hutchinson
Mother	Vicky Hutchinson
Half brothers	Dominic Reilly
Sons	Harry Thompson
Daughters	Grace Hutchinson

Anthony "Tony" Hutchinson is a fictional character from the long-running Channel 4 soap opera *Hollyoaks*, played by Nick Pickard. Tony is the only original character still on the show to the present day. Tony's on-screen half-brother, Dom Reilly, is played by John Pickard, the real life brother of Nick.

Character creation

Backstory

Tony's main backstory was never originally established. He comes from a British-German background, this was discovered in 2009 that his great-grandfather was a German, who fought against Britain in the First World War. Tony discovered his cousin Dom was in fact his half-brother.Tony is a bit of a player and has had relationships with most of the women who have been in hollyoaks. He had an affair with Mrs C on a boat.

Pickard is the longest serving cast member in the serial's history and the only original character left. In 2009 he also revealed that he had no plans to leave the serial.

Development

Personality and identity

Tony appears as a caring, kind and considerate businessman, however can be easily led. He has had a lot of heartbreak in his life and expects the worst of people, seen more recently on starting a relationship with Cindy Cunningham where he assumed she was only interested in him for his money, which will prove true. Tony has had many failed romances, but did find his soulmate in Jacqui McQueen, however, their love was short-lived when he slept with her sister, Mercedes. Tony is also a devoted father to Harry, Grace and Max, despite Grace's death and Max's true paternity. Tony is still listed on Max's birth certificate as his father.

Storylines

1995–2005

Tony comes up with a new scheme to save money, as he implements a recycling system in his house for the student tenants. He encourages them to eat a high fibre diet after learning that the more waste his new system collects, the more money he receives. He discovers that as a result of the system, he is drinking his own urine. Tony runs for council, but is defeated by Gordon Cunningham. Finn and Ruth tell Tony to buy out Lewis's share of The Loft because of his financial problems. Tony agrees and Finn repays the favour by investing into Tony's new restaurant. Moving away from Hollyoaks Village with Ruth and Finn, Tony focuses on his new business venture Gnosh, in *Hollyoaks: Movin' On*. He receives bad news that Ruth has been beaten up by Lewis, who then commits suicide due to guilt over his actions. Tony is asked by Lewis's mum, Helen, to perform the eulogy at Lewis's funeral.

After Lewis's death, Tony decides to make the most of life, and moves back to Hollyoaks Village to concentrate on running his businesses. Finn had decides to leave Hollyoaks, as does Ruth, leaving Tony lonely. Tony starts dating Izzy Cornwell. Tony then buys Deva from Andy Morgan. He ends up renaming it to Gnosh Village. Tony then receives a shock when ex-fiancée, Julie Matthews, returns to Hollyoaks. Tony is delighted to see her and offers her a job at Gnosh. Izzy gets suspicious and does not like the idea of Tony and Julie working together. Izzy suggests to Tony that they get married, which Tony agrees. However, he has a one-night stand with Julie and asks her to marry him, which she accepts. Tony makes Julie and Izzy promise to keep their engagement a secret. During filming for a cookery show, Julie and Izzy fight and discover Tony is engaged to both of them. Izzy and Julie both dump Tony. Tony realises he loves Julie and asks her to stay, however she reveals she wanted him so she could steal his money as she has a boyfriend in prison.

Tony becomes a supportive friend of Helen Cunningham, who is having a marriage crisis. He helps her with her new laundrette shop, Washed Up. The pair end up falling for each other and they start an affair. Sam "O.B." O'Brien catches them together. Tony tries to persuade OB not to tell anyone from the Cunningham family, but OB tells Max Cunningham. Tony promises Max that he has finished with Helen, Max agrees to keep their affair a secret. Tony continues his affair with Helen. Tony is then made homeless so Gordon insists he stays with the Cunningham family. The situation is uncomfortable for Tony, as Max puts pressure on him to find another home. Max has enough of Tony and Helen's lies and tells Gordon about the affair. Tony moves out, and moves onto the barge, but is shocked when Helen decides to move in with him. Tony does not want to cause any trouble and he tells Helen she belongs with Gordon. Eventually, he is persuaded to take Helen in with him. The whole village finds out about their affair and Tony tries to persuade Helen to move back in with Gordon for Tom and Mandy's sake, which she does

Tony then starts dating Mandy. The couple leave for Rome, where they marry on February 10 2005. After a miscarriage, Mandy gives birth to Grace Hutchinson. However, Grace sadly dies from suspected SIDS on a night where Hannah Ashworth and Nancy Hayton are babysitting. Tony struggles to accept Grace's death and places blame on many people, including Hannah and Nancy. Tony turns to alcohol, which turns Mandy into the arms of his half-brother, Dom Reilly. Tony gets counselling, however it is too late and Mandy leaves him.

2006—

Tony begins a relationship with Jacqui McQueen. The relationship has to remain secret due to Jacqui's fake marriage to Aleksander Malota. During Mercedes and Tina McQueen's double wedding to Russ Owen and Dom Reilly, Jacqui admits to Tony that she is pregnant. Sadly, she loses the baby. Alek then leaves for Albania. Jacqui goes off the rails and is arrested for shoplifting. Tony declares his love for Jacqui to her in Il Gnosh. Jacqui and Tony decide to adopt a child, however, Jacqui's criminal record is revealed to the social services, who tell them it is unlikely they will be able to adopt.

Tony turns thirty and Jacqui plans to reward him with a stripper pole and sexy lingerie. Tina throws a surprise party and invites everyone in his address book. Tony is tipped off when old friend Jambo sends him a text saying he could not make it. Sending invites to everyone meant Tony's ex-fiancées, Julie, Izzy, and Tessie. Julie tries to make amends but Tony sends her away. Jacqui is jealous of Izzy, however during a heart to heart, she tells him she cannot have children either. Tessie shows up in the middle of the party and reveals she had lied about not being pregnant and has an eight year old son called Harry Thompson. Jacqui grows jealous and forces Tony to choose between her and Harry, which results in him choosing Harry. A drunken Tony ends up sleeping with, and impregnating, Jacqui's sister, Mercedes. Tony and Jacqui reconcile and Jacqui tries to convince Mercedes to let them raise the baby after Mercedes books an abortion. However, Mercedes goes through with it.

Tina volunteers to have a baby for Jacqui and Tony. Dom finds out and tells her not to as he wants her to only have their children. Tina and Dom end their relationship soon after he does not support her when she is sexually harassed at work, which led to a one-night-stand with Russ. Tina inseminates herself with Tony's sperm. Dom returns and is not happy. Tina discovers she is pregnant. Dom tries to get her to have an abortion, however she refuses and he accepts her decision.

Tina goes to hospital for her 12-week pre-natal scan, it is then revealed that the baby is in fact 15 weeks old and therefore must have been conceived when she slept with Russ. Tina gives birth after being pushed down stairs by secret brother, Niall Rafferty. She has a baby son, Max McQueen, named after deceased Max Cunningham. Tony becomes over-protective of Max, not wanting to lose him after Grace. Tina, who has to undergo an emergency hysterectomy, decides to raise Max as her own son, leaving Tony and Jacqui devastated. Tony is more devastated to discover Russ is the father. After Tina dies and she finds out about his fling with Mercedes, Jacqui ends her relationship with Tony, who planned to propose, she then changes Max's second name to McQueen.

Tony and Russ go to the Loft at a 'school disco' themed night. Russ introduces Tony to a girl named Theresa and, after a few drinks, Tony takes her back to his flat, where they sleep together. The next day, Theresa begins following Tony, not realising it was just a one-night-stand. Tony tries to tell her this but she does not listen. Theresa then reveals she is only 15. A shocked Tony tells her to leave and never to return again. Theresa runs out in tears to her cousin - Jacqui. She wants advice from Michaela, who is not there. Theresa shows Myra and Jacqui who she slept with and point to Tony. Jacqui hits Tony and calls him a paedophile. Tony is then arrested, where he tries to lie by telling them nothing happened between him and Theresa. However, a witness from The Loft tells the police that Tony kept buying Theresa drinks, they then charge Tony for having sexual activity with children. After this, Tony becomes increasingly paranoid, thinking everyone is talking about him. Cindy Cunningham even stops her daughter Holly from seeing Tony.

Tony has a one-night-stand with his former wife, Mandy. Jacqui decides to apologise to Tony after the charges are dropped and Theresa admits she never told him her age. Tony then leaves Hollyoaks with Mandy and her daughter Ella after her affair with Warren Fox is revealed at his wedding to Louise

Summers.

Tony returns after three months away with Mandy. Tony began to have visits from Harry. After Max is taken by Russ, Jacqui asks Tony to hire a private investigator, which infuriates Dom. Jacqui then leaves for France to find Max. Tony grows closer with Cindy. The pair sleep together and begin a relationship. When Jacqui returns, she is horrified to find out about Tony and Cindy's relationship. Tony decides to take Cindy and Holly on holiday, however drops the plans when Holly hints that Cindy wants to get married. Dom then taunts Cindy about Tony finally seeing her true colours. Cindy is comforted by Darren Osborne in her flat. The pair begin to kiss and undress just as Tony walks in however they do get back together unbeknown to him Cindy and Darren are planning to scam him out of his money so Darren can buy back The Dog.

Cindy and Tony make up and later get in engaged, but he reveals to Dom that he does not really love Cindy. Cindy, Tony, Dom, Darren and Cindy's friend Savannah go to a hotel for the wedding. Darren continues his jealousy and pays a woman to seduce him before sending him to a farm in the middle of nowhere. Tony is found and confesses to sleeping with another woman to Cindy, who then reveals her plans to scam him. Cindy and Tony then agree to get married, which they do despite interruptions by Darren and Jacqui. After constantly struggling with Holly, Tony and Cindy discuss sending her to a boarding school. Holly overhears the conversation and is upset, blaming Tony for trying to get rid of her. Holly later catches Tony giving Theresa a friendly kiss and taunts him over it. He grabs Holly and she runs home. This led to Holly running away. Cindy blames Tony for her disappearance. However, she is eventually found. To get their marriage back on track, Tony and Cindy agree to move. Tony views properties in Wales. He witnesses Gabby Sharpe being run over. He helps her and stays by her bedside to care for her. During this time, Tony realises he does not love Cindy, so ends their marriage. After getting divorced, Cindy is convinced that Tony had been having an affair with Gabby, but he reassures her. Gabby and her child Taylor and Amber move into Tony's flat to get away from Gabby's husband Phil. Amber does not appear to like Tony, and gets her father when she catches Tony and Gabby kissing.

Reception

Pickard was nominated at the 2002 British Soap Awards in the category of 'Best Comedy Performance'. In her book *Soap Stars*, Debbie Foy refers to Leah as having lived through several dramatic episodes. At the awards the following year he was nominated for 'Best Actor' and again for 'Best Comedy Performance'. Website *Women Republic* stated that Tony was one of *Hollyoaks*' top five characters. In a 2009 poll by *Loaded* magazine, Tony was voted eighth in the 'Top Soap Bloke' of all time, losing to Australian soap opera *Neighbours* character Harold Bishop, played by Ian Smith respectively. In her book *Soap Stars*, Debbie Foy describes Tony as being famous for his "many on-screen relationships, affairs and engagements" but always has plenty of heartache.

External links

- Tony Hutchinson [1] on the E4 website [2]

Curlz

Curlz

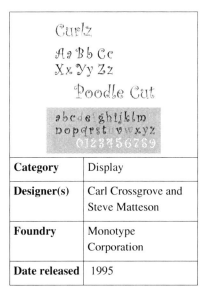

Category	Display
Designer(s)	Carl Crossgrove and Steve Matteson
Foundry	Monotype Corporation
Date released	1995

Curlz is a whimsical serif typeface designed by Carl Crossgrove and Steve Matteson in 1995 for Agfa Monotype. While decorative and without a historical model, the face bears comparison with the Emigre foundry's 1991 typeface **Remedy** designed by Frank Heine.

A TrueType version of Curlz shipped as part of the original Microsoft Project font set, and with Microsoft Office for Macintosh.

See also

- Samples of display typefaces
- Agfa Monotype

References

- Fiedl, Frederich, Nicholas Ott and Bernard Stein. *Typography: An Encyclopedic Survey of Type Design and Techniques Through History.* Black Dog & Leventhal: 1998. ISBN 1-57912-023-7.

Hayley Smith (American Dad!)

Hayley Smith (American Dad!)

American Dad! character	
Hayley Smith	
First appearance	Pilot
Created by	Seth MacFarlane
Portrayed by	Rachael MacFarlane (voice-actor)
Duration	1x01– (2005–)
Species	Human
Gender	Female
Family	Smith Family **Father**: Stan Smith **Mother**: Francine Smith **Brother**: Steve Smith **Half-Sister**: Liberty "Libby" Belle **Pets**: Klaus, Roger the Alien
Spouse(s)	**Ex-Husband**: Dill Shephard **Husband**: Jeff Fischer
Nationality	American

Hayley Dreamsmasher Fischer (*née* **Smith**) is the daughter of Stan and Francine Smith on the animated television series, *American Dad!*. She is voiced by Rachael MacFarlane, the younger sister of one of the series co-creators, Seth MacFarlane. Hayley and Stan were the first two characters that were conceived and created for the series, and is considered a hybrid of Michael Stivic from All in the Family and Meg Griffin of Family Guy.

Biography and personality

Hayley Smith is the daughter of Stan Smith, a CIA agent, and Francine Smith, a housewife. Hayley was born while her parents were on a safari in Africa, due to Stan refusing to believe the OB-GYN when she said Francine should not travel. Prior to her birth, Stan had been attempting to find Oliver North's gold hidden under their house; because her birth made him too busy to pursue this hobby, he gave her the middle name "Dreamsmasher." Hayley is considered the American Dad! version of Meg Griffin because they are both the least respected characters and both of their fathers verbally abuse them and do not treat them very well. They also get the least plots and sub-plots of the episodes. However, Hayley is shown to be treated considerably better than Meg by her peers, as Hayley is shown to have friends, a sex life, various lovers, and a family that loves her and cares for her. Also Hayley gets along with Steve Smith, much better than Meg does with her brother Chris Griffin. In the episode Merlot Down Dirty Shame, she states she has a telepathic connection with Klaus Heissler, but, nonetheless, she's not the most respected person in the world. In The American Dad After School Special, Stan said she's not pretty without make-up and, when she finally does wear it, he calls her a whore. And, in Office Spaceman, when she calls her mother a left-hand woman, Francine slaps her on purpose, but Hayley quickly forgave her. She also had a cancer of some sort that was totally ignored by the part of her family still at home while her parents were on a year long holiday trying to break George Clooney's heart. Unlike her father and her brother, Steve Smith, Hayley is ultra-liberal and possibly a member of the Green Party. She is a casual marijuana user and has stated to have smoked salvia (which led to her getting the *Ghostbusters* logo painted on her chest), often helps the homeless, and in favor of gun control. This causes a great amount of distrust for Stan, consistently having views being polar opposite of hers. When she was younger, Hayley and Stan got along very well, and indeed, they have similar personality traits, such as stubbornness and distrust of those they disagree with. She still lives with her parents and goes to Groff Community College, though she moved out temporarily after a bitter argument with Stan. As a college student, Hayley also majors in women's history and promotes women's rights. She also poses for nude paintings, and insists, "...I am a proud and evolved woman, and I have nothing to be ashamed of." Hayley is very often the rational and open-minded member of the family. For example, she helped to unionize the homeless men Stan paid to fight each other, helped free foster children that Roger had enslaved, and is the one most likely to stand up for people's rights when her family tries to exploit people. Nevertheless, she is also sometimes seen as hypocritical and has moments of weakness—for example, in "Camp Refoogee" she went to an African refugee camp and swore to help the starving people during the short time she expected to be there; however, after finding out they would be there for a few weeks, she went to the spa-like U.N. aid base and went so far as to eat steak, despite being a vegetarian (although she is seen eating meat in nearly every episode). She even admits to having thrown away more food than she ate. On another occasion in "American Dream Factory," after arguing for the rights of illegal immigrants, even going so far as to date one, she proved willing to have him deported, just to spite her father. Other members of the household seem to find her annoying, even Roger, one of the more apolitical characters, once shouted at her to just "let it go!" as she was ranting about his voting for President George W. Bush. Hayley replies: "Never!" She greatly dislikes Bush, and once attempted to create a scandal that would result in him being ejected from office, which she abandoned after he stood up to Stan on her behalf, causing her to decide that he's, "better than Dick Cheney".

The fourth season has started showing that Hayley is often prone to violent and uncontrollable mood swings. During puberty, she went through violent outbursts during every development, such as having to wear maxipads and her lack of developing breasts. These mood swings terrified her parents and they were fearful of the same problems in her brother, although it is shown Steve has had his temper more under control. In "Pulling Double Booty", it is shown that whenever Hayley gets dumped she goes on an insane and murderous rampage that often require twenty tranquilizer darts to stop her. After awakening, she strangles her mother, Francine, who then proclaims, "Shoot her! Shoot her in the face!"

In the episode "Haylias" it is revealed that her father Stan had her put in "Project Daycare" where she was trained and brainwashed to be a sleeper agent, so they could be the perfect father-daughter spy team. During the program she had to go through punishment for small things, such as accidentally coloring outside the lines of a picture, which resulted in intense electrical shock. The training stayed dormant in her mind until Stan said her "trigger phrase" (which meant he had to yell "I'm getting fed up with this orgasm!"), to stop her from getting on a plane to France. However Stan kept her active too long and she tried to kill him. This was the reason "Project Daycare" was stopped, as agents turned on their handlers and killed them after a week of activation.

Voice actors

According to a DVD special on the creation of *American Dad,* Laura Prepon (Donna on *That '70s Show*) was initially chosen to play Hayley, but Prepon was dropped and replaced by Rachael MacFarlane (younger sister of Seth MacFarlane).

Romance

Hayley has a on-and-off boyfriend named Jeff, who is a vegetarian as well (despite eating meat loaf and offering some to Hayley in the pilot), though apparently less so than Hayley.Hayley did once move out to move in with Jeff who it turns out lives in his van. They sometimes go hiking and use marijuana together. She once dumped Jeff, because he agrees with everything that she says. During this time, she slept with Stan's boss, Deputy-Director Bullock, a conservative. This happened after they had an argument; he apologized and she ended up sleeping with him at his house. At first, Stan was outraged, but he later ignored their relationship and decided it was a great chance to be promoted to "Deputy-Deputy Director". Hayley later dumped Bullock before announcing Stan's promotion. Bullock learned that a more assertive Jeff came back into her life. Being very upset, Bullock promised Stan the promotion if he killed Jeff. Stan didn't kill Jeff, but ended up battling his boss upon him insulting Hayley. Before Stan finished him off, Bullock gave him the job. Jeff was last seen in Phantom of the Telethon, where he was performing hacky-sack tricks on-stage at a telethon when a boat, pushed by Roger, fell on him. Hayley once mentioned Jeff and her may marry one day- although her father wasn't happy he came close to Jeff at the end of the episode. Jeff and Hayley sometimes live in Hayley's room or Jeff's van. Hayley and Jeff elope in the 100th episode after tricking Stan and Francine into giving them $50,000.

When the Smith family was relocated to Saudi Arabia, Hayley also slept with a man named Kazim who claimed to be a tormented, conflicted member of a terrorist group., but who was really a vendor for the restaurant chain *Shawarma King* who lied about his job in order to appear more interesting to women. She presumably did not tell Jeff of her infidelity. In "Dungeons and Wagons" the two are shown dating, but again Hayley dumps Jeff for being too clingy; he then goes on to develop a hobby of playing *Dragon Scuffle* (an MMORPG in a similar vein to World of Warcraft) with Steve instead of begging Hayley to get back together, as she had suspected he would. She becomes jealous and, with Klaus' help, kills Steve in the game. Rather than winning Jeff back, however, this makes Jeff horrified at how mean Hayley is, by destroying Steve in the one thing he was good at. Hayley tries to win Jeff back by finding a way to bring Steve's character back to life. The two of them succeed in resurrecting Steve's character, but then she loses interest in Jeff just when he wants to get back together with her and decides to date another player she met in the game instead. They are a couple again in the second season finale, though she breaks up with him yet again in season three.

She has also turned to exotic dancing in order to pay for her erased tuition and prostitution to supplement the family's income during hard times (and prostitution for drugs, according to "Helping Handis", when she grumbled "Damn it, Eddie! I slept with you!" after finding nothing but marijuana stems and seeds).

In "Haylias" she has expressed interest in having a love affair with a woman in a passing comment to her parents; whether this was sincere, or possibly merely meant to shock them, is unconfirmed at this time. While under mind-control, she also marries Dill Shephard, a rich senator's son, but their marriage is annulled shortly after the wedding as he is clearly gay. In season four, she began dating Bill, Stan's CIA body double. Stan, trying to break them up, posed as Bill and acted like a jerk to entice her into breaking up. At one point, he blatantly checked out another woman and talked about how he'd like to have sex with her. In response, Hayley suggested they should invite her, going so far as to say he could watch as they had a turn with each other, again, hinting at bisexuality.

In several episodes, it is implied she is into BDSM-type sex, likely as a dominant. Usually, it is shown that Jeff is her partner at the time, taking the role as the submissive. Although it is not clarified, it is implied that this is her fantasy more so than it is his.

Hayley may or may not be infertile due to repeated exposure to The Vacation Goo, a presumably CIA-invented substance used to keep the Smiths in suspended animation during simulated family vacations. Stan cautioned a female CIA employee not to expose herself to the Goo as it would "rot out her womb", and described his future grandchildren as family members that "only Steve will be able to give us".

Although in The Return of the Bling, Hayley claims to be going on a date with her boyfriend Ian. This may have fallen under a time when Hayley and Jeff were not dating.

Religion

In the episode "Roger Codger", Hayley says that the Christian God is fake, though it is unclear if she is an atheist or part of a non-Christian religion. However, in later in the episode, when Francine Smith started to become an atheist, Hayley was trying hard to revive Francine's faith in the Christian God; it is unclear if Hayley was acting out of some sense of faith herself or if she merely wanted to help Francine's sense of bitter disappointment. Two episodes later in "Deacon Stan, Jesus Man", when Roger asked how church was, she said it was a waste of time. This could mean she's not a devout Christian, that she is still an atheist, or that she simply does not like the institution of church, particularly the family's church with its completely apathetic pastor. It's worth noting that in "Dope and Faith", she finds it extremely offensive that Stan would pray to win a raffle prize in church. In "Tears of a Clooney," however, after contracting a terminal disease (presumably cancer), she makes a "promise to God" to call child services and stop Roger from enslaving orphans if she survives, which may mean that her sickness revived a sense of faith in her, at least temporarily (although she would usually call Child Services anyway). She once called on "Gaia" to help her protect a tree from destruction, which may indicate a Neopagan or Wiccan belief.

In Family Affair, she participated in a family prayer before games night. Also, it is worth noting that Hayley is seen ascending to Heaven and remaining there throughout the episode titled Rapture's Delight.

ICE 2

ICE 2

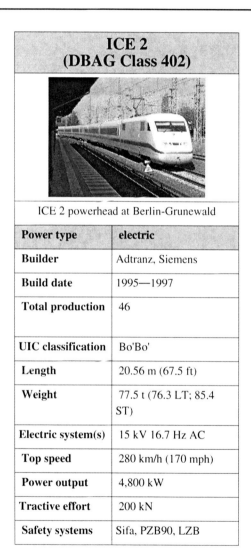

ICE 2 (DBAG Class 402)	
ICE 2 powerhead at Berlin-Grunewald	
Power type	**electric**
Builder	Adtranz, Siemens
Build date	1995—1997
Total production	46
UIC classification	Bo'Bo'
Length	20.56 m (67.5 ft)
Weight	77.5 t (76.3 LT; 85.4 ST)
Electric system(s)	15 kV 16.7 Hz AC
Top speed	280 km/h (170 mph)
Power output	4,800 kW
Tractive effort	200 kN
Safety systems	Sifa, PZB90, LZB

This article is about the train. For the Bridgman form of water ice, see Ice II.

The **ICE 2** is the second series of German high-speed trains and one of five in the Intercity-Express family since 1995.

The ICE 2 (half-)trains are even closer to a conventional push-pull train than the ICE 1, because each train consists of only one power car (**Class 402**, called *powerhead*), six passenger cars (**Classes 805 to 807**) and a cab car (**Class 808**).

Differences to ICE 1

ICE 2 powerhead with opened coupling cover

Two set ICE 2 block train on the Nuremberg-Munich high-speed track

Controls in the driver's cab

Except for the automatic coupling, ICE 2 powerheads are very similar to those of the ICE 1 and can actually be used in ICE 1 trains if strictly necessary.

Half-trains

Usually two ICE 2 half-trains are coupled to form a block train of similar dimensions to the original ICE 1 for serving the main routes, and separated again to operate on routes with less traffic or to provide the passengers two different destinations.

Until the class 808 cab cars have been tested and cleared for passenger service, two ICE 2 half-trains had been solidly coupled to form a permanent block train.

Cars

The passenger cars are very different from the ICE 1 cars, despite their similar exterior: The weight has been significantly reduced and the passenger compartments have been removed in favor of a seating arrangement similar to an airliner (due to reduced seat pitch). Also, the train has been equipped with air suspension to circumvent the wheel noise problems of the ICE 1, which led to the installation of rubber-buffered wheel rims on the ICE 1 units and therefore the Eschede train disaster.

ICE 2 trains have no service car as the class 803 on ICE 1 trains, on the other hand the class 808 cab car is unique to the ICE 2.

Service

ICE 2 trains usually run on the main east-west line, starting in Berlin with two unit block train. In Hamm the train is separated into two half-trains.

One half-train goes through the Ruhr area to Cologne Bonn Airport, while the other half-train continues through Wuppertal and Cologne to Bonn. In the opposite direction, both half-trains are coupled again at Hamm.

Some trains also serve the Munich—Hanover line with halves continuing to Hamburg and Bremen respectively.

Eurotrain

Main article: Eurotrain

Eurotrain was a joint venture formed by Siemens and GEC-Alsthom (today Alstom) in 1996 to market high-speed rail technology in Asia. In 1997, it was one of two competitors to supply the the core system of Taiwan High Speed Rail (THSR), and was awarded the status of preferred bidder by concessionaire THSRC.

In early 1998, the two companies created a demonstration train by combining cars of three existing French and German high-speed trains: ICE 2 powerheads 402 042 and 402 046, were joined at both ends to the articulated double-deck intermediate cars of TGV Duplex trainset #224. On 4 May 1998, the *Eurotrain* demonstration train made a presentation run on the Hanover—Würzburg high-speed railway in Germany, achieving a maximum speed of 316 km/h.

In December 2000, THSRC decided to award the contract to the rival Taiwan Shinkansen Consortium, leading to a legal battle ending in damage payments for Eurotrain in 2004.

External links

- ICE 2 [1] Siemens Page

Area code 360

Area code 360

Area code 360 is the area code for western Washington state outside of the greater Seattle metropolitan area. It began service on January 15, 1995. The area, which encompasses all of western Washington outside of urban King, Pierce, and Snohomish counties and Bainbridge Island, was previously part of area code 206. The 360 area code was one of the first two area codes that did not take the N1X or N0X form (*i.e.*, the middle digit is neither 0 nor 1) in the North American Numbering Plan, along with Alabama area code 334, which began service on the same day.

Cities and towns in area code 360 include:

- Aberdeen
- Arlington
- Bellingham
- Bremerton
- Camas
- Centralia
- Enumclaw
- Kelso
- Marysville
- Mount Vernon
- Oak Harbor
- Olympia
- Port Angeles
- Snohomish
- Vancouver
- Whidbey Island

In 1999, an overlay area code of 564 was to be introduced to the entire 360 area; however the implementation has been delayed indefinitely by order of the Washington Utilities and Transportation Commission. Currently, the Washington Utilities and Transportation Commission forecasts that supply of 360 area code numbers will not be exhausted until 2012.

See also

- Washington area codes
- List of NANP area codes

External links

- NANPA Washington area code map [1]
- List of exchanges from AreaCodeDownload.com, 360 Area Code [2]

State of Washington area codes: 206, 253, 360, 425, 509		
	North: 250, 604, 778	
West: Pacific Ocean, 250	**Area Code 360**	**East:** 206, 253, 425, 509
	South: 503, 971	
Province of British Columbia Area Codes: 250, 604, 778		
State of Oregon area codes: 458, 503, 541, 971		

RIM-900

RIM-900

The **RIM-900** was one of the first wireless data devices, marketed as a two-way pager. It operated on the Mobitex network. It was a clam shell device that could fit on your belt. It had a small keyboard for sending and receiving email and interactive messages.

The product was introduced as Inter@ctive Paging in 1995 by Research in Motion and RAM Mobile Data.

Inter@ctive Pager

Inter@ctive Pager

The **Inter@ctive Pager**, introduced in 1995 by Research In Motion (RIM), allowed users to receive and send messages over the internet via a wireless data network known as Mobitex. The US Operator of Mobitex, RAM Mobile Data operated the network and introduced the Inter@ctive Pager service as RAMfirst Interactive Paging(sm). The product was named the 1997 Top Product by Wireless for the Corporate User Magazine.[1] The Inter@ctive Pager was also known as the RIM-900.

In August 1998, BellSouth Wireless Data replaced the RIM-900 with the **RIM 950** and marketed the service as BellSouth Interactive Paging(sm).

The Interactive Paging service introduced wireless users to such features as peer-to-peer Delivery and Read Receipts and sending faxes and text to speech messages to a telephone. It also incorporated all the features of a traditional one way paging system (Interactive voice response, Telocator Alphanumeric input Protocol, etc..) and added two way extensions to those services. The devices communicated to the internet, peer users, and the PSTN via a Gateway which also served as the store and forward mailbox for the wireless user. Interactive Paging became known as Interactive Messaging Plus(sm) when BellSouth and SBC formed Cingular Wireless.

External links

*   Interactive Messaging Plus User's Guide [2]

Rayman

Rayman

Rayman (series)	
The original *Rayman* logo	
Genres	Platform game Action game 3rd person
Developers	Ubisoft
Publishers	Ubisoft
Creators	Michel Ancel
Official website	http://raymanzone.ubi.com/

Rayman is an action video game series developed by Ubisoft, originally under the direction of Michel Ancel.

Overview

Gameplay

Rayman games are typically platformer games, although spin offs have had radically different gameplay. The original Rayman was a 2D sprite based platformer similar to those of the 16 bit era. Rayman 2 moved the series into 3D, and added more variety to the gameplay with new actions such as riding a rocket, being pulled through a marsh by a snake, and an entire level where Rayman's hair allows him to fly instead of simply hover. Rayman 3: Hoodlum Havoc kept the same core platforming of Rayman 2, but added timed power ups and had a bigger emphasis on combat. The handheld entries in the series have remained similar to the sprite based original in gameplay in that they are 2D. Rayman DS, which was a port of Rayman 2, is an exception to that. Rayman Raving Rabbids, which was at first planned to be a traditional platformer, turned into a mini-game collection late in development after the developers got their hands on the Wii Remote and Nunchuck. Early trailers for the game and early information portray it having a darker atmosphere than is typical of a Rayman game, and show Rayman riding animals including a giant spider. Rayman could alter his appearance, and his dancing style with it, and dance to entrance the Rabbids. Ultimately this idea was scrapped, replaced with motion based mini-games similar to WarioWare: Smooth Moves. Rayman Raving Rabbids was also released on the Xbox 360, despite being made around the motion-sensing Wii controller, and simply replaced physical actions with traditional button presses. Rayman has two racing games (Rayman Arena and Rayman Rush) that feature Rayman characters racing on foot through platformer like stages, and battling in a separate arena mode. There have also been Rayman educational games, such as Rayman Brain Games, which focused less on gameplay and more on learning.

Characters

- **Rayman** is the main protagonist of the series. He has no arms and legs, though he has hands and feet that are able to move independently from his body. Rayman is able to launch long range punches at his enemies, and in some games, eject damaging balls of light from his gloves. He has the ability to use his hair to glide and float by spinning it at a rapid speed. He is typically found wearing white gloves, a red neckerchief on a purple shirt and a white ring on the chest, (which was replaced with a red and purple hoodie), and he wears yellow trainers. He is voiced by David Gasman and Steve Perkinson in the video games, and by Billy West in the animated series. He was awarded the Best New Character award of 1995 by Electronic Gaming Monthly.

- **Globox** is a gentle, sensitive glute, who acts as Rayman's sidekick. He is very cowardly, fleeing at the sight of any enemies, leaving Rayman alone to fight them. Globox's magic power is the ability to create a small cloud that rains over fire and machinery after performing a rain dance.

- **Ly the Fairy** is a fairy made by the godlike Polokus to help Rayman. She appears as a weak and serious character, but despite this, she's actually potentially dangerous if she has to be, though is an energetic, loving and playful character and hardly loses her patience. She likes activity and experimenting with magic.

- **Murfy** serves as a guide to Rayman. He has a really hasty nature unable to deal with failure. He appears bored with his job and can't be bothered with trivial details. His race is depicted as mischievous and described as "cultivated hedonists".

- The **Teensies** are a race of small Cyan skin colored creatures with elongated noses and beady black eyes. They exist in many forms and most of them have magical powers. Their purpose is to unveil all the roads in the world. They are led by Grand Minimus, who acts as caretaker of the Heart of the World, the Grand Minimus is the greatest little king of them all.

- **The Glosies** are two baby globoxes that were adopted by **teensies** and became their princes for the Grand Minimus. The Glosies are usually having trouble standing on each other though and when they do the one on bottom has trouble walking. The Glosies were thought to be royalty after they found out they didn't have watermelons in their mouths because their head were long in the opposite direction then the rest of them.

- **Mr. Dark** is Rayman's arch-nemesis and first primary antagonist of the series. Little is known about him, except that he is an incredibly talented yet evil sorcerer. After stealing the Great Protoon and imprisoning all the Electoons, Mr. Dark hides away in his lair, at the Candy Chateau, high above the Cave Of Skops. Once Rayman meets him, instead of them fighting directly, Mr. Dark flees the scene and sets fused versions of his main Henchmen upon Rayman. Ever since fleeing the scene, his location and even existence remain to be unanswered, although he appeared as the main antagonist in Rayman Brain Games.

- **Reflux** is a Knaaren, a race of invincible, ruthless warriors who cannot stand sunlight, who gives up his invincibility while stealing the scepter from the Leptys. He is voiced by Ziggy Marley.

- **Admiral Razorbeard** is Rayman's second enemy, the main villain in *Rayman 2* and the Game Boy Advance version of *Rayman 3*. He commands a force of Robo-Pirates and ships that plague over Rayman's World. He rules from a gigantic ship, known as the Buccaneer. Razorbeard is infamous for his attacks that have left over 100 peaceful planets to cosmic dust, making him a vicious and cruel mass murderer. His personality is mainly similar to a power-hungry dictator, a cruel and a sadistic villain. Razorbeard is also extremely frustrated and he has a short fuse, as he throws minor temper tantrums whenever one of his henchmen came to tell him bad news. Unlike Mr. Dark, Razorbeard fights Rayman at the game's climax, but after being beaten by Rayman, he flees the scene. In *Rayman 2*, he is voiced by Matthew Géczy.

- **Andre** is a maniacal dark lum and the main villain in *Rayman 3* and *Rayman: Hoodlum's Revenge*. Globox has a strange fondness of him. He is transformed from a red lum into a dark lum when Rayman's hands scare him with shadow puppets. At the beginning of the game, Globox accidentally swallows him, and the Teensies tell Rayman to take Globox to a doctor to get him out. After visiting three different doctors, Andre finds Reflux and makes a deal with him: that if he steals King Gumsi's sceptre, he will give him the opportunity to kill Rayman. At the end of the game, Reflux is defeated and Rayman turns Andre back into a red lum.

Games

Main series

The games in the main series have fairly distinct settings (sometimes described as different realms, etc. within Rayman's home world) and plots. Nonetheless, besides the titular hero, several characters (Globox, Murfy, Ly) and themes (freeing magical beings from cages, collecting magical energy, etc.) besides the titular hero do appear with some regularity.

Particularly, the universe featured in the original *Rayman* has largely been left unvisited in subsequent instalments, with the exception of cameos including the famous purple plums, small harmless versions of its boss Moskito, etc. Some elements from the original game (e.g. the hunters called Livingstones, and Betilla the Fairy) will feature in the upcoming *Rayman Origins*, although since in the new game these characters (and its world overall) bear some visual differences, and more obviously it features Rayman's friend Globox who first appeared in *Rayman 2*, it is likely to be more of a reboot.

See the following articles for synopses and other information on the main series games:

- *Rayman*
- *Rayman 2: The Great Escape*
- *Rayman 3: Hoodlum Havoc*
- *Rayman Origins*

Handheld series

The original *Rayman* has been rereleased on several handheld platforms, including the Nintendo Game Boy Advance, Nintendo DSi (via DSiWare) and smartphones. As well as this, handheld tie-ins to the main series games have been released; however, these often resemble the 2D cage-hunting gameplay of the first game more than their 3D counterparts. Particularly, the Game Boy Color version of *Rayman* featured music and box art based on *Rayman 2*, but the gameplay, graphics and settings of the first game.

- *Rayman* (Handheld version)
- *Rayman 2: The Great Escape* (Game Boy Color version)
- *Rayman 3* (GBA Version)
- *Rayman: Hoodlums' Revenge*
- *Rayman Raving Rabbids* (GBA and DS Versions)

Raving Rabbids

The Raving Rabbid series is based around Rabbids, a species of maniacal anthropomorphic rabbits that serve as the primary antagonists. Their most well known traits feature various slapstick comedy elements; running around wielding various household objects, dressing up as various other fictional characters, and most of all, constant screaming. Although essentially the "villain" in the game, they have gained a considerable popularity and fanbase through viral videos and media appearances. Many people even suspect them to overshadow Rayman, despite hints that there could be a *Rayman 4*. The Rabbids left the Rayman series to form a series of their own with the release of *Rabbids Go Home* in November 2009 and *Raving Rabbids: Travel in Time*. In October 2010, Ubisoft and Aardman announced a partnership to produce a TV series pilot and several shorts based on the franchise.

A rabbid model at Otakon in 2007.

The Rabbids appear as humanoid, stout, usually white lagomorphs with big round eyes and a large mouth with two large incisors. Rabbids tend to be somewhat mentally unstable, and often experience strange adrenaline rushes, where their eyes turn red and they emit a loud yell: DAAAAAAAAH! (although spelled "BWAAAAAAAH!") Other than this, their only communication seems to be random gibberish. This is also often a precursor of the bunny smashing something or attacking someone with its tool of choice, usually a toilet plunger or something plunger-related, such as a plunger-shooter, or other household items, such as feather dusters, ladles, toilet brushes, toy shovels, tennis rackets, sausages and other objects. Rabbids also have a penchant for dressing up. These outfits include French maid outfits, snorkels with duck-shaped swim rings, ninja suits, pirate outfits, and various other pop culture costumes. The Rabbids have made several appearances in non-Rayman games as well, such as Red Steel and Teenage Mutant Ninja Turtles: Smash-Up.

- *Rayman Raving Rabbids*
- *Rayman Raving Rabbids 2*
- *Rayman Raving Rabbids TV Party*
- *Rabbids Go Home*
- *Raving Rabbids: Travel in Time*

Spin-offs

- *Rayman Arena/Rayman M/Rayman Rush*
- *Rayman Brain Games*
- *Rayman Golf*
- *Rayman Designer*

Ports and remakes

- *Rayman Advance* - A port of Rayman 1 on Game Boy Advance.
- *Rayman Gold* - A game with no plot that has the PC version of Rayman 1 in the disc.
- *Rayman Forever* - Expansion pack of Rayman Gold, it contained a bundle of 50+ new levels, a level editor and a fridge magnet.
- *Rayman DS* - Nintendo DS port of Rayman 2 on N64.
- *Rayman Revolution* - Remake of Rayman 2 for PS2 that has exclusives such as new music tracks, bosses amongst other things.
- *Rayman DSi* - Remake of Rayman 1 for Nintendo DSi.

Development

The earliest *Rayman 4* trailers depicted menacing and zombie-like rabbits, simply appearing from underground with a blank stare in various shapes and forms, smaller eyes and furry. At this point, trailers showed the game as an adventure game with fight stages, where Rayman would need to punch and kick himself kung fu style through a horde of zombie-bunnies. As the game concept evolved, from one of a central objective to minigames, and viral videos were created, the rabbits slowly evolved into the Rabbid figures, which were much more conscious and amusing, changing from merely being enemies to fight through into more memorable characters with various traits and quirks. *Rayman* creator Michel Ancel described the bunnies as *"vicious, but at the same time [...] totally stupid"*. In a recent video review, project lead Loïc Gounon confirmed the possibility of splitting the Rayman and Rabbid series apart, mentioning that the Rabbids seem to appeal more to younger gamers, due to its slapstick humor and minigames deviating from the Rayman series' more fantasy-oriented gameplay.

Reception

Since his debut in 1995 on the Atari Jaguar, Sega Saturn, PlayStation and on the MS-DOS, Rayman has become a popular and recognizable video game character over the past decade, along with his trademark lack of limbs and Helicopter power, having appeared in several titles up for many platforms until the present day. Since the first game's release in 1995, the Rayman games have become highly successful and popular with many fans.

The Rabbids from the Raving Rabbids series became massively popular both through the teaser trailers and the game itself. IGN has stated that the Rabbids have *"more personality and charisma than 10 of the most popular video game mascots combined"*, and that the bunnies have literally *"upstaged Rayman himself"*. GameSpot has noted, *"The Rabbids themselves are almost exclusively responsible for [selling the game's humor], as they are, without a doubt, hysterical. They're adorably designed, with their dumb stares, high-pitched shrieks, and a penchant for taking comedic bumps."* There has been speculation by reviewers that the success of the Rabbid character will probably inspire the developers to create more games of the franchise, possibly even without Rayman. This was first hinted in the launch trailer of the first game, where Rayman, despite being the title character, only appears for a fraction of a second, only to be squashed flat by a couch taken over by the bunnies, and became evident in *Rayman Raving Rabbids 2,* in which case Rayman disguises himself as a Rabbid, causing the game to put more emphasis on them than on Rayman himself. This was then proven to be true with the announcement of *Rabbids Go Home.*

Before the game's release, the director Jacques Exertier was asked about why Rayman was omitted, Exertier confirmed that after *Rabbids Go Home*, Rayman WILL return for more action-adventure video games. And it looks like Exertier was true to his word, because a Rayman-only game was released on March 1, 2010. However, it was only another re-release of Rayman 2 (this time on the iPhone OS.)

At the end of May 2010, as a result of rumors that *Rayman* creator Michel Ancel was leaving Ubisoft and the Beyond Good & Evil 2 project, fellow game designer and close colleague Nicolas Choukroun posted on Ancel's unofficial Facebook page stating that Ancel had instead moved into another studio to work on a new Rayman game . The game was revealed as *Rayman Origins* at Ubisoft's E3 2010 conference.

External links

- Rayman Pirate-Community [1]
- RayWiki, a free wiki encyclopedia about Rayman [2]
- Rayman Fanpage [3] (in French, English and German)

Everson Mono

Everson Mono

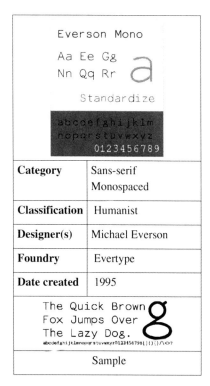

Category	Sans-serif Monospaced
Classification	Humanist
Designer(s)	Michael Everson
Foundry	Evertype
Date created	1995
Sample	

Everson Mono is a monospaced humanist sans serif Unicode font whose development by Michael Everson began in 1995. At first, Everson Mono was a collection of 8-bit fonts containing glyphs for tables in ISO/IEC 10646; at that time, it was not easy to edit cmaps to have true Unicode indices, and there were very few applications which could do anything with a font so encoded in any case. The original "Everson Mono" had a MacRoman character set, and other versions were named with suffixes: "Everson Mono Latin B", "Everson Mono Currency", "Everson Mono Armenian" and so on. A range of fonts with the character set of the ISO/IEC 8859 series were also made. A large font distributed in 2003 was named "Everson Mono Unicode", but since 2008 the font has been named simply "Everson Mono". There are at present no bold or bold-italic styles, but an italic style was added in July 2010.

Range, Characters, Version

Everson Mono version 5.1.5, dated 2008-12-07, contains 6,343 characters (6,350 glyphs). Its previous major version (version 4.1.3, dated 2003-02-13) contained 4,893 characters (4,899 glyphs).

In short, this font covers following scripts: Armenian, Canadian Syllabics, Cherokee, Cyrillic, Georgian, Greek (excepting Coptic), Hebrew, Latin, Ogham, Runic, see below for details.

Characters included in Unicode Ranges / Blocks

Block Name (Range)	Chars. v.5.1.5	Chars. v.4.1.3
Basic Latin (0000–007F)	95	95
Latin-1 Supplement (0080–00FF)	96	96
Latin extended-A (0100–017F)	128	128
Latin extended-B (0180–024F)	208	183
IPA Extensions (0250–02AF)	96	96
Spacing Modifier Letters (02B0–02FF)	80	80
Combining Diacritical Marks (0300–036F)	112	107
Greek and Coptic (0370–03FF)	120	118
Cyrillic (0400–04FF)	256	246
Cyrillic Supplement (0500–052F)	40	16
Armenian (0530–058F)	86	86
Hebrew (0590–05FF)	87	82
Arabic (0600–06FF)	0	3
Syriac (0700–074F)	0	0
Arabic Supplement (0750–077F)	0	0
Thaana (0780–07BF)	0	0
Devanagari (0900–097F)	0	0
Bengali (0980–09FF)	0	0
Gurmukhi (0A00–0A7F)	0	0
Gujarati (0A80–0AFF)	0	0
Oriya (0B00–0B7F)	0	0
Tamil (0B80–0BFF)	0	0
Telugu (0C00–0C7F)	0	0
Kannada (0C80–0CFF)	0	0

Malayalam (0D00–0D7F)	0	0
Sinhala (0D80–0DFF)	0	0
Thai (0E00–0E7F)	0	0
Lao (0E80–0EFF)	0	0
Tibetan (0F00–0FFF)	0	0
Myanmar (Burma) (1000–109F)	0	0
Georgian (10A0–10FF)	83	80
Hangul Jamo (1100–11FF)	0	0
Ethiopic (Ge'ez) (1200–137F)	0	0
Ethiopic Supplement (1380–139F)	0	0
Cherokee (13A0–13FF)	85	85
Unified Canadian Aboriginal Syllabics (1400–167F)	640	630
Ogham (1680–169F)	29	29
Runic (16A0–16FF)	81	81
Tagalog (Baybayin) (1700–171F)	0	0
Hanunoo (1720–173F)	0	0
Buhid (1740–175F)	0	0
Tagbanwa (1760–177F)	0	0
Khmer (1780–17FF)	0	0
Mongolian (1800–18AF)	0	0
Limbu (1900–194F)	0	0
Tai Le (1950–197F)	0	0
Tai Lue (1980–19DF)	0	0
Khmer Symbols (19E0–19FF)	0	0
Buginese (1A00–1A1F)	0	0
Phonetic Extensions (1D00–1D7F)	128	107
Phonetic Extensions Supplement (1D80–1DBF)	64	0
Combining Diacritical Marks Supplement (1DC0–1DFF)	42	0
Latin extended additional (1E00–1EFF)	256	246
Greek Extended (1F00–1FFF)	233	233
General Punctuation (2000–206F)	107	97
Superscripts and Subscripts (2070–209F)	34	29

Currency Symbols (20A0–20CF)	25	18
Combining Diacritical Marks for Symbols (20D0–20FF)	33	27
Letterlike Symbols (2100–214F)	80	74
Number Forms (2150–218F)	58	49
Arrows (2190–21FF)	112	112
Mathematical Operators (2200–22FF)	256	256
Miscellaneous Technical (2300–23FF)	219	207
Control Pictures (2400–243F)	39	39
Optical Character Recognition (2440–245F)	11	11
Enclosed Alphanumerics (2460–24FF)	160	159
Box Drawing (2500–257F)	128	128
Block Elements (2580–259F)	32	32
Geometric Shapes (25A0–25FF)	96	96
Miscellaneous Symbols (2600–26FF)	183	125
Dingbats (2700–27BF)	174	160
Miscellaneous Mathematical Symbols-A (27C0–27EF)	27	0
Supplemental Arrows-A (27F0–27FF)	16	0
Braille Patterns (2800–28FF)	0	0
Supplemental Arrows-B (2900–297F)	110	111
Miscellaneous Mathematical Symbols-B (2980–29FF)	0	62
Supplemental Mathematical Operators (2A00–2AFF)	195	21
Miscellaneous Symbols and Arrows (2B00–2BFF)	0	0
Glagolitic (2C00–2C5F)	0	0
Latin Extended-C (2C60–2C7F)	32	0
Coptic (2C80–2CFF)	0	0
Georgian Supplement (2D00–2D2F)	38	0
Tifinagh (2D30–2D7F)	55	0
Ethiopic Extended (2D80–2DDF)	0	0
Cyrillic Extended-A (2DE0–2DFF)	16	0
Supplemental Punctuation (2E00–2E7F)	50	0
CJK Radicals Supplement (2E80–2EFF)	0	0
Kangxi Radicals(Kangxi) (2F00–2FDF)	0	0

Ideographic Description Characters (2FF0–2FFF)	0	0
CJK Symbols and Punctuation (3000–303F)	0	0
Hiragana (3040–309F)	0	90
Katakana (30A0–30FF)	0	94
Bopomofo (3100–312F)	0	0
Hangul Compatibility Jamo (3130–318F)	0	0
Kanbun (3190–319F)	0	0
Bopomofo Extended (31A0–31BF)	0	0
CJK Strokes (31C0–31EF)	0	0
Katakana Phonetic Extensions (31F0–31FF)	0	0
Enclosed CJK Letters and Months (3200–32FF)	0	0
CJK Compatibility (3300–33FF)	0	0
CJK Unified Ideographs Extension A (3400–4DBF)	0	0
Yijing Hexagram Symbols (4DC0–4DFF)	0	0
CJK Unified Ideographs (Han Unification) (4E00–9FFF)	0	0
Yi Syllables (A000–A48F)	0	0
Yi Radicals (A490–A4CF)	0	0
Lisu (A4D0–A4FF)	0	0
Cyrillic Extended-B (A640–A69F)	80	0
Modifier Tone Letters (A700–A71F)	0	0
Latin Extended-D (A720–A7FF)	115	0
Syloti Nagri (A800–A82F)	0	0
Hangul Syllables (AC00–D7AF)	0	0
High Surrogates (D800–DB7F)	0	0
High Private Use Surrogates (DB80–DBFF)	0	0
Low Surrogates (DC00–DFFF)	0	0
Private Use Area (E000–F8FF)	1	0
CJK Compatibility Ideographs (F900–FAFF)	0	0
Alphabetic Presentation Forms (FB00–FB4F)	58	58
Arabic Presentation Forms-A (FB50–FDFF)	0	0
Variation Selectors (FE00–FE0F)	16	1
Vertical Forms (FE10–FE1F)	0	0

Combining Half Marks (FE20–FE2F)	7	4
CJK Compatibility Forms (FE30–FE4F)	0	0
Small Form Variants (FE50–FE6F)	0	0
Arabic Presentation Forms-B (FE70–FEFF)	0	0
Halfwidth and Fullwidth Forms (FF00–FFEF)	0	0
Specials (FFF0–FFFF)	5	5
Linear B Syllabary (10000–1007F)	88	0
Linear B Ideograms (10080–100FF)	123	0
Aegean Numbers (10100–1013F)	57	0
Ancient Greek Numbers (10140–1018F)	43	0
Ancient Symbols (10190–101CF)	12	0
Phaistos Disc (101D0–101FF)	46	0
Lycian (10280–1029F)	29	0
Old Italic (10300–1032F)	35	0
Gothic (10330–1034F)	27	0
Deseret (10400–1044F)	80	0
Shavian (10450–1047F)	48	0
Cypriot Syllabary (10800–1083F)	55	0
Ancient Greek Musical Notation (1D200–1D24F)	70	0

See also

- List of typefaces
- Unicode typefaces (Information and comparison on major fonts)

External links

- Evertype: Everson Mono [1]

Canon PowerShot

Canon PowerShot

The **PowerShot** products are a line of consumer and prosumer grade digital cameras, launched by Canon in 1995. The PowerShot line has been successful for Canon, and is one of the best-selling digital camera lines worldwide. On the photo sharing website Flickr, in the point-and-shoot category, as of March 2010 all five of the top used cameras are Canon.

Free software from the Canon Hack Development Kit (CHDK) project allows nearly complete programmatic control of PowerShot cameras, enabling users to add features, up to and including BASIC & Lua scripting.

Some models of Powershot cameras were affected by third party CCD sensors with a design flaw which caused them to fail and display severely distorted images. Canon has offered to repair affected cameras free of charge.

Products

Current

- **A series**: "Easy and Fun" budget cameras ranging from point-and-shoot to prosumer cameras
- **D series**: waterproof, freeze- and shock-resistant
- **E series**: design-oriented budget cameras
- **G series**: flagship cameras with advanced features
- **S/SD series** (*also known as* **PowerShot Digital ELPH, Digital IXUS** and **IXY Digital***)*: "Performance and Style" ultracompact point-and-shoot cameras

Front view of Canon PowerShot A720 IS.

- **S/SX series**: ultra-zoom cameras
- **S series**: originally a series of compact point-and-shoot cameras, currently a series of prosumer cameras slotting beneath the G series

Discontinued

- **Pro series**: semi-professional-level cameras slotting right beneath Canon's dSLRs, consisting of the Pro70 (1998), Pro90 IS (2001), and Pro1 (2004).
- **TX series**: hybrid camera/camcorders

See also

- List of Canon products

External links

- Official Canon PowerShot page [1]
- Canon PowerShot Digital Camera Product Advisories [2]

Cray T90

Cray T90

The **Cray T90** series (code-named *Triton* during development) was the last of a line of vector processing supercomputers manufactured by Cray Research, Inc, superseding the Cray C90 series. The first machines were shipped in 1995, and featured a 2.2 ns (450 MHz) clock cycle and two-wide vector pipes, for a peak speed of 1.8 gigaflops per processor; the high clock speed arises from the CPUs being built using ECL logic. As with the Cray J90, each CPU contained a scalar data cache, in addition to the instruction buffering/caching which has always been in Cray architectures.

Configurations were available with between four and 32 processors, and with either IEEE 754 or traditional Cray floating point arithmetic; the processors shared an SRAM main memory of up to eight gigabytes, with a bandwidth of three 64-bit words per cycle per CPU (giving a 32-CPU STREAM bandwidth of 360 gigabytes per second). The clock signal is distributed via a fibre-optic harness to the processors.

The T90 series was available in three variants, the **T94** (one to four processors), **T916** (eight or 16 processors) and **T932** (16 or 32 processors).

It is widely considered as being slightly ahead of the state of the art at the time it was shipped; the systems were never particularly reliable. At launch, a 32-processor T932 cost $39 million.

Cray T90 systems were installed, amongst other places, at least three US government sites, at NAVOCEANO in Mississippi (Bay St. Louis) USA, at NTT and NIED in Japan, at the Ford Motor Company and at General Motors, at NOAA's Geophysical Fluid Dynamics Laboratory, at Forschungszentrum Jülich in Germany, and at the Commissariat à l'Energie Atomique in France.

The system chassis weighs ten tons and contains four tons of fluorinert coolant; it is approximately the shape and size of a very large chest freezer, and panelled in black and gold plastic.

Its successor, some years after the last T90s shipped, was the Cray X1.

References

- Armari, Seymour Cray and a giant gold sarcophagus [1]
- Top 500 Supercomputer sites [2] (PDF)

Time Out (confectionery)

Time Out (confectionery)

Type	Confectionery
Owner	Cadbury plc
Introduced	1992
Related Brands	Cadbury products

Cadbury **Time Out** is a chocolate based snack introduced in 1992 in the UK and the Republic of Ireland and 1995 in Australia. The Time Out bar includes a thin layer of Cadbury Flake chocolate.

Time Out available for the Irish and UK markets is produced by Cadbury Ireland.

The bar is sold in the United Kingdom and has been sold in Australia for a number of years, as well as various other Australasian countries. It was introduced to Canada and South Africa in 2001, but was discontinued three years later due to lagging sales. It is available in Japan.

When it first came out, it was a substantial snack (about 25 grams), then suddenly it was down-sized to 20.5g. The new single-finger bar, just released, shrunk into 16g.

The current 2 finger bar has a combined weight of 32g and is suitable for vegetarians.

Digital-S

Digital-S

D-9 Videotape

D-9 or **Digital S** as it was originally known, is a professional digital videotape format created by JVC in 1995. It is a direct competitor to Digital Betacam. Its name was changed to D-9 in 1999 by the SMPTE. It is used mostly inside Europe and Asia, though has seen some use in the US, most notably by the FOX news channel.

Technical details

D-9 uses a tape shell of the VHS formfactor, but the tape itself uses a much higher quality metal particle formulation. The recording system is digital and for video uses DV compression at a 50 Mbit/s bitrate. Video is recorded in 4:2:2 component format at a variety of standard definition resolutions, in either 4:3 or 16:9 aspect ratios. Audio is recorded as 16bit/48 kHz pcm with up to 4 separate channels.

HD recording

For HD recording, JVC developed an extension to D-9 called D-9 HD. D-9 HD uses twice the number of recording heads to record a 100Mbit/s video bitstream at resolutions of 720p60, 1080i60 and 1080p24. This variant is also able to record 8 channels of PCM audio at 16bit/48 kHz. This is ideal for mastering to AC3 or other multichannel audio compression formats used for broadcasting. The higher data rate means that the recording time of any given tape is cut in half.

Video quality

Video quality is generally very high; at standard definition resolutions, quality is higher than that of Betacam SP and comparable to Digital Betacam. At HD resolutions, based on specifications, quality is higher than HDCAM but lower than HDCAM SR; unfortunately, no objective tests have been done comparing these formats.

Additional information

Although D-9 uses the same video codec (DV) as MiniDV, the video bitrate of D-9 is significantly higher than that of the "pro-sumer" format. DVCPRO achieves bitrate parity with D-9 and D-9 HD, but has a slower tape speed, making it less reliable. Some of the D-9 studio gear is capable of recording with pre-read and is provided with 4 channel audio like digital betacam. SDI interfaces are also provided. There is only one dockable recorder for docking to other cameras and that is the JVC BR-D40.

External links

- JVC's japanese D-9 product page [1]

See also

- Betacam
- Digital Betacam
- HDCAM

Gene Marshall

Gene Marshall

Gene Marshall is a 15.5 inches tall collectible fashion doll inspired by Hollywood's Golden Age. It was created by the illustrator Mel Odom. Each doll features an intricate movie-styled theme based upon fashions from the 1930s, 40s and 50s as well as Hollywood's version of historical costuming.

When the Gene Marshall doll appeared on the market in 1995, it was the first large fashion doll primarily intended for adult collectors. Its success sparked the creation of similar dolls from other companies.

History

When the Gene Marshall doll appeared on the market in 1995, it was the first item of its type and size: a large fashion doll primarily intended for display by adult collectors. Until then, the standard fashion doll had been the 11.5" Barbie, which is still primarily sold as a children's plaything; while some collectors were attracted to limited-edition specialty Barbies, most collectible dolls at the time were constructed with neotenous baby-doll proportions instead of with mature, nubile ones. The popular success of Gene Marshall sparked the invention of an entire genre of similar collectible large fashion dolls from other companies, such as Tyler Wentworth from Tonner Doll Company, Alexandra Fairchild Ford from Madame Alexander and Clea Bella from Bella! Productions.

Three years after Gene Marshall's introduction, over half a million had been sold, and a Gene subculture had sprung up including collectibles clubs, magazines, and conventions. Her design is "an amalgam of all the larger-than-life actresses of Hollywood's Golden Era", and costumes that evoke the work of Edith Head are supposed to represent her appearances in specific but fictional films.

Odom's illustration work has been compared to dolls, and though his career progressed beyond the men's magazines for which he is still best known (he has done book and magazine covers including TIME magazine), he believes that Gene is the "something significant" he has felt bound to do after watching 2/3 of his friends die during the AIDS epidemic. After a its debut at the 1995 Toy Fair, Gene became a hit among adult collectors, among them actress Demi Moore ("the world's most high-profile doll collector", according to the *New York Times*).

Between 1995 and 2005 the dolls were manufactured by the Ashton-Drake Galleries. Since 2005 they are produced by Jason Wu and made by Integrity Toys. They have a dedicated following and have inspired other characters in the line: Madra Lord, Violet Waters, Ivy Jordan and Trent Osborn. These dolls are also popular for artists' one of a kind (OOAK) repaints.

Backstory

The doll comes with a detailed backstory, eventually expressed in the novelization *Gene Marshall, Girl Star*. The character Gene Marshall was born in Cos Cob, Connecticut in 1923, and was discovered by the filmmaker Eric von Sternberg while working in New York City as an usherette. Cast in his next film, she was thrust into a major role when the star fell through a trapdoor during a musical number called "You Floor Me". By the 1950s she was a Hollywood "powerhouse".

Further reading

- Mel Odom and Michael A. Sommers (2000). *Gene Marshall, Girl Star*. Hyperion. ISBN 0786865571. - Fictional backstory
- Carolyn Cook (1998). *Gene*. Hobby House Press. ISBN 0875885233. - Doll's history and accessorization options

External links

- Mel Odom's Gene produced by Jason Wu [1]

Super A'Can

Super A'Can

Manufacturer	Funtech
Type	Video game console
Generation	Fourth generation (16-bit era)
Retail availability	1995
Media	Cartridge
CPU	16-bit Motorola 68000, 8-bit MOS 6502

The **Super A'can** is a console that was released exclusively in Taiwan in 1995 by Funtech Entertainment. At first glance it appears to be a Super Nintendo clone with the case and controllers bearing a strong similarity to the Japanese version, but inside is a Motorola 68000, similar to the Sega Genesis/Mega Drive and Neo Geo. Twelve games have been confirmed to exist for the system.

Although the A'can is a powerful console that had the support of several of Taiwan's largest firms developing software for it, it ultimately failed on the market for a few reasons: its initial cost was too high for most interested parties to afford, and newer, more powerful systems with 3D technology were appearing on the market at the same time (such as the Sony PlayStation). Also, as the developers were pushed to finish their games as quickly as possible (and using a rather stubborn and poorly documented development kit to do so), the resulting A'can games were, by far, nothing special.

In fact, the A'can did so very poorly on the market during its short appearance there that it lost its company over USD$6M (6 million US dollars). In the end, the company destroyed all development and production materials related to the machine, and sold off the remaining systems to the United States as scrap parts.

Technical specifications

CPU

Hardware specifications

Processor	Motorola 68000 (or equivalent) clocked at 10.74 MHz
Secondary processor	8-bit MOS 6502, clocked at 3.58 MHz

Graphics

Palette:	32,768 colors

Input and output

Control pad inputs	Two DE-9M (9-pin male D-connectors) on front of console, identical to those of the Sega Genesis/Mega Drive (though not compatible with Genesis/Mega Drive control pads)

List of games

- F001: *Formosa Duel*
- F002: *Sango Fighter*
- F003: *The Son of Evil*
- F004: *Speedy Dragon/Sonic Dragon*
- F005: *Super Taiwanese Baseball League*
- F006: *Journey to the Laugh (aka C.U.G.)*
- F007: *Super Light Saga - Dragon Force*
- F008: *Monopoly: Adventure in Africa*
- F009: *Gambling Lord*
- F010: *Magical Pool*
- F011: *Boomzoo*
- F012: *Rebel Star*

External links

- Fan site [1] (via archive.org)
- Video Game Console Library page [2]

R-Zone

R-Zone

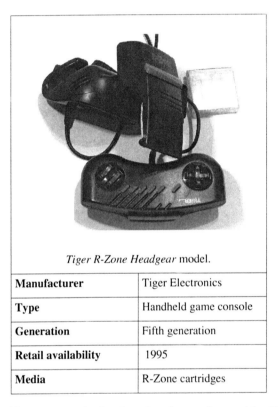

Tiger R-Zone Headgear model.

Manufacturer	Tiger Electronics
Type	Handheld game console
Generation	Fifth generation
Retail availability	1995
Media	R-Zone cartridges

The **R-Zone** was a handheld game console developed and manufactured by Tiger Electronics, released in 1995. The R-Zone was a largely unsuccessful handheld console and would only be manufactured for a short period of time. Although the R-Zone was not designed to compete directly with any other handhelds, it marked Tiger Electronics' first multi-game entry into the portable electronic game market.

The original R-Zone unit consisted of a headset and a separate controller containing batteries. Each game cartridge contained its own transparent LCD display screen which was projected onto a mirrored surface held in front of the player's eye. It is thought that this original design, including the red color scheme, was designed to capitalize on popular buzz for the Nintendo Virtual Boy at the time.

Features

Games

- R-Zone games varied only in title and subject; gameplay within the R-Zone's gaming library was almost identical from title to title.
- Popular franchises released one or more games on the R-Zone: Star Wars, Virtua Fighter, Men in Black, Jurassic Park, Batman, etc.

Controls

The R-Zone's controls are located on the lower top front face of its body and are positioned on the left, right, and bottom sides.

- The R-Zone has ten face buttons. The buttons on the right are labeled "A", "B", "C", and "D". The functions of these face buttons vary from game to game but typically the buttons correspond to a four-direction attack scheme (whereas the "C" button would attack to the left, the "D" button would attack up, the "B" button would attack right, and the "A" button would attack down or do nothing at all. The buttons on the bottom are labeled "ON", "START", "SELECT", "SOUND", "PAUSE", and "OFF". The functions of these face buttons are universal and do not vary from game-to-game. The "ON" button simply turned on the console but was largely un-used as inserting a game cartridge would automatically turn the unit on. The "START" button was required to begin all games. The "SOUND" button turned the audio from on-to-off and vice versa. The "PAUSE" button would allow for any game to be stopped at the exact point in which gameplay was taking place. Pressing this button again resumed gameplay. The "OFF" button was used to turn the console off.
- The R-Zone also features a directional pad, allowing four directions of movement in its games.

Display

- The R-Zone game cartridges were transparent in the center. - This allowed light to pass through and reflect off a specialized mirror to the gamer's eyes.
- The LCD in each cartridge operated identically to Tiger's earlier handheld LCD game units. All of the "graphics" were pre-drawn and permanently set into the LCD itself. Different portions of the display were darkened/activated at different times to provide the illusion of motion or action.
- The mirror had minor tilt adjustment and could be pushed up against the unit for protection and storage.
- The games only displayed a dark red color.

Input/Output

The R-Zone contains the following input/output connectors:

- The bottom side of the console shows two ports (one on the left side, the other on the right). Each port was accessible with a screwdriver and held two AAA batteries or two AA batteries. The units manufactured from 1995 to late 1996 held a total of four AA batteries whereas the units manufactured there after utilized a total of four AAA batteries.
- A single speaker allowed for mono audio output.
- An input for R-Zone cartridges is situated on top of the R-Zone.

Sales and Competition

Variations

A few variations of the R-Zone were produced:

R-Zone X.P.G. Model

- The R-Zone Headgear (1995) was largely different from later units in that the game cartridge was inserted into a device that was strapped onto the user's head. The user would flip down a transparent lens that was designed to reflect the game images into the user's right eye. The head unit held the game being played and was connected to a controller with a cable approximately 2.5 feet (0.76 m) long. The controller required 4 AAA batteries, sported a cartridge storage slot (for keeping an additional game protected and available), volume adjustment dial, and brightness adjustment dial. This unit as a whole is sometimes thought to have been designed to compete against the Virtual Boy. The very first game to be distributed with this console was Batman Forever, based on the 1995 movie of the same name.

- The R-Zone Super Screen (1995–1996) allowed R-Zone games to have color for the first time. Some games allowed for a special lens to be used with this particular R-Zone and simply provided the user with a non-animated color background. Game movement on screen was black. The screen was considerably larger than the other R-Zone models, because of this and the fact that the user was not required to look at a mirror (at a precise angle) to see the gameplay, other people could also see gameplay. Because of its size, the R-Zone Super Screen was often not considered a handheld at all. The unit changed the layout yet again and required 4 C batteries to run. In this model the D-pad was swapped out for four directional buttons (up, down, left, and right).

- "X.P.G. Xtreme Pocket Game" (1997) was a completely handheld version of the console. It lacked a headset, and instead projected the game's display onto a mirrored surface directly above the game controller area on the unit.

External links

- R Zone Head Gear commercial [1](link goes to commercial on retrojunk.com)
- El Museo de los 8 Bits [2] with a list of games
- miniarcade.com [3]
- Review by Dr. Ashens [4]
- Info and pictures of the R Zone DataZone game console and organizer [5]

Gerald "T-Bones" Tibbons

Gerald "T-Bones" Tibbons

Gerald "T-Bones" Tibbons is a comedic fictional character played by David Koechner. He has appeared on two television series and alongside his partner, The Naked Trucker, performed live, and recorded a musical album. As of March 2007, a film based on T-Bones was also in the works.

When asked what the inspiration behind the character was, Koechner explained, "He's a truth teller, we crafted these characters with a lot of truth, and Gerald purely lives for every moment." Koechner also stated that he based Gerald "T-Bones" Tibbons off a Midwestern muse drifter named "Four Way George." The character dates back to 1995, when Koechner filmed a short television pilot based on T-Bones' misadventures. The character became so popular that Koechner would go to auditions, only to find that directors were always demanding his stage persona.

Saturday Night Live

T-Bones made his first major TV appearance as an executioner, hospital orderly and barber during the 1995-1996 season of *Saturday Night Live*, when Koechner was a cast member on the long-running comedy program. He made numerous appearances there and served as the focal point of the sketches, making sly jokes and showcasing his redneck mentality as he annoyed others around him. T-Bones became recognizable by his signature appearance of a slicked comb over, long mutton chop sideburns, tight brown T-shirt, and underbite. In the midst of making clever comments, T-Bones often reveals his utter foolishness and speaks with a hint of southern accent.

The Naked Trucker and T-Bones Show

It was during Koechner's brief tenure on *Saturday Night Live* that he met Dave "Gruber" Allen who, too, had developed a sketch comedy character known as Naked Trucker. The duo formed a musical comedy act in 1999 with T-Bones serving as the vocalist and Trucker on guitar and vocals. They have performed frequently at the Largo nightclub and alongside Tenacious D as well as garnering some TV appearances. The stage act, a mix of stand-up comedy and off-color country songs, became a hit on the Hollywood improv circuit, ultimately landing television performances on *Late Night with Conan O'Brien*, *The Late Late Show with Craig Ferguson*, *Jimmy Kimmel Live*, and *Real Time with Bill Maher*. Their popularity also lead to several offers to bring their act to television, though many early deals never came to fruition. The musical act also helped shed light on T-Bones' background with songs like "My Daddy Is An Astronaut," which describes his fatherless childhood and believing that

Buzz Aldrin is his dad, not Neil Armstrong as often reported.

On January 17, 2007, over a decade after T-Bones's *Saturday Night Live* debut, Comedy Central premiered *The Naked Trucker and T-Bones Show*. While a number of movies have been based on *SNL* characters, this was an extremely rare case of one getting its own TV series. In contrast to his barbershop position on *SNL*, T-Bones was now portrayed as a freeloading drifter and con artist alongside his counterpart, Naked Trucker, who usually served as the more sensible straight man. He also claimed to have had experience as a carny and was frequently seen in promotional photos with an American flag draped over his shoulder as a sign of his patriotism. Between performing in front of a live studio audience, the team presented pre-taped sketches showing them getting in trouble with the law or incidents with hitchhikers they picked up off the highway. The series lasted only eight episodes to mixed reviews.

Film in development

Following the release of *Naked Trucker and T-Bones: Live at the Troubador* in March 2007, Koechner revealed that he has a T-Bones film in development. Will Ferrell and Adam McKay's Gary Sanchez Productions will produce the film through Paramount Vantage. Koechner is currently working on the film with screenwriter/producer Norm Hiscock, who was a writer for *The Naked Trucker and T-Bones Show*, in addition to past work on *Saturday Night Live*, *Kids in the Hall*, and *King of the Hill*.

See also

- Recurring Saturday Night Live characters and sketches

External links

- *The Naked Trucker and T-Bones Show* Official Site [1]
- *The Naked Trucker and T-Bones Show* Comedy Central Site [2]
- *The Naked Trucker and T-Bones Show* Reviews [3] at Metacritic
- *The Naked Trucker and T-Bones Show* [4] at the Internet Movie Database
- *The Naked Trucker and T-Bones Show* [5] at TV.com
- Audio interview with Koechner & Allen [6] on public radio program The Sound of Young America
- 2007 SuicideGirls interview with David Koechner by Daniel Robert Epstein [7]

Jambo Bolton

Jambo Bolton

Jambo Bolton	
Hollyoaks character	
Portrayed by	Will Mellor
Created by	Phil Redmond
Duration	1995–98, 2004
First appearance	23 October 1995
Last appearance	22 December 2004
Classification	Former; regular
Family	
Mother	Janice Bolton

James "Jambo" Bolton is a fictional character from the long-running Channel 4 soap opera *Hollyoaks*, played by Will Mellor. He first appeared as an original character in 1995.

Storylines

Jambo was an individualist, putting his unique stamp on anything that came his way, from his formula for salty vinegar and his devotion to Margaret the cow. Jambo had a penchant for climbing through windows, yet, as he argued, "Why walk round to the door when the window is right in front of you?". Jambo was good friends with Kurt Benson and Tony Hutchinson and, whilst they were often confused by his odd behaviour, the three formed a strong bond, providing one another with support and, very often, humour needed to get through their rather tumultuous lives.

Meanwhile, Kurt was soon paired off with Ruth Osborne and Tony was hopelessly in love with Julie Matthews. Jambo was often left on the sidelines, unlucky in love and unable to act on the feelings he had for Dawn Cunningham. After countless missed opportunities as well as Jambo's brief relationship with Carol Groves's sister, Anita and his stepmother Lisa, Dawn and Jambo finally admitted their feelings for each other. The other woman in Jambo's life was his Bond Bug Beryl, whom he loved and cherished almost as much as Dawn! Tragically, Jambo's romance with Dawn was short-lived, as she was diagnosed with leukaemia. She eventually lost her battle against the disease, leaving Jambo devastated over the loss of his girl he wanted more than anything else in the world. Jambo never got over the death of Dawn and, although he tried to persevere with his new landscaping business, "Dig It!', he decided that there were too many memories of Dawn in Hollyoaks and he wanted to move on.

However, Jambo certainly left the female population of Hollyoaks with a memory they would cherish, when he was the unwilling stripper at Jude's opening night at the Parkers! The irrepressible Jambo finally bid farewell to Hollyoaks to begin a new life in Anglesey in 1998 but made one final visit to Hollyoaks to put flowers on Dawn's grave and vowed never to return. We saw Jambo again when the gang went to a trip to Anglesey to visit him. As they left Jambo in Wales, it was clear that Hollyoaks would never be quite the same without him.

At Christmas 2004, Jambo reappeared as a vision to Tony Hutchinson in a unique take on A Christmas Carol. Tony later confirmed that it was just as vision, not a ghost, and that he had contacted Jambo in Wales who was very much alive.

Jambo hasn't been seen since, although in October 2007, Tina McQueen threw a surprise birthday party for her brother-in-law Tony. She invited all the people in his address book, including Jambo. Tony later told Izzy he had known about the party all along because Jambo had sent him a text saying, "Thanks for the invitation to your surprise birthday party, Tony, sorry I can't make it."

194

350 nanometer

350 nanometer

Semiconductor manufacturing processes
• 10 μm — 1971
• 6 μm — 1974
• 3 μm — 1975
• 2 μm — 1979
• 1.5 μm — 1982
• 1 μm — 1985
• 800 nm (0.80 μm) — 1989
• 600 nm (0.60 μm) — 1994
• 350 nm (0.35 μm) — 1995
• 250 nm (0.25 μm) — 1998
• 180 nm (0.18 μm) — 1999
• 130 nm (0.13 μm) — 2000
• 90 nm — 2002
• 65 nm — 2006
• 45 nm — 2008
• 32 nm — 2010
• 22 nm — approx. 2011
• 16 nm — approx. 2013
• 11 nm — approx. 2015

The **350 nm** process refers to the level of semiconductor process technology that was reached in the 1995–1996 timeframe, by most leading semiconductor companies, like Intel and IBM.

Products featuring 350 nm manufacturing process

- Intel Pentium Pro (1995), Pentium (P54CS, 1995), and initial Pentium II CPUs (Klamath, 1997).
- AMD K5 (1996) and original AMD K6 (Model 6, 1997) CPUs.
- NEC VR4300, used in the Nintendo 64 game console.

Gordon Cunningham

Gordon Cunningham

Gordon Cunningham	
Hollyoaks character	
Portrayed by	Bernard Latham
Created by	Phil Redmond
Duration	1995, 1996, 1997, 1999–2004
First appearance	23 October 1995
Last appearance	2 February 2004
Spin-off appearances	*Hollyoaks: The Good, the Bad and the Gorgeous*
Profile	
Date of birth	1953
Occupation	Businessman
Family	
Wife	Angela Cunningham Helen Richardson (1999–2004)
Sons	Max Cunningham Tom Cunningham
Daughters	Dawn Cunningham Jude Cunningham Cindy Cunningham
Stepsons	Lewis Richardson
Stepdaughters	Mandy Hutchinson
Granddaughters	Bethany Cunningham Holly Cunningham
Cousins	Benny Cunningham

Gordon Hilton Cunningham (commonly referred to as **Mr. C**) is a fictional character from the long-running Channel 4 soap opera *Hollyoaks*, played by Bernard Latham. He first appeared as one of the original characters on the show when it started, he left in 2004.

Development

Personality and identity

Gordon was an irascible though kind-hearted man who often displayed an amazing tendency to infuriate those that loved him the most. Gordon often had to deal with family problems including daughter Dawn's leukaemia, Cindy's teenage pregnancy and his ill-fated marriage to Helen. Gordon had four children to first wife Angela, they are Max, Dawn, Cindy and Jude. In 1999, Gordon married Helen Richardson, who then gave birth to Tom.

Storylines

1995–2004

Gordon begins to comfort his daughter Dawn when she struggles to fend off the advances of her mother's new boyfriend, Terry. Gordon tries to help his ex-wife, Angela overcome her crippling debts and tries to inject some discipline into the lives of their wayward children. Gordon soon builds up a witty repartee with Tony Hutchinson, when he becomes landlord of Got it Taped, and finds himself in various scrapes in his desperate attempts to keep Max and Cindy on the straight and narrow. However, things get bad for Gordon as he loses Dawn to leukaemia, and also is saddened when Jude runs off the next year after getting herself in trouble with the police.

Gordon opens his own mini supermarket called Drive 'n' Buy. He rediscovers the joys of romance later in life, falling for the recently divorced Helen Richardson. When he discovers that Helen is pregnant with his child, he does the honourable thing and asks her to marry him. With Helen come her children, Mandy and Lewis Richardson, promoting the merging of the Cunningham and Richardson families. Soon, Gordon becomes "Councillor of Chester", after he beats tough competition from Tony Hutchinson and Matt Musgrove. With the Richardson family comes considerable angst, culminating in Lewis's suicide, yet Gordon proves himself as the rock to his wife and together they have a son called Tom. Gordon began to become self-conscious. After he turns fifty, he begins a 'new look' to make himself look younger with the help of student, Nick O'Connor.

Gordon's world ruptures when Max tells him that Helen is having an affair with Tony. Gordon is shattered even more when Helen decides to leave him for Tony, but Gordon is convinced that Helen will come back to him. Struggling to cope without Helen, Gordon receives comfort from David "Bombhead" Burke. Gordon becomes a father figure to Bombhead. Eventually, Helen returns back to Gordon and with some match fixing from Mandy and Max, the pair are reunited. However, tragedy strikes for Gordon when he is distracted by Tom and ends up crashing the car. Gordon takes a heart attack immediately and dies in hospital. Helen also dies a few days later and Tom is left as an orphan. In Helen and Gordon's wills, Tom is supposed to live with Mandy but instead he goes to live with Max.

After death

Bombhead takes the news of Gordon's death badly. When his mum dies, he starts to see Gordon's ghost (reprised by Bernard Latham) who tries to convince him to tell his friends about his mum's death and that he needs help. After he gets help, his visions of Gordon's ghost stop.

Max dies on June 27, 2008. Two days later, when the show is replayed on the omnibus edition, the show is followed by a dream sequence on *T4*, which shows Max being reunited with Gordon in heaven. Whilst father and son are overcome with emotion at being reunited, Max tells his father that he has sold Drive 'n' Buy. Gordon's joy of the reunion vanishes, as he smacks Max around the head and calls him a "berk".

In a 2009 non-canon special entitled *Hollyoaks: The Good, the Bad and the Gorgeous*, Latham returns to reprise the role of Gordon once again from beyond the grave, where he runs a cinema showing previous *Hollyoaks* clips.

Cindy Longford

Cindy Longford

Cindy Longford	
Stephanie Waring as Cindy (2010)	
Hollyoaks **character**	
Portrayed by	Laura Crossley (1995–96) Stephanie Waring (1996—)
Introduced by	Phil Redmond (1995) Jo Hallows (2002, 2004) Bryan Kirkwood (2008)
Duration	1995–2001, 2002, 2004, 2008–10
First appearance	30 October 1995
Last appearance	24 September 2010
Classification	Former; regular (returning)
Spin-off appearances	*Hollyoaks Later* (2009)
Profile	
Date of birth	11 May 1981
Occupation	Boutique owner

Family	
Husband	Tony Hutchinson (2009–10) Alistair Longford (2010—)
Father	Gordon Cunningham
Mother	Angela Cunningham
Stepmother	Helen Cunningham
Brothers	Max Cunningham
Sisters	Dawn Cunningham Jude Cunningham
Half brothers	Tom Cunningham
Daughters	Holly Cunningham
Nieces	Bethany Cunningham

Cindy Longford (née **Cunningham**, previously **Hutchinson**) is a fictional character from the Channel 4 soap opera *Hollyoaks*, played by Stephanie Waring. The youngest daughter of Gordon (Bernard Latham) and Angela Cunningham (Liz Stooke), She made her first on-screen appearance on 30 October 1995, then played by Laura Crossley. In 1996, Crossley quit the serial and the role was recast to actress Stephanie Waring. Waring remained with the soap until 2001, when she quit the role. Waring reprised the role briefly in 2002 and 2004. She returned to *Hollyoaks* as a full time character in June 2008, reintroduced by series producer Bryan Kirkwood. In 2010, Waring became pregnant and her character was temporarily written out for Waring's maternity leave.

Creation

Auditions were held for the part of Cindy with actress Laura Crossley going onto secure the part in 1995. Crossley quit the show the following year and the decision was made to recast the part so actress Stephanie Waring stepped into the role with immediate effect and remained with the show until 2001. In 2002 Waring admitted she would like to return to the series and later reprised the role in with 2004 for a brief stint. In 2008 news surfaced that the character was to be reintroduced to the series. It was later confirmed producer Bryan Kirkwood had asked Stephanie to reprise her role along with Sarah Jayne-Dunn for the exit of their on-screen brother Max Cunningham on an initial six month contract. This was because at the time the series had lost many of its long term characters and he felt it was time to bring some characters from the past back. She remained with the series until 2010, when Waring took maternity leave.

Development

Characterisation

The Channel 4 publicity website for *Hollyoaks* have described the character as having a manipulative personality, not being even curbed by the death of her brother. Also that she constantly enjoys stirring up other people's lives.

In an interview with *PA*, Stephanie Waring, who plays the character, said she wanted to see Cindy tackle more emotional storylines. She stated, "It's really fun to play the comedy and the manipulative bitch, but for me personally I feel more at home doing the drama — so it was really nice to get scripts again that show that. As much as I love doing the comedy, this is where I feel at home so I'm hoping there is more to come."

Waring also admitted that growing older has helped her cope better with *Hollyoaks*. "There is a different vibe since I was here last time", she continued, "I'm a lot older as well so my life is completely different so I'm handling it a lot better than I probably did when I was 18. When you're 18 and start a new show you don't know anything about life. It will be difficult for anybody. But now after being away, doing other things and growing up you approach it from a different angle. It's work at the end of the day and you go home and you've got your family. And that's what it's about. Doing what you love."

In 2010, a new plot saw Cindy's daughter Holly run away. During an interview with Digital Spy, Waring was asked whether she felt the storyline would change Cindy permanently, she replied: "Definitely. I hope so. I hope not to the extent that they stop making her fun. She says what she thinks but she's got a vulnerable side as well. She doesn't want to be seen as joker all the time. I hope they keep that but that she becomes a better mother because of it. I just hope we don't lose the essence of Cindy." Waring claimed that the plot made her emotional, she told PA: "I'm a mother myself so I have to put myself in that position and think how I'd feel how if it happened to me. Going there even a little bit made me break down completely. I can't even think about it. Even when I'm watching stuff on TV involving kids being hurt I get a lump in my throat and have to give her a cuddle when she's asleep!" Despite promising Cindy would change, in an interview with Radio Times, Waring stated that viewers have not seen the last of her unpleasant side, which she dubbed "uber-Cindy". She commented: "I'm excited about [it]. It's so much more exciting to play a character with character. I see [her] as a 'fun bitch' rather than a nasty one like [*Coronation Street's*] Tracy or [*Hollyoaks*] Clare Devine. Cindy has a swagger and delusions of grandeur and I think people love to hate that."

Return (2008)

In 2008, it was announced *Hollyoaks* producer Bryan Kirkwood had decided to bring back Stephanie Waring to reprise her role as Cindy for the wedding, and funeral, of her on-screen brother Max.

Speaking to *Digital Spy* in 2009 of her return, Waring stated: "It's flattering to think the return's been successful because I was a bit worried. At first I thought, 'How are we going to make this work?' but Bryan [Kirkwood] was very clear with what he wanted. He was going to bring Cindy back as this larger than life character. We don't actually know what went on in Spain and what changed her over these last few years and we find out a little bit why in *Hollyoaks Later* which kind of brings it round full circle."

She continued about her future with the soap: "I don't have any plans to leave — I'm very, very happy. I say bring it on to whatever the producers want to give me. I do have a couple of projects that I'm working on myself. I have something that I'm currently writing — I wrote something a few years ago and I'm currently working on that. I like having something of my own as well as *Hollyoaks*." During 2009, Waring signed an 18-month contract to stay on the soap. She told *PA*: "I am contracted until next April so a long time yet. I'd love to stay as long as they want me. I got an 18-month contract, which they offered me last September. I was really surprised. They are usually six months or a year."

Cindy's 'gold-digging' personality became clearer after her return. Cindy and Darren Osborne decided to scam Tony Hutchinson out of his money. However, the character changed her plans and decided not to marry Tony for his money. Talking about the conclusion of the storyline, Waring stated: "I think she's definitely out for what she can get — she's always going to be up to something! We're going to have to see what happens with this but I don't think she'll change who she's become over the last eight years in Spain. It's important that we see she's not this one-dimensional gold-digging tart, though. There were some episodes in normal *Hollyoaks* where we saw this a little bit when she thought Tony was just with her for her looks and Holly didn't want to be like her. In *Later* this spills out again and we get to see more of the Cindy there once was before moving to Spain." In another interview, she said: "She uses her outer image to hide who she really is inside and in Later we discover she's just a normal girl who wants to find love and security and have a secure life with her daughter and have a family — she's found that in Tony." After their postponed wedding, Cindy admitted her plans to Tony and the pair split up, however they agreed to get married, which they did in *Hollyoaks Later*.

In 2010, it was announced that Waring was pregnant and would leave *Hollyoaks* to go on maternity leave, returning in early 2011.

Storylines

1995–2001

Originally, Cindy had minor storylines. However, on the character's sixteenth birthday, she was given her first major one. Cindy succumbs to the charms of Lee Stanley (Nathan Valente) and falls pregnant. Cindy conceals this, and after giving birth, abandons the child. Gordon (Bernard Latham) tells Cindy she has responsibilities and forces her to look after the baby, named Holly (Lydia Waters). Cindy grows depressed and tries to suffocate Holly; however, her sister Jude (Davinia Taylor) stops her from going through with it and makes her realise that she truly loves her daughter.

After an uneasy few years of looking after Holly, Cindy and local decorator Sean Tate begin a relationship. Behind Cindy's back, Sean begins to mistreat Holly. He is caught locking her in a fridge by Max Cunningham (Matt Littler). The social services get involved in Cindy's motherhood when Holly is burnt by a firework. Cindy sees no other option but to leave the country with Holly and Sean to get the social services off of her back. However, Holly does not have a passport and therefore Sean abandons the pair. Cindy returns to the village and begins to adapt to the life of a single mother.

Cindy settles into her new business venture, "Steam Team" and she falls head over heels for fire-fighter Ben Davies (Marcus Patric). Cindy and Ben's relationship is on and off for a year after her cheating with Dan Hunter (Andrew McNair) and Sam "O.B." O'Brien (Darren Jeffries). After beginning work at The Loft, Cindy leaves Holly asleep in the cloak room, where she finds and swallows an ecstasy tablet. After Holly is rushed to hospital, Cindy realises the social services will soon be involved. Cindy then decides to flee the country to avoid having Holly taken from her. On her dash to the airport, Cindy runs over Anna Green (Lisa Kay) with her car. Shocked, Cindy leaves Anna for dead and leaves for Spain.

2002, 2004

Cindy returns from Spain in May 2002 with Holly. She secretly needs money but keeps her agenda for returning secret, she then decides to scam Max and O.B. out of their money. During her minor return, Cindy is involved in an affair with Scott Anderson (Daniel Hyde), who is cheating on Steph Dean (Carley Stenson). After two months, Cindy manages to clear Max and O.B.'s bank accounts and leaves for Spain once more. When she returns to Spain, Cindy begins working as a pole dancer in a nightclub, where she befriends fellow worker Savannah Madeiros (Nicola Stapleton).

In October 2004, Cindy returns to Hollyoaks once again for her father Gordon's funeral. During this time, Cindy reveals she has a bar in Spain. After several arguments, Cindy gives Max and O.B. their money back, which helps them save their business. Cindy then vows never to return and departs for Spain. Back in her normal life, Cindy is deceived by Savannah, who uses Holly to smuggle drugs and scams her out of a large amount of money. Cindy begins a relationship with a wealthy man named Phillip. However, he begins to be violent towards her, so she leaves Spain, taking his money with her.

2008–2010

Cindy and Holly return to Hollyoaks in June 2008 after escaping from Phillip with his money. Cindy moves in with Max and has her doubt about his fiancée Steph, believing she is only interested in his money. Cindy turns up at Steph and Max's wedding despite not being invited. After making a remark to stepsister Mandy Richardson (Sarah Jayne Dunn), she ends up throwing a drink on Cindy's dress. Whilst cleaning it, Cindy and Darren Osborne (Ashley Taylor Dawson) begin to flirt. After Max dies, Cindy uses his death as an excuse to get sympathy.

Cindy begins to flirt with Warren Fox (Jamie Lomas); however, he turns her advances down due to his engagement to Louise Summers (Roxanne McKee). After this, Cindy and Darren begin a relationship. After he is sent to prison, he sends her a letter explaining their relationship is over. Cindy then starts going out with Rhys Ashworth (Andrew Moss). Holly does not get along with him to start with, but later does. After a visit with Darren, Cindy reconciles with Darren and dumps Rhys. Cindy discovers that Mandy and Warren are having an affair. Louise tells Cindy to stay away after Mandy's underwear are found in Warren's flat and he blames Cindy. Cindy tries to blackmail Warren, but is unsuccessful when he threatens Holly.

After starting work at Il Gnosh, Cindy begins a relationship with Tony Hutchinson (Nick Pickard). Darren becomes jealous of their relationship; however, Cindy is also jealous on discovering Darren's drunken marriage to Hannah Ashworth (Emma Rigby). Holly accidentally makes Tony think Cindy wants to marry him, so he postpones their relationship. Cindy sleeps with Darren behind Tony's back; however, Tony walks in as they get changed. Cindy tries to explain to Tony, who walks out. Darren then tells Cindy he loves her and the pair come up with a plan for Cindy to marry and scam Tony as Darren runs The Dog into the ground so they can buy it cheaply. Cindy and Tony eventually get back together. Cindy tries her hardest to make Tony believe she is not just interested in his money, which he believes. After telling Tony she wants him to love her because of who she is and not her looks, Cindy leaves Tony. Tony then tries to apologise and ends up asking her to marry him.

Cindy gets into a fight with Tony's ex-fiancée Jacqui McQueen (Claire Cooper), who is desperate to expose her money scheme. Savannah appears and attacks Jacqui, who then leaves. Cindy then brawls Savannah for her deceit in Spain. Tony and Cindy set off for their wedding along with Darren, Dom (John Pickard) and Savannah. Savannah discovers Cindy and Darren's plan to scam Tony and tries to blackmail them. Darren sends a drunken Tony, who had slept with another woman, to a farm. Cindy is angry to be stood up and sets off after him. They find each other and confess his one-night-stand and her plans to scam him. They then agree to get married, which they do, despite Darren and Jacqui's attempt to stop the wedding. Cindy forgives Savannah, who leaves again for Spain. Cindy settles into married life, and enjoys spending Tony's money. At Christmas, Cindy wants to make the day special, and assumes she is getting an expensive gift from Tony. However, this turns out to be funding for a private school for Holly. The day is ruined when Cindy forgets to turn on the oven and cook the turkey and the Christmas tree falls onto the table. Cindy discovers Tony has bought back Tan & Tumble.

When he plans to rent it, she takes over and turns it into a clothing shop, despite Tony's negative view on the venture, and decides to prove Tony wrong. Cindy decides to enter Holly for a competition for children to advertise Cincerity. Holly decides to be a dancer and is trained by Loretta Jones (Melissa Walton) in a talent competition. Tom also enters as a comedic act. Holly is nervous and does not want to participate. However, Cindy forces her, not wanting to lose to Tom. Despite this, Holly cannot perform and runs off the stage.

Holly runs away from home after seeing Tony give Theresa McQueen a friendly kiss and assuming that Tony and Cindy did not want her anymore. Cindy believes her disappearance is just for attention. However, after police find Holly's school bag battered and left in a dustbin, Cindy begins to fear the worst and assumes Holly has been abducted. A nationwide search goes underway. Holly, who had been hiding at Spencer Gray's flat, is found by Jake Dean. He chases her and she ends up falling and hitting her head, which knocks her unconscious. Jake takes Holly to hospital, where Cindy accuses him of abducting her. Jake is arrested as Holly lies in a coma. Cindy feels Tony is not supportive at this time and turns to Darren for comfort, believing her marriage is over. When Holly wakes up, Tony has a heart to heart with her, which Cindy overhears. She then gives him a second chance. To get their marriage back on track, Cindy suggests they move to North Wales. Tony disagrees, but begins to view properties in the area. While there, he helps Gabby Sharpe, who is run over. After a week caring for Gabby, Tony realises that he does not really love Cindy. He returns to Hollyoaks and tells her he wants a divorce.

Cindy meets Alistair Longford, the grandfather of India and Texas Longford, who assumes she saved him from choking to death when it was in fact Myra McQueen. Alistair flirts with Cindy, and after only a few days of knowing each other, he proposes marriage. Cindy is taken aback, but accepts when she discovers he is a multi-millionaire. However, Jacqui McQueen blackmails Cindy, threatening to tell Alistair that it was Myra who saved his life. The McQueens then plan Cindy's wedding. Steph is horrified to discover Cindy is marrying Alistair, who is in his seventies. Furthermore, things become even more complicated when Alistair's mother Blanche Longford arrives in Hollyoaks after being called by India and Texas in an attempt to sabotage the wedding. Her plans fail, but she refuses to believe Cindy truly loves Alistair. Carmel Valentine eventually makes Cindy tell Alistair that Myra had actually been the one who saved his life. However, this does not hinder Alistair's decision to marry Cindy. On the day of the wedding, Darren tries to talk Cindy out of it and asks her to marry him. She rejects him and he is heartbroken. Blanche sees Darren leaving Cindy's shop and during the wedding, she tells Alistair that they are having an affair. Both Darren and Cindy deny this and the wedding goes ahead. Before she leaves for her honeymoon, Cindy apologises to Steph and says goodbye, knowing it may be the last time she sees her as Steph is terminally ill with cancer. Alistair and Cindy then leave, although she seems displeased when he reveals he has taken viagra.

External links

- Cindy Hutchinson [1] on the E4 website [2]

Ruth Osborne

Ruth Osborne

Ruth Osborne	
Hollyoaks character	
Portrayed by	Terri Dwyer
Introduced by	Phil Redmond (1995) Jo Hallows (2003) Bryan Kirkwood (2008)
Duration	1995–2001, 2003–04, 2008
First appearance	23 October 1995
Last appearance	5 August 2008
Classification	Former; regular
Profile	
Home	London
Occupation	Journalist

Family	
Father	Jack Osborne
Mother	Celia Osborne
Brothers	Darren Osborne
Half sisters	Bethany Cunningham
Grandfathers	Bert Andersen
	Mr Osborne
Grandmothers	Beryl Andersen
	Mrs Osborne
Uncles	Greg Andersen
	Kenneth Osborne
Cousins	Natasha Andersen
	Sarah Andersen
	Natalie Osborne
	Rachel Osborne

Ruth Osborne (previously **Benson**) is a fictional character from the long-running Channel 4 soap opera *Hollyoaks*, played by Terri Dwyer. She first appeared in 1995 before leaving in 2001. Since then, she has made guest appearances between 2003-2004 and 2008.

Storylines

Ruth arrived as a student and began to date heartthrob Kurt Benson. Ruth's father Jack Osborne And with mother Celia Osborne and younger brother Darren Osborne had moved into Hollyoaks and owned the local pub **The Dog in the Pond**. Soon, Ruth had a shocking discovery when she caught her father and best friend Dawn Cunningham were together, and they both confessed to all. Ruth's reaction was that she didn't want to see Dawn ever again.

Ruth than started getting hassle from Spike who tried to entrap her, but Kurt intervened and accidentally pushed Spike off the scaffolding. This caused more hassle in the relationship, when Kurt was charged. Kurt became paranoid that Ruth thought he was guilty and he broke up with her and went away to Hull and Ruth followed him and they ended up getting married in true Benson style. Ruth's troubles had still continued with Spike, when she found out that Spike was one of the builders doing repairs at the College. Spike trapped Ruth in a room and tries to force himself on her, but Rob Hawthorne stepped in to rescue her.

Ruth's marriage with Kurt was on the rocks as they argued, especially about spending Christmas with Ruth's family. It went from bad to worse when Rob organised a hill walk in Wales and when Ruth had another argument with Kurt, she ended up going with Lewis Richardson. Ruth and Lewis both took refuge in a cave and ended up kissing. Ruth than decided to go off to London for some work placement, leaving Kurt home alone. When Ruth returned, she was devastated to learn that Kurt is having an affair with Kate Patrick and Ruth told Kurt their marriage is over. Ruth gets into a fight with Kate that ended with Kate trying to drown her. In a fit of rage, Kurt intervened, trying to teach Kate a lesson by drowning her. In a wake of the fight, Ruth and Kurt do some soul searching and realised that they were not right for each other, promoting Kurt to leave Hollyoaks.

Ruth than began to rekindle her affair with Lewis, but they both agreed to keep their relationship under wraps. Ruth then took a break from her relationship with Lewis and met Luke Morgan who seduced her. However, Ruth was embarrassed to discover he was only 16 and on top of that when she confessed to Lewis about what happened he dumped her. Ruth decided that there was nothing left for her to say and decide to move to the states, but Lewis made a mad dash to the airport to stop her and Ruth decided to stay. During the first late night special Lucy Benson was kidnap by Rob Hawthorne and taken to a disused watertank, with Ruth, Lewis and Tony in pursuit but the gang end up surviving and rescuing Lucy.

From than, Ruth's life took a turn when she found out that she was pregnant and without Lewis knowing, she had an abortion. Ruth than discovered that Lewis had lied about how big his debt to Lorraine Wilson was and Ruth hit Lewis making Lewis hit her back. Ruth got more heartache when Lewis told her that he had slept with Lorraine to pay of his debt, which left Ruth heartbroken. In all this trouble Ruth and Lewis finally broke up and Ruth than began to date John Stuart, her colleague, but that never worked out either. In a special 16 part late night show *Hollyoaks: Movin' On*, Viewers saw Lewis beat-up Ruth before trying to force himself on her and he left Ruth for dead. Ruth was badly hurt in hospital and Lewis had died after committing suicide. Ruth left Hollyoaks and started a fresh start in London, with a new life away from Lewis.

Ruth briefly returned in 2008 for the 'funeral' of Jack, unaware that the whole thing is an insurance scam. Ruth told Frankie she was engaged.

Maddie Parker

Maddie Parker

Maddie Parker	
Hollyoaks character	
Portrayed by	Yasmin Bannerman
Created by	Phil Redmond
Introduced by	Phil Redmond
Duration	1995–97
First appearance	23 October 1995
Last appearance	10 March 1997
Profile	
Occupation	Restaurateur

Madeline "Maddie" Parker is a fictional character from the Channel 4 soap opera *Hollyoaks*, a long-running serial drama about life in a fictional suburb of Chester. The character is no longer part of current storylines. She was played by actress Yasmin Bannerman between 1995 and 1997. Maddie was created by screenwriter Phil Redmond as one of *Hollyoaks'* original characters. She made her debut in the soap on 23 October 1995, and remained for one year and six months with Bannerman making her final appearance on 10 March 1997.

Storylines

1995–97

Maddie was the streetwise and sassy siren who ran Parker's restaurant. Maddie was young, free and single and always lookout for a man. Maddie's earlier storylines started when she received a creepy Valentine's card, which leads to Maddie being worried that someone might be following her. Soon, Michael, an old flame of Maddie's turns up and gets an unwelcome reception. Maddie began to rekindle her love for Michael, as the pair begins to date and reminisce about better times. However, Maddie gets a bit concerned over his jealous behaviour and dumped him. Maddie later discovered that

Michael was mentally ill, after he became highly obsessed with Maddie becoming his wife.

Things begin to get increasingly out of hand, when Michael kidnapped Maddie and her friend Jude Cunningham (Davinia Taylor), and took them hostage. He then drove them to Scotland, ready to marry Maddie. Maddie refused to put on the wedding dress and go through the charade of marriage to Michael, which made Micheal mad and he took Jude up to the roof as revenge. For a moment it looked as if Michael was going to push Jude off the roof, but Maddie came up dressed in a wedding dress, and he was distracted. As Jude manages to escape his clutches, Michael fell to his death. Jude than tried to console Maddie over Michael's death but Maddie decided to go away to come to terms with it all. When Maddie returns, she told Jude that she wanted a fresh start by expanding the Parkers. Yet, Maddie still found it hard to get over Michael's death and became increasingly insecure about her safety. Maddie decided the only way she could make a new start was by leaving *Hollyoaks*, and leaving Parkers in the hands of Jude. She left the village to live with her mother.

Threatened Species Protection Act 1995

Threatened Species Protection Act 1995

The **Threatened Species Protection Act 1995**, is an act of the Parliament of Tasmania that provides the statute relating to conservation of flora and fauna. Its long title is **An Act to provide for the protection and management of threatened native flora and fauna and to enable and promote the conservation of native flora and fauna**. It received the Royal Assent on 14 November 1995.

See also

- Environment Protection and Biodiversity Conservation Act 1999, federal legislation
- Wildlife Conservation Act 1950, Western Australian legislation

References

- Threatened Species Protection Act 1995 [1]

Tōyō Rapid 1000 series

Tōyō Rapid 1000 series

Tōyō Rapid 1000 series	
 Withdrawn 1000 series at Kawasaki City Pier yard prior to shipping abroad, January 2007	
In service	1995 - December 2006 (Tōyō) May 2007 - Current (Jabotabek)
Number built	120 vehicles (12 sets)
Formation	10 cars per trainset
Operator	Tōyō Rapid Railway KRL Jabotabek (3 trainsets)
Line(s) served	Tōyō Rapid Railway
Specifications	
Car body construction	Stainless steel
Car length	20,000 mm
Width	2,870 mm
Maximum speed	100 km/h
Acceleration	3.5 km/h/s
Deceleration	4.0 km/h/s (5.0 km/h/s for emergency)
Power output	100 kW x 4 per motor car
Electric system(s)	1,500 V DC overhead catenary
Gauge	1,067 mm

The **Tōyō Rapid 1000 series** (東葉高速鉄道1000系) was an electric multiple unit formerly operating on the Tōyō Rapid Railway, an extension of the Tokyo Metro Tōzai Line. A total of twelve 10-car sets were converted in 1995 from former Tōkyō Metro 5000 series sets. The fleet was retired from service in December 2006, replaced by the Tōyō Rapid 2000 series.

The last three sets to be withdrawn (1006, 1008, 1009) were sold to Indonesia in 2006 and 2007, where they now operate on suburban services in the Jakarta area.

Lines used

(Until December 2006)

- Tōyō Rapid Line
- Tokyo Metro Tōzai Line

(After May 2007)

- KRL Jabotabek

References

- *Japan Railfan Magazine*, March 1996 issue (No. 419): "東葉高速鉄道１０００形", p. 60-61

External links

- ⚙ Media related to Tōyō Rapid 1000 series at Wikimedia Commons

DVD

DVD

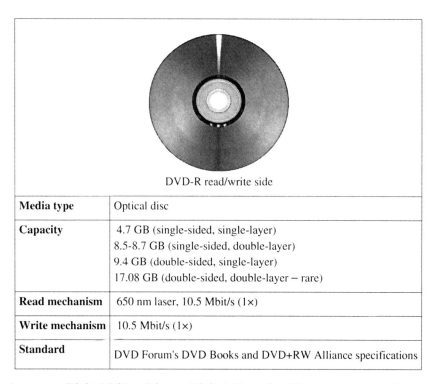

DVD-R read/write side

Media type	Optical disc
Capacity	4.7 GB (single-sided, single-layer) 8.5-8.7 GB (single-sided, double-layer) 9.4 GB (double-sided, single-layer) 17.08 GB (double-sided, double-layer – rare)
Read mechanism	650 nm laser, 10.5 Mbit/s (1×)
Write mechanism	10.5 Mbit/s (1×)
Standard	DVD Forum's DVD Books and DVD+RW Alliance specifications

DVD, also known as **Digital Video Disc** or **Digital Versatile Disc,** is an optical disc storage media format, and was invented and developed by Philips, Sony, Toshiba, and Time Warner in 1995. Its main uses are video and data storage. DVDs are of the same dimensions as compact discs (CDs), but are capable of storing just under seven times as much data.

Variations of the term *DVD* often indicate the way data is stored on the discs: DVD-ROM (read only memory) has data that can only be read and not written; DVD-R and DVD+R (recordable) can record data only once, and then function as a DVD-ROM; DVD-RW (re-writable), DVD+RW, and DVD-RAM (random access memory) can all record and erase data multiple times. The wavelength used by standard DVD lasers is 650 nm; thus, the light has a red color.

DVD-Video and DVD-Audio discs refer to properly formatted and structured video and audio content, respectively. Other types of DVDs, including those with video content, may be referred to as DVD Data discs.

History

Optical discOptical disc driveOptical disc authoringOptical disc authoring softwareAuthoring softwareOptical disc recording technologiesRecording technologiesOptical disc recording modesRecording modesPacket writing
Optical media types
Blu-ray Disc (BD): Blu-ray Disc recordableBD-R, BD-REDVD: DVD-R, DVD+R, DVD-R DL, DVD+R DL, DVD-R DS, DVD+R DS, DVD-RW, DVD+RW, DVD-RAM, DVD-D, High-Definition Versatile DiscHVD, EcoDiscCompact Disc (CD): Red Book (audio Compact Disc standard)Red Book, CD-ROM, CD-R, CD-RW, 5.1 Music Disc, Super Audio CDSACD, PhotoCD, CD Video (CDV), Video CD (VCD), SVCD, CD+G, CD-Text, CD-ROM XA, CD-iUniversal Media Disc (UMD) Enhanced Versatile Disc (EVD) Forward Versatile Disc (FVD) Holographic Versatile Disc (HVD) China Blue High-definition Disc (CBHD) HD DVD: HD DVD-R, HD DVD-RW, HD DVD-RAMHigh definition Versatile Multilayer Disc (HD VMD) VCDHDGD-ROMMiniDisc (MD) (Hi-MD) Laserdisc (LD) Video Single Disc (VSD) Ultra Density Optical (UDO) Stacked Volumetric Optical Disk (SVOD) 5D DVDFive dimensional discs (5D DVD) Nintendo optical disc (NOD)
Standards
Rainbow BooksFile systems ISO 9660Joliet (file system)JolietRock Ridge / SUSP El Torito (CD-ROM standard)El ToritoApple ISO 9660 ExtensionsUniversal Disk Format (UDF) Mount Rainier (packet writing)Mount Rainier
See also
History of optical storage mediaHigh definition optical disc format war

In 1993, two optical disc storage formats were being developed. One was the MultiMedia Compact Disc (MMCD) also called CDi, backed by Philips and Sony, and the other was the Super Density (SD) disc, supported by Toshiba, Time Warner, Matsushita Electric, Hitachi, Mitsubishi Electric, Pioneer, Thomson, and JVC.

Representatives of the SD camp approached IBM, asking for advice on the file system to use for their disc as well as seeking support for their format for storing computer data. Alan E. Bell, a researcher from IBM's Almaden Research Center received that request and also learned of the MMCD development project. Wary of being caught in a repeat of the costly videotape format war between VHS and Betamax in the 1980s, he convened a group of computer industry experts, including representatives from Apple, Microsoft, Sun, Dell, and many others. This group was referred to as the Technical Working Group, or TWG.

The TWG voted to boycott both formats unless the two camps agreed on a single, converged standard. Lou Gerstner, president of IBM, was recruited to apply pressure on the executives of the warring factions. Eventually, the computer companies won the day, and a single format, now called DVD, was agreed upon. The TWG also collaborated with the Optical Storage Technology Association (OSTA) on the use of their implementation of the ISO-13346 file system (known as Universal Disc Format [UDF]) for use on the new DVDs.

Philips and Sony decided it was in their best interest to avoid another format war over their MultiMedia Compact Disc, and agreed to unify with companies backing the Super Density Disc to release a single format with technologies from both. The specification was mostly similar to Toshiba and Matsushita's Super Density Disc, except for the dual-layer option (MMCD was single-sided and optionally dual-layer, whereas SD was single-layer but optionally double-sided) and EFMPlus modulation.

EFMPlus was chosen because of its great resilience to disc damage, such as scratches and fingerprints. EFMPlus, created by Kees Immink (who also designed EFM), is 6% less efficient than the modulation technique originally used by Toshiba, which resulted in a capacity of 4.7 GB, as opposed to the original 5 GB. The result was the DVD specification, finalized for the DVD movie player and DVD-ROM computer applications in December 1995.

The DVD Video format was first introduced by Toshiba in Japan in November 1996, in the United States in March 1997 (test marketed), in Europe in October 1998, and in Australia in February 1999.

In May 1997, the DVD Consortium was replaced by the DVD Forum, which is open to all other companies. DVD specifications created and updated by the DVD Forum are published as so-called *DVD Books* (e.g. DVD-ROM Book, DVD-Audio Book, DVD-Video Book, DVD-R Book, DVD-RW Book, DVD-RAM Book, DVD-AR Book, DVD-VR Book, etc.).

Some specifications for mechanical, physical and optical characteristics of DVD optical discs can be downloaded as *freely available standards* from the ISO website. Also, the DVD+RW Alliance publishes competing DVD specifications such as DVD+R, DVD+R DL, DVD+RW or DVD+RW DL. These DVD formats are also ISO standards.

Some of DVD specifications (e.g. for DVD-Video) are not publicly available and can be obtained only from the DVD Format/Logo Licensing Corporation for a fee of US $5000. Every subscriber must sign a non-disclosure agreement as certain information in the DVD Book is proprietary and confidential.

Etymology

A newsgroup FAQ written by Jim Taylor (a prominent figure in the industry) claims that four years later, in 1999, the DVD Forum stated that the format name was simply the three letters "DVD" and did not stand for anything.

The DVD Forum website has a section called "DVD Primer" in which the answer to the question, "What does DVD mean?" reads, "The keyword is 'versatile.' Digital Versatile Discs provide superb video, audio and data storage and access—all on one disc."

Identification (MID)

The DVD is made of a spiral groove read or written starting at the center. The form of the groove encodes unalterable identification data known as Media Identification Code (MID). The MID contains data such as the manufacturer and model, byte capacity, allowed data rates (also known as speed), etc.

Capacity

Capacity and nomenclature

SS = single-sided, DS = double-sided, SL = single-layer, DL = dual-layer

Designation		Sides	Layers (total)	Diameter (cm)	Capacity (GB)	(GiB)
DVD-1	SS SL	1	1	8	1.46	1.36
DVD-2	SS DL	1	2	8	2.66	2.47
DVD-3	DS SL	2	2	8	2.92	2.72
DVD-4	DS DL	2	4	8	5.32	4.95
DVD-5	SS SL	1	1	12	4.70	4.37
DVD-9	SS DL	1	2	12	8.54	7.95
DVD-10	DS SL	2	2	12	9.40	8.75
DVD-14	DS SL+DL	2	3	12	13.24	12.33
DVD-18	DS DL	2	4	12	17.08	15.90

Capacity and nomenclature of (re)writable discs

Designation		Sides	Layers (total)	Diameter (cm)	Capacity (GB)	(GiB)
DVD-R	SS SL (1.0)	1	1	12	3.95	3.68
DVD-R	SS SL (2.0)	1	1	12	4.70	4.37
DVD-RW	SS SL	1	1	12	4.70	4.37
DVD+R	SS SL	1	1	12	4.70	4.37
DVD+RW	SS SL	1	1	12	4.70	4.37
DVD-R	DS SL	2	2	12	9.40	8.75
DVD-RW	DS SL	2	2	12	9.40	8.75

DVD+R	DS SL	2	2	12	9.40	8.75
DVD+RW	DS SL	2	2	12	9.40	8.75
DVD-RAM	SS SL	1	1	8	1.46	1.36*
DVD-RAM	DS SL	2	2	8	2.65	2.47*
DVD-RAM	SS SL (1.0)	1	1	12	2.58	2.40
DVD-RAM	SS SL (2.0)	1	1	12	4.70	4.37
DVD-RAM	DS SL (1.0)	2	2	12	5.16	4.80
DVD-RAM	DS SL (2.0)	2	2	12	9.40	8.75*

The basic types of DVD (12 cm diameter, single-sided or homogeneous double-sided) are referred to by a rough approximation of their capacity in gigabytes. In draft versions of the specification, DVD-5 indeed held five gigabytes, but some parameters were changed later on as explained above, so the capacity decreased. Other formats, those with 8 cm diameter and hybrid variants, acquired similar numeric names with even larger deviation.

The 12 cm type is a standard DVD, and the 8 cm variety is known as a MiniDVD. These are the same sizes as a standard CD and a mini-CD, respectively. The capacity by surface (MiB/cm^2) varies from 6.92 MiB/cm^2 in the DVD-1 to 18.0 MiB/cm^2 in the DVD-18.

As with hard disk drives, in the DVD realm, gigabyte and the symbol GB are usually used in the SI sense (i.e., 10^9, or 1,000,000,000 bytes). For distinction, gibibyte (with symbol GiB) is used (i.e., 2^{30}, or 1,073,741,824 bytes). Most computer operating systems display file sizes in gigabytes, megabytes, and kilobytes, labeled as gigabyte, megabyte, and kilobyte, respectively.

Each DVD sector contains 2,418 bytes of data, 2,048 bytes of which are user data. There is a small difference in storage space between + and - (hyphen) formats:

Size comparison: a 12 cm DVD+RW and a 19 cm pencil.

Capacity differences of writable DVD formats

Type	Sectors	Bytes	KB	MB	GB	KiB	MiB	GiB
DVD-R SL	2,298,496	4,707,319,808	4,707,319.808	4,707.320	4.707	4,596,992	4,489.250	4.384
DVD+R SL	2,295,104	4,700,372,992	4,700,372.992	4,700.373	4.700	4,590,208	4,482.625	4.378
DVD-R DL	4,171,712	8,543,666,176	8,543,666.176	8,543.666	8.544	8,343,424	8,147.875	7.957
DVD+R DL	4,173,824	8,547,991,552	8,547,991.552	8,547.992	8.548	8,347,648	8,152.000	7.961

Technology

DVD uses 650 nm wavelength laser diode light as opposed to 780 nm for CD. This permits a smaller pit to be etched on the media surface compared to CDs (0.74 μm for DVD versus 1.6 μm for CD), allowing for a DVD's increased storage capacity.

In comparison, Blu-ray Disc, the successor to the DVD format, uses a wavelength of 405 nm, and one dual-layer disc has a 50 GB storage capacity.

Writing speeds for DVD were 1×, that is, 1350 kB/s (1,318 KiB/s), in the first drives and media models. More recent models, at 18× or 20×, have 18 or 20 times that speed. Note that for CD drives, 1× means 153.6 kB/s (150 KiB/s), approximately one ninth as fast.

DVD-RW Drive operating with the protective cover removed.

DVD drive speeds

Drive speed	Data rate			~Write time (min)	
	(Mbit/s)	(MB/s)	(MiB/s)	SL	DL
1×	10.80	1.35	1.29	61	107
2×	21.60	2.70	2.57	31	54
2.4×	25.92	3.24	3.09	25	45
2.6×	28.08	3.51	3.35	23	41
4×	43.20	5.40	5.15	15	27
6×	64.80	8.10	7.72	10	18
8×	86.40	10.80	10.30	8	13

10×	108.00	13.50	12.87	6	11
12×	129.60	16.20	15.45	5	9
16×	172.80	21.60	20.60	4	7
18×	194.40	24.30	23.17	3	6
20×	216.00	27.00	25.75	3	5
22×	237.60	29.70	28.32	3	5
24×	259.20	32.40	30.90	3	4

Internal mechanism of a drive

See also: optical disc drive

This mechanism is shown right side up; the disc is above it. The laser and optical system "looks at" the underside of the disc.

With reference to the photo, just to the right of image center is the disc spin motor, a gray cylinder, with its gray centering hub and black resilient drive ring on top. A clamp (not in the photo, retained in the drive's cover), pulled down by a magnet, clamps the disc when this mechanism rises, after the disc tray stops moving inward. This motor has an external rotor – every part of it that you can see spins.

The gray metal chassis is shock-mounted at its four corners to reduce sensitivity to external shocks, and to reduce drive noise when running fast. The soft shock mount grommets are just below the brass-colored washers at the four corners (the left one is obscured). Running through those grommets are screws to fasten them to the black plastic frame that's underneath.

Two parallel precision guide rods that run between upper left and lower right in the photo carry the "sled", the moving optical read-write head. As shown, this "sled" is close to, or at the position where it reads or writes at the edge of the disc.

A dark gray disc with two holes on opposite sides has a blue lens surrounded by silver-colored metal. This is the lens that's closest to the disc; it serves to both read and write by focusing the laser light to a very small spot. It's likely that this disc rotates half a turn to position a different set of optics (the other "hole") for CDs vs. DVDs.

Under the disc is an ingenious actuator comprising permanent magnets and coils that move the lens up and down to maintain focus on the data layer. As well, the actuator moves the lens slightly toward and away from the spin-motor spindle to keep the spot on track. Both focus and tracking are relatively quite fast and very precise. The same actuator rotates the lens mount half.a turn as described.

To select tracks (or files) as well as advancing the "sled" during continuous read or write operations, a stepping motor rotates a coarse-pitch leadscrew to move the "sled" throughout its total travel range. The motor, itself, is the gray cylinder just to the left of the most-distant shock mount; its shaft is parallel to the support rods. The leadscrew, itself, is the rod with evenly-spaced darker details; these are the helical groove that engages a pin on the "sled".

The irregular orange material is flexible etched copper foil supported by thin sheet plastic; these are "flexible printed circuits" that connect everything to the electronics (which is not shown).

DVD recordable and rewritable

Main article: DVD recordable

HP initially developed recordable DVD media from the need to store data for backup and transport.

DVD recordables are now also used for consumer audio and video recording. Three formats were developed: DVD-R/RW, DVD+R/RW (plus), and DVD-RAM. DVD-R is available in two formats, General (650 nm) and Authoring (635 nm), where Authoring discs may be recorded with encrypted content but General discs may not.

Although most DVD writers can nowadays write the DVD+R/RW and DVD-R/RW formats (usually denoted by "DVD±RW" and/or the existence of both the DVD Forum logo and the DVD+RW Alliance logo), the "plus" and the "dash" formats use different writing specifications. Most DVD readers and players will play both kinds of discs, although older models can have trouble with the "plus" variants.

Dual-layer recording

Dual-layer recording (sometimes also known as **double-layer recording**) allows DVD-R and DVD+R discs to store significantly more data—up to 8.54 gigabytes per disc, compared with 4.7 gigabytes for single-layer discs. Along with this, DVD-DLs have slower write speeds as compared to ordinary DVDs and when played on a DVD player, a slight transition can be seen between the layers. DVD-R DL was developed for the DVD Forum by Pioneer Corporation; DVD+R DL was developed for the DVD+RW Alliance by Philips and Mitsubishi Kagaku Media (MKM).

A dual-layer disc differs from its usual DVD counterpart by employing a second physical layer within the disc itself. The drive with dual-layer capability accesses the second layer by shining the laser through the first semitransparent layer. In some DVD players, the layer change can exhibit a noticeable pause, up to several seconds. This caused some viewers to worry that their dual-layer discs were damaged or defective, with the end result that studios began listing a standard message explaining the dual-layer pausing effect on all dual-layer disc packaging.

DVD recordable discs supporting this technology are backward-compatible with some existing DVD players and DVD-ROM drives. Many current DVD recorders support dual-layer technology, and the price is now comparable to that of single-layer drives, although the blank media remain more expensive. The recording speeds reached by dual-layer media are still well below those of single-layer media.

DVD-Video

Main article: DVD-Video

DVD-Video is a standard for content on DVD media. The format went on sale in Japan on November 1, 1996, in the United States on March 1, 1997, in Europe on October 1, 1998 and in Australia on February 1, 1999. DVD became the dominant form of home video distribution in Japan when it first went on sale in 1996, but did not become the dominant form of home video distribution in the United States until June 15, 2003, when weekly DVD-Video in the United States rentals began outnumbering weekly VHS cassette rentals, reflecting the rapid adoption rate of the technology in the U.S. marketplace. Currently, DVD-Video is the dominant form of home video distribution worldwide, although in Japan it was surpassed by Blu-ray Disc when Blu-ray first went on sale in Japan on March 31, 2006.

Although many resolutions and formats are supported, most consumer DVDs use either 4:3 or anamorphic 16:9 aspect ratio MPEG-2 video, stored at a resolution of 720/704×480 (NTSC) or 720/704×576 (PAL) at 29.97, 25, or 23.976 FPS. Audio is commonly stored using the Dolby Digital (AC-3) or Digital Theater System (DTS) formats, ranging from 16-bits/48 kHz to 24-bits/96 kHz format with monaural to 6.1-channel "Surround Sound" presentation, and/or MPEG-1 Layer 2 and/or LPCM Stereophonic. Although the specifications for video and audio requirements vary by global region and television system, many DVD players support all possible formats. DVD Video also supports features such as menus, selectable subtitles, multiple camera angles, and multiple audio tracks.

Security

Main article: Content Scramble System

Consumer rights

The rise of filesharing and "piracy" has prompted many copyright holders to display notices on DVD packaging or displayed on screen when the content is played that warn consumers of the illegality of certain uses of the DVD. It is commonplace to include a 90 second advert warning that most forms of copying the contents is illegal. Many DVDs prevent skipping past or fast-forwarding through this warning, forcing the consumer to watch.

Arrangements for renting and lending differ by geography. In the U.S., the right to re-sell, rent, or lend out bought DVDs is protected by the first-sale doctrine under the Copyright Act of 1976. In Europe, rental and lending rights are more limited, under a 1992 European Directive that gives copyright holders broader powers to restrict the commercial renting and public lending of DVD copies of their work.

DVD Audio

Main article: DVD Audio

DVD Audio is a format for delivering high fidelity audio content on a DVD. It offers many channel configuration options (from mono to 5.1 surround sound) at various sampling frequencies (up to 24-bits/192 kHz versus CDDA's 16-bits/44.1 kHz). Compared with the CD format, the much higher-capacity DVD format enables the inclusion of considerably more music (with respect to total running time and quantity of songs) and/or far higher audio quality (reflected by higher sampling rates and greater sample resolution, and/or additional channels for spatial sound reproduction).

Despite DVD Audio's superior technical specifications, there is debate as to whether the resulting audio enhancements are distinguishable in typical listening environments. DVD Audio currently forms a niche market, probably due to the very sort of format war with rival standard SACD that DVD Video avoided.

Security

Main article: Content Protection for Recordable Media

DVD Audio discs employ a DRM mechanism, called Content Protection for Prerecorded Media (CPPM), developed by the 4C group (IBM, Intel, Matsushita, and Toshiba).

Although CPPM was supposed to be much harder to crack than DVD Video's CSS, it too was eventually cracked in 2007 with the release of the *dvdcpxm* tool. The subsequent release of the libdvdcpxm library (which is based on dvdcpxm) allowed for the development of open source DVD-Audio players and ripping software, such as DVD-Audio Explorer. As a result, making 1:1 copies of DVD-Audio discs is now possible with relative ease, much like DVD-Video discs.

Improvements and succession

HD DVD/Blu-ray Disc

In 2006, two new formats called HD DVD and Blu-ray Disc were released as the successor to DVD. HD DVD competed unsuccessfully with Blu-ray Disc in the format war of 2006–2008. A dual layer HD DVD/Blu-ray Disc can store up to 30/50GB.

However, unlike previous format changes, e.g., audio tape to compact disc or VHS videotape to DVD, there is no immediate indication that production of the standard DVD will gradually wind down, as they still dominate, with around 87% of video sales and approximately one billion DVD player sales worldwide. In fact experts claim that the DVD will remain the dominant medium for at least another five years as Blu-ray technology is still in its introductory phase, write and read speeds being poor as well as the fact of necessary hardware being expensive and not readily available.

This situation can be best compared to the changeover from 78 rpm shellac recordings to 45 rpm and 33⅓ rpm vinyl recordings; because the medium used for the earlier format was virtually the same as the latter version (a disc on a turntable, played using a needle), phonographs continued to be built to play obsolete 78s for decades after the format was discontinued. Manufacturers continue to release standard DVD titles as of 2010, and the format remains the preferred one for the release of older television programs and films, with some programs such as *Star Trek: The Original Series* requiring remastering and replacement of certain elements such as special effects in order to be better received in high-definition viewing. In the case of *Doctor Who*, a series primarily produced on videotape between 1963 and 1989 (and thus expected to be difficult to upconvert to high definition), BBC Video reportedly intends to continue issuing DVD-format releases of that series until at least November 2013.

Holographic Versatile Disc

The Holographic Versatile Disc (HVD) is an optical disc technology that may one day hold up to 4 terabytes (TB) of information, although the current maximum is 500GB. It employs a technique known as collinear holography.

5D DVD

The 5D DVD, being developed in the Swinburne University of Technology in Melbourne, Australia, uses a multilaser system to encode and read data on multiple layers. Disc capacities are estimated at up to 10 terabytes, and the technology could be commercially ready within ten years.

Use as backup medium

There are two considerations for a backup medium: obsolescence and durability. If the specifications of the DVD format are not preserved and there is no device that can read the medium, it might be hard to re-create devices that can read DVDs, making it very hard to retrieve the data.

Durability of DVDs is measured by how long the data may be read from the disc, assuming compatible devices exist that can read it: that is, how long the disc can be stored until data is lost. Five factors affect durability: sealing method, reflective layer, organic dye makeup, where it was manufactured, and storage practices.

The longevity of the ability to read from a DVD+R or DVD-R, is largely dependent on manufacturing quality ranging from 2 to 15 years, and is believed to be an unreliable medium for backup unless great care is taken for storage conditions and handling.

According to the Optical Storage Technology Association (OSTA), "manufacturers claim life spans ranging from 30 to 100 years for DVD, DVD-R and DVD+R discs and up to 30 years for DVD-RW, DVD+RW and DVD-RAM".

See also

- Book type
- Content Scramble System
- Digital video recorder (DVR)
- DVD authoring
- DVD region code
- DVD TV game
- Evita (First film to be ever released on DVD.)
- IFO, BUP and VOB

Further reading

- Bennett, Hugh (April 2004). "Understanding Recordable & Rewritable DVD" [1]. Optical Storage Technology Association. Retrieved 2006-12-17.
- Labarge, Ralph. *DVD Authoring and Production*. Gilroy, Calif.: CMP Books, 2001. ISBN 1-57820-082-2.
- Taylor, Jim. *DVD Demystified, 2nd edition*. New York: McGraw-Hill Professional, 2000. ISBN 0-07-135026-8.

External links

- DVD [2] at the Open Directory Project
- Dual Layer Explained [3] – Informational Guide to the Dual Layer Recording Process
- DVD Frequently Asked Questions (and Answers) [4]
- DVD Burning and Ripping: A Primer, A Glossary [5]
- YouTube: Segment from 1997 Toshiba DVD demo disc [6] – Technical information about the then-new DVD format, from "DVD Gallery," an in-store demonstration disc from Toshiba.

pnb:⬚ یو ی⬚ ی

Keiō 1000 series

Keiō 1000 series

Keiō 1000 series	
 Keiō Inokashira Line 1000 series, May 2006	
In service	1995-Present
Manufacturer	Tokyu Car Corp, Nippon Sharyo
Replaced	Keiō 3000 series
Number in service	135 vehicles (27 sets)
Formation	5 cars per trainset
Operator	Keio Corporation
Depot(s)	Fujimigaoka Depot
Line(s) served	Keiō Inokashira Line
Specifications	
Car body construction	Stainless steel
Car length	20 m (65 ft 7 in)
Doors	4 pairs per side
Maximum speed	90 km/h (56 mph)
Acceleration	2.6 km/h/s (Type I), 3.3 km/h/s (Type II/III)
Deceleration	3.7 km/h/s (4.0 km/h/s for emergency brake)
Power output	180 kW (241 hp) per motor, 160 kW (215 hp) for Type III
Electric system(s)	1,500 V DC

Current collection method	Overhead
Safety system(s)	ATS-SN
Gauge	1067 mm (3 ft 6 in)

The **Keiō 1000 series** (京王1000系) is a DC commuter EMU type operated by Keio Corporation in Tokyo, Japan. As of January 2010, 27 5-car trainsets are in operation.

Variants

Type I

Sets 1701 to 1710. Formation consists of two motor and three trailer cars.

Type II

Sets 1711 to 1715. Formation consists of three motor and two trailer cars. Raised driver's position.

Type III

Sets 1721 to 1732. Formation consists of three motor and two trailer cars. Beadless stainless steel bodysides. Full-colour LED destination indicator panels. Interior 17-inch colour LCD information panels.

History

The 1000 series were initially built by Tokyu Car Corp. The type was introduced in 1995, and was the first new rolling stock introduced on the Keiō Inokashira Line in 33 years, after the 3000 series of 1962. It was the first type on the Inokashira Line to feature 20 m cars with four pairs of doors per side.

Type II sets from 1711 onward, built from 2003, incorporate system and interior modifications.

A new batch of 12 (Type III) 5-car 1000 series sets built by Nippon Sharyo were delivered from fiscal 2008 to replace ageing rolling stock on the Inokashira Line. These new trains feature full-colour LED destination indicators.

Additional technical details

- Motor/trailer ratio: 2M3T (2 motor cars and 3 trailers (up to set 1710); 3M2T (set 1711 onward)
- Drive mechanism: Parallel cardan
- Control system: IGBT-VVVF (1702, 1704, 1706, 1708, 1710 to 1715); GTO-VVVF (1701, 1703, 1705, 1707, 1709)
- Headlights: Sealed beam
- Destination indicators: 3-colour LED
- Passenger information displays: 3-colour LED (4 per car)
- Seating: All longitudinal

Driver's cab

- T-shape single-handle controller
- Analogue speedometer
- TNS (Train Navigation System)
- Dead man system
- Acceleration: 4 notches
- Braking: 7 notches + emergency

Livery variations

The cab ends are painted one of several different pastel colours as shown below. The colour is also used for bodyside lining.

Colour	Set numbers				
Blue-green	1701	1708	1715	1722	1729
Ivory white	1702	1709		1723	1730
Salmon pink	1703	1710		1724	1731
Light green	1704	1711		1725	1732
Lilac	1705	1712		1726	1733
Beige	1706				
Orange-beige		1713		1727	1734
Light blue	1707	1714	1721		

External links

- Tokyu Car Corp - 1000 series [1]

Odakyū 2000 series

Odakyū 2000 series

Odakyū 2000 series	
Odakyū 2000 series at Shin-Yurigaoka (29 June 2006)	
In service	1995 – Present
Number built	72 cars (9 sets)
Formation	8-car sets
Operator	Odakyu Electric Railway
Specifications	
Car length	20 m (65 ft 7 in)
Maximum speed	100 km/h (62 mph)
Acceleration	3.0km/h/s
Deceleration	4.0km/h/s (service)
Electric system(s)	1,500 V DC
Current collection method	Overhead lines
Gauge	1067 mm (3 ft 6 in)

The **Odakyū 2000 series** (小田急2000形) is a commuter EMU operated by the Odakyū Electric Railway in Japan.

A total of nine 8-car sets were manufactured between 1995 and 2001 in three batches. The design was based on the earlier 1000 series sets, with the passenger doors increased in width from 1300 to 1600 millimetres (4 ft 3 in to 5 ft 3 in) to help reduce station dwell times.

2000 Series in culture

The Odakyu 2000 Series is also featured as a player-driveable train in the computer game Microsoft Train Simulator.

References

- Nippon Sharyō information page [1]
- Tōkyū Car information page [2]
- Tetsudō Daiya Jōhō Magazine, June 2007 issue, p21

Spatial twist continuum

Spatial twist continuum

The **spatial twist continuum** is a dual representation of an all hexahedral mesh that defines the global connectivity constraint.

Discovered by Dr. Peter Murdoch on the 16th September 1993, the spatial twist continuum is a method that can be used in automatic and semi-automatic mesh generation methods to create all hexahedral meshes for both computational fluid dynamics and finite element method applications.

The name is derived from the description of the surfaces that define the connectivity of the hexahedral elements. The surfaces are arranged in the three principal dimensions such that they form orthogonal intersections that conicide with the centroid of the hexahedral element. They are arranged predominately coplanar to each other in their respective dimensions yet they can twist into the other dimensional planes through transitions. The surfaces are unbroken throughout the entire volume of the mesh hence they are continuums.

One of the areas where the STC finds application is CFD computational fluid dynamics which is a field of Science and analysis that involves simulating the flow of fluids such as air over and through bodies defined by boundary surfaces. The procedure involves building a mesh and solving the same on a computer using a finite volume approach.

An analyst has many choices available for creating a mesh that can be used in a CFD or CAE simulation, one is to use a Tetrahedral, Polyhedral, Trimmed Cartesian or Mixed of Hybrid of Hexahedra called hex dominate, these are classified as non-structured meshes, which can all be created automatically, however the CFD and FEA results are both inaccurate and prone to solution divergence, (the simulation fails to solve). The other option for the analyst is to use an all-hexahedral mesh that offers far greater solver stability and speed as well as accuracy and the ability to run much more powerful turbulence solvers like Large eddy simulation LES in transient mode as opposed to the non-structured meshes that can only run a steady state RANS model.

The difficulty with generating an all-hexahedral mesh on a complex geometry is that mesh needs to take into consideration the local geometric detail as well as the global connectivity constraint. This is the STC, and it is only present in an all-hexahedral mesh. This is the reason why it is relatively easy to automate a non-structured mesh, the automatic generator only needs to be concerned with the local cell size geometry.

The tradeoffs and relative benefits of using either mesh method to build and solve a CFD or CAE model are best explained by looking at the total work flow.

1) CAD cleanup. This involves fixing the gaps and holes in the CAD data. Usually the forgotten task that can consume a lot of time and energy and not something any experienced analyst looks forward too.

2) Mesh generation: The two main choices are to use an automated non-structured mesh or build a full hexahedral mesh.

a) Non-Structured: If one chooses to build a non-structured mesh then it is not as easy as first perceived. The process involves automatically building the mesh then manually fixing the regions of very poor cell quality. This process can take a considerable amount of time, another hidden time cost.

b) All-Hexahedral: As of mid-2009 there are a few all-hexahedral mesh generating tools. Some of them are (in alphabetical order)

- GridPro(1985)-a pure multiblock meshing tool ... with really good inter and intra block smoothing .For more details visit www.gridpro.com
- Moceon(1995)-based on the STC ... just released .. and has generated good interest among the community. For more details www.moceon.com
- IcemCFD www.ansys.com/products/icemcfd.asp
- Pointwise (primarily a multiblock meshing tool .. but can also produce tetrahedrons) www.pointwise.com
- TrueGrid (multiblock meshing tool) www.truegrid.com

However there are ways of quickly building a hexahedral mesh such as using a 2D quad mesh and projecting into the z-direction. Another method is building a block structured mesh by using a CAD based program to create logically connected splines. After the blocks are built the cell factors are added to the blocks and the mesh created. One significant advantage of using a block based hexahedral mesh is the mesh can be smoothed very quickly. For large complex geometric models the process of building a hexahedral mesh can take days, weeks and even months depending on the skill level and tool sets available to the analyst.

3) Set up the model and assign the boundary conditions: This is a rather trivial step and it is usually taken care of by GUI assisted menus.

4) Running the Simulation: This is where the nightmares for the non-structured mesh begin. Since it takes six tetrahedrals to represent one hexahedral the tet mesh size will be considerably larger and will require a lot more computing power and RAM to solve an equivalent hexahedral mesh. The tetrahedral mesh will also require more relaxation factors to solve the simulation by effectively dampening the amplitude of the gradients. This increases the number of sub-cycle steps and drives the courant number up. If you built a hexahedral mesh this is where the tortoise passes the hare.

5) Post processing the results: The time required in this step is highly dependent on the size of the mesh (number of cells).

6) Making design changes: If you build a non-structured mesh this is where you go back to the beginning and start all over again. If you build a hexahedral mesh then you make the geometric change,

re-smooth the mesh and restart the simulation.

7) Accuracy: This is the major difference between a non-structured mesh and a hexahedral mesh, and the main reason why it is preferred.

The "spatial twist continuum" addresses the issue of complex mesh model creation by elevating the structure of the mesh to a higher level of abstraction that assists in the creation of the all-hexahedral mesh.

References

Murdoch P.; Benzley S.1; Blacker T.; Mitchell S.A. "The spatial twist continuum: A connectivity based method for representing all-hexahedral finite element meshes." *Finite Elements in Analysis and Design*, Volume 28, Number 2, 15 December 1997, Elsevier, pp. 137–149(13)

Murdoch, Peter and Steven E. Benzley. "The Spatial Twist Continuum." *Proceedings, 4th International Meshing Roundtable*, Sandia National Laboratories, pp. 243–251, October 1995

Major League Baseball Wild Card

Major League Baseball Wild Card

The wild card was established for Major League Baseball's playoffs in 1994 with the intention of helping the best teams that did not win their division to still have a chance to win the World Series. The restructuring of both the American and National Leagues from two divisions each to three made it necessary to either (A) give one team a bye in the first round of playoffs or (B) create the wild card for the best second-place team. In addition, the wild card guarantees that the team with the second-best record in each league will qualify for the playoffs, even if it is in the same division as the team that has the best record.

The "wild card" rule was first used in the 1981 Major League Baseball season after a players' strike wiped out the middle third of the season. The owners decided that the winners of both "halves" of the abbreviated season from each division would qualify for the playoffs, with the caveat that if the same team won both halves then the team with the second best record from the second half would enter the playoffs as a wild card. However, in none of the then four MLB divisions did same team win both halves, so no club entered the 1981 playoffs as a "wild card" team.

There were no division or wild-card winners in 1994, due to the 1994 Major League Baseball strike.

Wild-card winners by year and by most wild-card titles

For each league's list of wild-card winners by year and teams with most wild-card titles, see:

- List of AL Wildcard winners
- List of NL Wildcard winners

Combined division-series, LCS, and World Series record as wild-card winners

Wild-card team	Series record	Playoffs
Florida Marlins	6-0	Won 1997 World Series and 2003 World Series
Anaheim Angels	3-0	Won 2002 World Series, 4-3
Boston Red Sox	6-6	Won 2004 World Series
New York Mets	3-2	Lost 2000 World Series to New York (AL), 4-1
San Francisco Giants	2-1	Lost 2002 World Series to Anaheim, 4-3
Houston Astros	3-2	Lost 2005 World Series to Chicago (AL), 4-0
Detroit Tigers	2-1	Lost 2006 World Series to St. Louis Cardinals, 4-1
Colorado Rockies	2-3	Lost 2007 World Series to Boston Red Sox, 4-0
Baltimore Orioles	1-1	Lost 1996 ALCS
Seattle Mariners	1-1	Lost 2000 ALCS
New York Yankees	0-3	Lost 1995 American League Division Series
Los Angeles Dodgers	0-2	Lost 1996 National League Division Series
Chicago Cubs	0-1	Lost 1998 National League Division Series
Oakland Athletics	0-1	Lost 2001 American League Division Series
St. Louis Cardinals	0-1	Lost 2001 National League Division Series
Milwaukee Brewers	0-1	Lost 2008 National League Division Series

Facts

- The following teams have won the World Series as a wild-card winner: Florida Marlins (1997 and 2003), Anaheim Angels (2002), Boston Red Sox (2004).
- The World Series was won by a wild-card team in three consecutive years: 2002, 2003, and 2004.
- A wild-card team appeared in the World Series in six consecutive years: 2002, 2003, 2004, 2005, 2006, and 2007.
- 2002 is the only year that both wild-card teams played in the World Series: the Anaheim Angels and San Francisco Giants.
- The Baltimore Orioles were the first wild-card team to win a Division Series.
- The Florida Marlins were the first wild-card team to reach the World Series.
- The Florida Marlins were the first wild-card team to win the World Series.
- The Florida Marlins were the first team to win two World Series as a wild-card team.
- The Boston Red Sox have the most wild-card appearances: seven (as of 2010). Second — at four appearances — is the New York Yankees. Third - at three appearances- is the Colorado Rockies.

- The following teams have won the wild card in consecutive years: Boston Red Sox (1998, 1999; 2003, 2004, 2005; 2008, 2009), Houston Astros (2004, 2005), New York Mets (1999, 2000).

See also

- Wild card (sports)#Major League Baseball
- Wild card (sports)#Record disparities
- Major League Baseball division winners (and wild-card winners)

External links

- MLB.com [1]
- ESPN.com [2]

Big Hardee

Big Hardee

The Big Hardee is a hamburger sandwich offered by Hardee's. The original Big Hardee was introduced in 1995 and was designed to compete against McDonald's Big Mac or Burger King's Whopper.

The Big Hardee was re-released in September, 2009. The sandwich features three 9:1 beef patties, two slices of American cheese, shredded lettuce and Big Twin Sauce on a 4-inch seeded bun. The sandwich averages 730 calories, 51g of fat and 1120 mg of sodium.

Additionally, Hardee's sister chain, Carl's Jr. also introduced its version of the Big Hardee, The Big Carl, though unlike Hardee's only has two patties and is priced at $2.49.

The Big Hardee was reintroduced in response to McDonald's inclusion of Angus beef into its own sandwich lineup. The Big Hardee costs approximately $2.29, 70 cents less than a Big Mac.

External links

- Hardee's unsaddles Roy's, hits back-to-basics trail [1]
- Hardee's taps El Pollo's Perry as chief officer [2]
- Official Hardee's Menu [3]

Lone Star Card

Lone Star Card

The **Lone Star Card** is an Electronic Benefit Transfer pin-based card. The card is used for Food Stamp and Temporary Assistance for Needy Families programs for the State of Texas, United States of America. When the program was implemented in 1995 the system became and still remains the largest EBT system in the United States of America. However this distinction is shared with New York state, alternating the position year to year.

External links

* Texas Food Stamp Program [1]

Fender Roscoe Beck Bass

Fender Roscoe Beck Bass

Roscoe Beck Bass	
Manufacturer	Fender
Period	1995 - 2005 / 2004 - 2009
Construction	
Body type	Solid
Neck joint	Bolt-on
Woods	
Body	"Modern-Vintage" Select Alder
Neck	Maple
Fretboard	Maple, Rosewood or Pao Ferro
Hardware	
Bridge	Gotoh Dual-Access (5-string), Fender 4-Saddle Locking Convertible (4-string)
Pickup(s)	Special Design Side By Side Bass Humbuckers
Colors available	
3-Color Sunburst, Candy Apple Red, Shoreline Gold, Teal Green Metallic, Lake Placid Blue, Crimson Red Transparent, Honey Burst	

The **Roscoe Beck Bass** is an Artist Signature Series electric bass guitar made by Fender for Texas bass veteran Roscoe Beck. Modeled after a custom-made 6-string bass built for Beck himself by luthier **Michael Stevens** of Stevens Guitars, this one-of-a-kind design came in 4 and 5-string versions and features a special-design "modern-vintage" select alder body, 3-ply mint green, 3-ply parchment or 4-ply brown tortoise pickguard, an asymmetrical oval shaped 6-bolt graphite-reinforced maple neck featuring rosewood, maple or pao ferro fingerboard with 22 Dunlop 6105 jumbo frets, two special-design side-by-side bass humbuckers, Hipshot UltraLite tuning machines (with a Drop D-tuner for the E string on the 4-string model), Gotoh (5-string) and Fender 4-Saddle Locking Convertible (4-string) strings-through-body/top-load bridges. Controls include a master volume, a master tone with push/pull midrange shaping feature and a 3-way pickup selector with two 3-way mini toggle switches for series/parallel/humbucking/single-coil wiring. The five-string version was introduced in 1995 and discontinued ten years later. The four-string was introduced in 2004, and saw its last production in 2009. Its master volume and tone/mid shaping controls feature knurled chrome-plated dome Tele knobs. Early prototypes had an abalone dot-inlaid neck, Schaller StrapLock-Ready buttons, lacked of Drop D-tuner on the E string and utilised a standard Fender round string tree. The production model sports black or white dot position markers on the fingerboard, vintage strap buttons and a custom Hipshot string tree.

For purposes of technical reference. Features and Technical Specifications:

Roscoe Beck V (5-String)

- BODY: Special Design "Modern-Vintage" Select Alder Body
- COLOURS: 3-Color Sunburst, Candy Apple Red, Shoreline Gold, Teal Green Metallic (Polyurethane Finish)
- NECK: Maple, Asymmetrical Oval Shape (Gloss Polyurethane Finish)
- MACHINE HEADS: Hipshot Ultralite Tuning Machines
- FINGERBOARD: Pao Ferro or Maple (9.5" Radius)
- NO. OF FRETS: 22 Dunlop 6105 Medium Jumbo Frets
- PICKUPS: 2 Special Design Side By Side 5-String Bass Humbuckers
- CONTROLS: Master Volume, Master Tone (with Push/Pull Mid Shaping Feature)
- BRIDGE: Gotoh Bridge (Strings-through-body/top-load)
- PICKUP SWITCHING: 3-Position Blade Pickup Selector Switch:
- **Position 1.** (Bridge Side), Bridge Pickup
- **Position 2.** (Middle), Bridge and Neck Pickups
- **Position 3.** (Neck Side), Neck Pickup, 2-Mini-Toggle Coil Selector Switches.

Mini-Toggle Switch 1:
- **Position 1.** (Bridge Side), Both Coils of Neck Pickup in Series Humbucking
- **Position 2.** (Middle), Front Coil of Neck Pickup
- **Position 3.** (Neck Side), Both Coils of Neck Pickup in Parallel Humbucking

Mini-Toggle Switch 2:
- **Position 1.** (Bridge Side), Both Coils of Bridge Pickup in Series Humbucking
- **Position 2.** (Middle), Front Coil of Bridge Pickup
- **Position 3.** (Neck Side), Both Coils of Bridge Pickup in Parallel Humbucking, Push/Pull Mid-Shaping Tone Switch/Pot

- HARDWARE: Chrome
- PICKGUARD: 3-Ply Mint Green, 4-Ply Brown Tortoise Shell
- SCALE LENGTH: 34" (864 mm)
- WIDTH AT NUT: 1.875 (47.6 mm)

- UNIQUE FEATURES: Posiflex Graphite Neck Support Rods, Asymmetrical Neck Profile, 6-Bolt Neck Plate, Locking Strap Buttons

Roscoe Beck IV (4-String)

- BODY: Special Design "Modern-Vintage" Select Alder Body
- COLOURS: 3-Color Sunburst, Lake Placid Blue, Crimson Red Transparent, Honey Burst (Polyurethane Finish)
- NECK: Maple, Asymmetrical Oval Shape (Gloss Polyurethane Finish)
- MACHINE HEADS: Hipshot Ultralite Tuning Machines with Drop-D Tuner on E-String
- FINGERBOARD: Rosewood or Maple, 12" Radius (305 mm)
- NO. OF FRETS: 22 Medium Jumbo Frets
- PICKUPS: 2 Special Design Side By Side Bass Humbuckers
- CONTROLS: Master Volume, Master Tone (with Push/Pull Mid Shaping Feature)
- BRIDGE: Fender 4-Saddle Locking Convertible Bridge
- PICKUP SWITCHING: 3-Position Blade Pickup Selector Switch:
- **Position 1.** (Bridge Side), Bridge Pickup
- **Position 2.** (Middle), Bridge and Neck Pickups
- **Position 3.** (Neck Side), Neck Pickup, 2-Mini-Toggle Coil Selector Switches.

Mini-Toggle Switch 1:

- **Position 1.** (Bridge Side), Both Coils of Neck Pickup in Series Humbucking
- **Position 2.** (Middle), Front Coil of Neck Pickup
- **Position 3.** (Neck Side), Both Coils of Neck Pickup in Parallel Humbucking

Mini-Toggle Switch 2:

- **Position 1.** (Bridge Side), Both Coils of Bridge Pickup in Series Humbucking
- **Position 2.** (Middle), Front Coil of Bridge Pickup
- **Position 3.** (Neck Side), Both Coils of Bridge Pickup in Parallel Humbucking, Push/Pull Mid-Shaping Tone Switch/Pot
- HARDWARE: Chrome
- PICKGUARD: 3-Ply Parchment
- SCALE LENGTH: 34" (864 mm)
- WIDTH AT NUT: 1.50" (38 mm)
- UNIQUE FEATURES: Posiflex Graphite Neck Support Rods, Asymmetrical Neck Profile, Neck Plate with Roscoe Beck's Signature, Knurled Chrome Control Knobs, Black or White Dot Position Inlays, Vintage Strap Buttons

Literature

- Peter Bertges: *The Fender Reference*; Bomots, Saarbrücken 2007, ISBN 978-3-939316-38-1

Charlie Schneider

Charlie Schneider

Charlotte Schneider	
Gabriele Metzger as Charlie Schneider (2008)	
Verbotene Liebe	
Portrayed by	**Gabriele Metzger**
First appearance	Episode 1 2 January 1995
Created by	Reg Watson (originally as Charlie Barlett for *Sons & Daughters*)
Profile	
Nickname(s)	Charlie
Gender	Female
Occupation	Owner of the bistro Schneiders Silent partner in the construction company Brandner Bau *Formerly*: • Manager and waitress at the No Limits • Gallery owner
Residence	Apartment Charlie Schneider Düsseldorf, Germany

Relationships	
Sibling(s)	Thomas Schneider
	Henriette Sabel
	Lars Schneider
Romances	Ludwig von Lahnstein
	Roberto Fiorani
	Peter Kaufmann
	Lukas Roloff
	David McNeil
	Johannes von
	Lahnstein
	Bernd von Beyenbach
	Sascha Göbel
	Stella Mann
Nieces and nephews	Oliver Sabel
	Olivia Schneider
	(deceased)
	Sophia von Lahnstein

Charlotte 'Charlie' Schneider is a fictional character from the German soap opera *Verbotene Liebe*, portrayed by actress Gabriele Metzger. She made her first appearance on screen in the series premiere on 2 January 1995. Together with Konrad Krauss, who plays Arno Brandner, Metzger is the only remaining original cast member.

Creation

Introduction

Charlie is introduced as a secondary character and best friend of Clarissa von Anstetten, played by Isa Jank. She is rarely seen in the beginning and when only as sidekick of Clarissa. She is the one who Clarissa can talk to and the only one Clarissa is really honest about everything. Charlie doesn't judge her no matter what and even supports Clarissa by her lies and schemes. It's also revealed that Charlie has a thing for younger men, when she leaves a party of the Anstetten family in company with a man, saying to Clarissa that she has plans with him for the night. The character of Charlie Schneider is also an adaption of the *Sons & Daughters*, where the character was named Charlie Barlett, played by Sarah Kemp. The original and the adaption share the minor role during the show's early months, before they both soon emerged as key characters.

Personality

Charlie is a dizzy socialite in the beginning that loves it to gossip about everything and everyone. She has a favor for younger man, even though she wants something more in life. With time, we find Charlie often as the tragicomic character of the show. While she entertains us with her love to gossip and some embarrassing situations, Charlie is also a character that has tragic moments when it comes to her relationship. Her believe in love and the urge for something more puts her in relationships with lousy men, who hurts her sooner or later. Even though she supports Clarissa's schemes in the beginning, Charlie later becomes a very warm and hearty person. She is also a very forgiven woman, which can also be her biggest weakness.

Development

Upon her arrival, Charlie was quickly established as gossip factory. A characteristic she keeps through to the years. But Charlie is also a character that goes to changes in her personality. Always shown on-screen and mentioned, she deals with her past and the person she has become now. While she is Clarissa's "partner in crime" in the beginning of the show, she develops as a participant, before Charlie becomes a good soul that helps others. But that her past isn't rewritten is last shown, when her niece Olivia, played by Kristina Dörfer arrives in 2006 and blackmails her aunt with one of her mistakes in the past. Back then in scenes with Olivia we see more of Charlie's old self. When the secret [that she paid the ex-girlfriend of her younger brother to get an abortion] comes out, she later forgives Olivia for her blackmail and leaves her old self once again in the past.

Love in Charlie's life

In the beginning Charlie is shown as a woman who loves it to have affairs with younger men. With the time, Charlie tries for something more; wants to find love and even a husband. She fails miserably a few times. Most of the men seem to have falling in love with Charlie's wealthy life instead with her. Others betray Charlie, like David McNeal, played by Sam Eisenstein, who cheated on her with Tanja von Anstetten, played by Miriam Lahnstein. In her relationship with Johannes von Lahnstein, played by Thomas Gumpert invested she to much in a time, where he wasn't ready for a new love in his life. With time, Charlie tries to give up on love. But then Bernd von Beyenbach, played by Ron Holzschuh, seems to have true feelings for her. But once again he is a men that is after her money. At least at first until he really begins to fall for her. But when Bernd cheats on her with Olivia, she breaks up with him. Bernd hopes for her forgiveness - with success. Charlie tries to speak with him, before Bernd wants to leave town, but then he is already gone. After this heartbreak, Charlie is once again shown as a woman how loves uncomplicated affairs, whichever while how long the last. With this side of Charlie, the viewers see her again in parts of her old self. When Sascha Göbel, played by Tobias Fries, is introduced Charlie is once again shown on the side of a younger man. But Sascha wants to get serious with Charlie and has descent feelings for her. This time we see that Charlie isn't this trustful in men anymore and she dumps him, not believing that it could work out. Even though she ended it, Charlie is left heartbroken once again. Then the character takes a drastic turn, when Stella Mann, played by Anne Wis, is introduced and shows interest in Charlie. Which begins for the viewers as a set-up to build a lesbian relationship between Stella and Carla von Lahnstein, played by Claudia Hiersche, gets more serious with time. A plotline that doesn't approved with most of the viewers, showing Charlie with a desperate past with men that is now pushed into a potential love affair with another woman.

Friendships

Since the beginning of the show, Charlie always has a friend on the show and with the start of being a key character also to a group of characters. Charlie's best friend was the devious Clarissa for the first years. Even though Clarissa betrayed Charlie a couple of times, the two remain as friends until Clarissa's exit in 2001. The friendship between the two woman was very unequal. While Clarissa was scheming, Charlie became a good person. And even in the beginning, Charlie was portrayed as little bit dumb and quirky, while Clarissa seemed intelligent and elegant. Over the years Charlie changed and has proved that she has become an intelligent businesswoman. After Clarissa's exit, Charlie's sudden stupidity was gone too. Cécile de Maron, played by Yvonne Burbach, becomes Charlie's new best friend. Charlie rises as good soul and loyal friend to Cécile and also to Clarissa's stepson Henning, last played by Patrick Fichte. She is shown as someone who likes to play amour and a very good listener. Charlie also becomes friends with other characters, most notable Arno Brandner, played by Konrad Krauss and Elisabeth von Lahnstein, played by Martina Servatius. In 2008, Charlie becomes friends with Nathalie von Lahnstein, played by Jenny Winkler, a woman that had committed hit and run by Charlie. Also involved in this was her friend Elisabeth, who kept Nathalie's crime as a secret. Charlie forgives both of them, which once again shows the mentioned weakness in her personality.

Storylines

In the beginning, Charlie owns a gallery and enjoys a luxurious lifestyle. She likes young men and has zippy being. For many years she is the best friend of Clarissa von Anstetten and supports her schemes, but changes her character later to the better and becomes a good soul. The friendship lasted to Clarissa's presumed death in 2001. After she decides to take a break from art and closes her gallery, she opens her own bistro - the Schneiders, which becomes a good address for the high society of Düsseldorf. Charlie only would need a man in her life to complete her happiness. But she always seems to meet the wrong guys. Most of them use Charlie because of her wealthy life and she is left heartbroken many times.

Charlie begins an affair with David McNeal and falls in love with him. They get into a relationship, but when Charlie's worst enemy, Tanja von Anstetten, who was supposed to be dead, returns, she wants to get back at Charlie. She threatens her with her life and begins an affair with David. Tanja makes sure Charlie finds out about it and Charlie catches David with Tanja in bed. Charlie breaks up with him, but Tanja isn't finished with her old "friend" - she wants to drive Charlie crazy. And her plans work, as not even her brother Lars (Herbert Ulrich) eventually believes or trusts her anymore. Charlie engages a professional murderer who should kill Tanja. But she already knows about Charlie's plan and blackmails her. Charlie has to give her all of her possession. And Charlie end up working at the No Limits.

But Charlie wins everything back, reopens the Schneiders and is very happy when her nephew Oliver Sabel (Jo Weil) comes back to town from working as a steward on cruise ships for a few years. He finds out Charlie hasn't the best relationship with Olivia and he wants to change that. He finds out that Olivia slept with Charlie's fiancé Bernd von Beyenbach. But when Olivia tells him that she regrets that, Oliver wants to help make peace between them. But what Oliver doesn't know is, that Olivia is blackmailing her aunt about a secret from her past. Then Charlie finds out that Olivia faked a pregnancy and made Andi Fritzsche (Dominic Saleh-Zaki) and Ansgar von Lahnstein (Wolfram Grandezka) both believe they are the father of the baby. Olivia warns Charlie not to tell anyone about that. But she can't shut her mouth and gives Andi a hint. When Olivia finds out that Charlie is involved in the fact that Andi had left her, she wants to get back at her and tells in front of anyone that Charlie paid Lars ex-girlfriend for an abortion years ago. Lars breaks ties with his sister and Charlie is left heartbroken. Oliver tries to help his aunt and sets up a big family reunion. Lars forgives his sister for the mistake she made years ago and Charlie is even willing to forgive Olivia. Since then, Charlie has a good relationship with Olivia and again to her brother Lars.

In fall of 2008, Charlie starts dating again. She meets the young and attractive Sascha Göbel (Tobias Fries) in a gallery, which she visits with her good friend Elisabeth (Martina Servatius). Charlie tries to take things slowly and doesn't want to rush in anything with her history with men. But Sascha really seems like a nice guy and Oliver and Olivia seem to like him too. But when Charlie sees Sascha with Olivia, old memories come back to her mind and she thinks about how her relationship with Bernd turned out. Charlie gets a little paranoid and assumes that Sascha is flirting with Olivia. But he isn't and tells Charlie that he wants her and then even confesses his love to her. But this is too much for Charlie and she tells him she isn't ready to say it back to him yet. Sascha is okay with it, but things get more complicated when he becomes more and more an important part in Charlie's life. Thinking that she isn't ready for a serious relationship she ends things with Sascha.

Single again, Charlie enjoys her life and is invited to a masked-ball on Castle Königsbrunn. Set up to dance with Eduard von Tepp (Hubertus Regout), she soon needs to see that he is a boring character. When Eduard wants to have another dance with Charlie, Stella Mann is rescuing her. Charlie thanks Stella and has a nice chat with her, before she wants to leave the ball. But her driver is already gone. Stella offers her to take her home. The two ladies end up in the Schneiders, have another glass of champagne and dance together.

Sentricon

Sentricon

The **Sentricon** Termite Colony Elimination System is a subterranean termite control product developed and manufactured by Dow AgroSciences. It was introduced in 1995 as a termite baiting system, the first major alternative to liquid termiticide soil barriers. It has been proven to eliminate termite colonies, even those of the Formosan subterranean termite, or super termite.

The baiting technique employed by the Sentricon System relies on termite biology and behavior. Subterranean worker termites forage for cellulose food sources 24 hours a day, ranging abroad from their underground nest, or colony, through tunnels in the soil up to 350 feet long. When any termite finds a food source, it leaves a pheromone scent trail to summon nestmates. Worker termites chew and digest cellulose, and then regurgitate it to share with other termites in the colony.

When foraging, worker termites find Sentricon bait stations placed in the soil by an Authorized Operator of the Sentricon System. These stations are baited with a cellulose material impregnated with noviflumuron, an insect growth regulator. The termites share this bait with colony nestmates, which later die when they are unable to molt. As they die, the colony is eliminated. The Authorized Operator, who is trained and certified by Dow AgroSciences, provides an ongoing station monitoring service.

The Sentricon System has environmental benefits. Less of its active ingredient is needed to achieve control than in traditional liquid chemical treatments. In addition, in 2000, the Sentricon System received the Presidential Green Chemistry Challenge Award, an environmental honor from the U.S. government.

External links

- Presidential Green Chemistry Challenge Award [1]
- Sentricon Termite Colony Elimination System [2]
- Sentricon System Web site [3]
- University of Kentucky Entomology Study about Termite Control Methods [4]

Hunter Van Pelt

Hunter Van Pelt

Hunter Van Pelt, often referred to simply as **Van Pelt**, is a fictional hunter and villain from the 1995 film *Jumanji*, as well as the spin-off cartoon series. He is portrayed by Jonathan Hyde in the film and by Sherman Howard in the TV series. He was also one of several exclusive characters not from the original book by Chris Van Allsburg, having been created especially for the film.

Film

In the film, Van Pelt was a hunter from the game *Jumanji*, appearing as the stereotypical hunter inspired by those in jungle fiction stories such as Allan Quatermain from *King Solomon's Mines* or Captain Hamilton from *Sanders of the River*. In all depictions, Van Pelt is always seen dressed in hunting garb with a spiked pith helmet.

Despite being a hunter and the film's primary antagonist, Van Pelt is an honorable man who respects the rules of Jumanji. His only target is Alan, because Alan rolled the dice to let him out. He does not harm Sarah, Judy or Peter, although he is prepared to use them as bait to attract Alan. He does not even fire at the armed (but inexperienced) Carl, though he destroys his police car. When he finally has Alan cornered, he gives him a running chance, expecting him to flee like a coward as he always has done before, and is genuinely impressed when Alan says he's finally prepared to face what he's afraid of.

Van Pelt initially uses an elephant gun as his weapon, but about halfway through the film it runs out of ammunition, forcing him to purchase a modern semi-automatic sniper's rifle (bribing the store owner with antiquated gold coins to skip the formalities). He also steals the *Jumanji* game to trap Alan and hopefully kill him. His plans are thwarted by the efforts of Judy and Peter, two children who began playing the game Alan had started before he was trapped in the game. At the end of the film, Van Pelt is sucked back into the game once Alan wins, along with everything else (strangely, including the sniper's rifle).

It is never made clear why Van Pelt wished to kill Alan Parrish in the jungle. Van Pelt is an elapsed metaphor of Alan's fear of his father, with both Van Pelt and Sam Parrish being played by actor Jonathan Hyde (a similar metaphor is used in most stage and film productions of *Peter Pan (1953 film)*, with Captain Hook and Wendy's father played by the same actor). Both Van Pelt and his father admonished Alan for being "cowardly", and Van Pelt's description is that of making Alan feel like a child. In addition, he is apparently the only person with which Alan alone grew up in Jumanji.

The origins of Van Pelt are unclear. Despite his appearance as a stereotypical character from British Empire fiction and his name *Van* Pelt implying Dutch origins, Van Pelt himself has no nationality, being just a component of the Jumanji game and not a *real* person. His face is on the box of Jumanji on the first circle on the top left, He shows no great difficulty adapting from a jungle set in the late 1800s into the present day (he shows no confusion when he is informed that his elephant-gun has been obsolete for 60 years, simply stating that he will require a replacement) and was probably created with the game as an antagonist for players to face along with the other obstacles from the games. His statement to Sarah that "You didn't roll the dice - Alan did." suggests that he is aware of this.

TV series

Like many other characters of the series, Van Pelt was altered for the cartoon series, although not to any great extent. In the TV series, Van Pelt is still a hunter, but this time with a light-blue skin tone, and has built a lodge in the jungle where he keeps various trophies of animals he has hunted and killed.

In the first episode, Van Pelt escorts Judy and Peter (who have just arrived in the game) to his lodge, but is furious at the idea of *Jumanji* being nothing but a game, and tries to kill them. Throughout the rest of the series, Van Pelt returns as a recurring villain (like Prof. Ibsen, Trader Slick and Captain Squint) and was given a large traction engine in the series to get about the jungle, the preliminary sketches of which appear in the ending credits of the series.

In the episode "*The Law Of Jumanji*", Alan, Judy and Peter seem to finally kill him by luring him into falling off a cliff, but Jumanji simply replaces him by turning Peter into a miniature replica of Van Pelt, who claims "There must always be a Van Pelt. It's a Law of Jumanji/the rules of the game". This ends up being reversed by solving the game clue, at which point the original Van Pelt simply climbs back up the cliff after Peter tosses his staff down it. Also, Alan states that Van Pelt is indestructible so he cannot actually be killed.

Friends & Enemies

The episode *Night of the Hunters* introduced a rival to Van Pelt, named Ludwig Von Richter. Like Van Pelt, Von Richter was a hunter resembling pre-WWI caricatures (in this case, the game hunters of the German Empire). Van Pelt and Von Richter ultimately compete for the favour to kill Alan Parrish, with Alan rescuing Van Pelt from quicksands, believing that Van Pelt would have merely been replaced by Von Richter. They don't like each other, but have respect and would never kill the other.

The only *friends* of the big game hunters are eventually Trader Slick (who supplies him with new weapons) and Prof. Ibsen (which also threatened Alan's life). The animals in Jumanji are hostile to him, but seem to fear his weapon - except the monkeys, which often annoy him.

See also

- Jumanji (film)
- Human hunting
- Trophy hunting

External links

- Van Pelt [1] at the Internet Movie Database

10 Złotych

10 Złotych

The **Polish 10 Złotych note** is a denomination of Polish currency, and is also the most common.

External links

- NBP [1]

20 Złotych

20 Złotych

The **Polish 20 Złotych note** is a denomination of Polish currency.

External links

* NBP [1]

50 Złotych

50 Złotych

The **Polish 50 Złotych note** is a denomination of Polish currency.

External links

- NBP [1]

100 Złotych

100 Złotych

The **Polish 100 Złotych note** is a denomination of Polish currency.

External links

- NBP [1]

200 Złotych

200 Złotych

The **Polish 200 Złotych note** is currently the highest denomination of Polish currency. It is also the only current Polish bill to feature a hologram. The bill's dimensions are 144 x 77 mm.

The obverse of the note features a likeness of King Sigismund I the Old. The reverse depicts the white eagle wrapped in the letter S, inscribed in a hexagon, from the Sigismund's Chapel at the Wawel Castle.

External links

- NBP [1]
- Official description of the 200 złotych note (In English) [1]

Rayman (character)

Rayman (character)

Rayman

Series	*Rayman* series
First game	*Rayman*
Created by	Michel Ancel
Voiced by	David Gasman

Rayman is the protagonist of the Rayman series, a video game created by Ubisoft. He is limbless and attacks by throwing his fists (although he shoots energy spheres in Rayman 2 and M). First appearing in 1995, Rayman debuted on the Atari Jaguar, PlayStation, Saturn and MS-DOS in *Rayman* where he had to defend his home from the clutches of Mr. Dark. Rayman reappeared in 1999, this time having to fight off Admiral Razorbeard in *Rayman 2*. In *Rayman 3: Hoodlum Havoc* Rayman has had to deal with André, the leader of the Black Lums. Soon afterwards, Rayman had to rescue his good friend Globox in *Rayman: Hoodlums' Revenge*. Rayman is a major character in the *Rayman Raving Rabbids series*. He is Ubisoft's mascot.

Appearance

Rayman is typically found wearing white gloves, a red scarf on a purple shirt (which was replaced with a red and purple hoodie) with a white Ring on it, and yellow sneakers. The Ring appears to have magical properties. Whenever he earned a new power in *Rayman*, sparkles would appear around the Ring; in *Rayman 2*, it was used to open the stones holding the masks. One part of his character design is he has no neck, arms or legs, but rather his head, torso, hands and feet appear to float in midair relative each other as though they were attached. His hands and feet usually act like normal appendages (running, using objects, etc.), but some of his abilities involve separating them from his body.

He has however been known to change outfits, beginning from his third adventure against the Black Lum André in *Rayman 3: Hoodlum Havoc*. Players in *Rayman Raving Rabbids* can dress Rayman in a variety of costumes. They start with the choices of Disco, Gangsta, and Granny; as they unlock more minigames, more costumes, such as Rock 'n' roll, DJ, Gothic and eventually a bunny suit, become available.

In Japanese versions, Rayman's suit is changed from purple to blue, since purple is seen as the color of death in Japan.

Abilities

Rayman's abilities consist of attacking his enemies by winding up his fists and throwing them at his enemies, floating through the air and descending slowly by using his hair as a helicopter propeller, and the ability to live and survive without his body parts attached. In Rayman 2: The Great Escape, he was granted the ability to attack his enemies with energy balls, rather than throwing his fists. Late in Rayman 3: Hoodlum Havoc, the Leptys granted Rayman the ability to turn Black Lums into Red Lums with a grimace. Also, there were combat fatigues in the game with could give Rayman Heavy Metal Fists that could increase his attack power, a propeller that could make him fly into the air, a missile attack that could make turn Rayman's fist into a powerful missile, a chain that could latch onto anything it could latch on to, and many more.

Biography

Not much is known about Rayman's past. Supposedly he was found by fishermen on a beach by the Sea of Lums. In *Rayman 2* this idea is further elaborated on when Rayman is revealed to be the only creature living in the world who was not dreamed up by Polokus, as well as the only person who can convert the Silver Lums made by the Fairies into powers. It is speculated (in the game) that Rayman could in fact be a 'chosen one' selected by all the gods of all the worlds, destined to fight against evil. Despite this, Rayman has not allowed it to dampen his views on life and continues to be witty and rather energetic.

The games take place in seemingly unconnected areas. The original, 2-D Rayman games take place in what is called Rayman's home world - a world that is kept stable by the Great Protoon. Most of the games after that take place in a seemingly different, more realistic world of a god named Polkus, while the Raving Rabbids take place in more contemporary settings and eventually Earth itself. The Protoon has not been spoken of in the games since, so whether or not these settings are of the same world or different ones remains a mystery.

Throughout his adventures, Rayman has accumulated a number of allies. These include bumbling Globox, helpful flying greenbottle Murfy, the numerous Teensies, and mystical Ly the Fairy, who has oddly not been seen since Rayman 2 except in handheld spin-offs.

Concept and creation

The original story from the Atari Jaguar version of Rayman claims he was originally a boy named Jimmy, brought into his game and set in a world called Hereitscool to fight the evil. This idea was quickly abandoned in enough time for the game's Jaguar release, and Rayman would remain a mysterious figure in his own world in the releases of the other versions of the game. (Saturn, PlayStation, etc.)

Gameplay

Rayman games are typically platformer games, although spin offs have had radically different gameplay. The original Rayman was a 2D sprite based platformer similar to those of the 16 bit era. Rayman 2 moved the series into 3D, and added more variety to the gameplay with new actions such as riding a rocket, being pulled through a marsh by a snake, and an entire level where Rayman's hair allows him to fly instead of simply hover. Rayman 3: Hoodlum Havoc kept the same core platforming of Rayman 2, but added timed power ups and had a bigger emphasis on combat. The handheld entries in the series have remained similar to the sprite based original in gameplay in that they are 2D. Rayman DS, which was a port of Rayman 2, is an exception. Rayman Raving Rabbids, which was at first planned to be a traditional platformer, turned into a mini-game collection late in development after the developers got their hands on the Wii Remote and Nunchuck. Early trailers for the game and early information portray it having a darker atmosphere than is typical of a Rayman game, and show Rayman riding animals including a giant spider. Rayman could alter his appearance, and his dancing style with it, and dance to entrance the Rabbids. Ultimately this idea was scrapped, replaced with motion based mini-games similar to *WarioWare: Smooth Moves*. Rayman: Raving Rabbids was also released on the Xbox 360, despite being made around the motion-sensing Wii controller, and simply replaced physical actions with traditional button presses. Rayman had two racing games (Rayman Arena and Rayman Rush) that saw characters from the Rayman universe racing on foot through platformer like stages, and battling in a separate arena mode. There have also been Rayman educational games, which focused less on gameplay and more on learning.

Games

Rayman games

* Rayman
* Rayman 2: The Great Escape
* Rayman 3: Hoodlum Havoc
* Rayman 3 (GBA Version)
* Rayman: Hoodlums' Revenge
* Rayman Raving Rabbids (GBA and DS Versions)

* Rayman Origins

Raving Rabbids

* Rayman Raving Rabbids
* Rayman Raving Rabbids 2
* Rayman Raving Rabbids TV Party

Spin-offs

* *Rayman Arena/Rayman Rush*
* *Rayman Brain Games*
* *Rayman Golf*
* *Academy of Champions*
* *Rayman Designer*
* *Rayman Kart*
* *Rayman: The Animated Series*

Remakes

* Rayman Advance
* Rayman Gold
* Rayman Forever
* Rayman DS
* Rayman Revolution

Reception

Since his debut in 1995 on the Atari Jaguar, Sega Saturn, PlayStation and on the MS-DOS, Rayman has become a popular and recognizable video game character over the past decade, along with his trademark lack of limbs and Helicopter power, having appeared in several titles up for many platforms until the present day.

The Rabbids from the Raving Rabbids series became massively popular both through the teaser trailers and the game itself. IGN has stated that the Rabbids have *"more personality and charisma than 10 of the most popular video game mascots combined"*, and that the bunnies have literally *"upstaged Rayman himself"*. GameSpot has noted, *"The Rabbids themselves are almost exclusively responsible for [selling the game's humor], as they are, without a doubt, hysterical. They're adorably designed, with their dumb stares, high-pitched shrieks, and a penchant for taking comedic bumps."* There has been speculation by reviewers that the success of the Rabbid character will probably inspire the developers to create more games of the franchise, possibly even without Rayman. This was first hinted in the launch trailer of the first game, where Rayman, despite being the title character, only appears for a fraction of a second, only to be squashed flat by a couch taken over by the bunnies, and became evident in *Rayman Raving Rabbids 2,* in which case Rayman disguises himself as a Rabbid, causing the game to put more emphasis on them than on Rayman himself. This was then proven to be true with the announcement of *Rabbids Go Home.*

External links

- Rayman Pirate-Community [1]
- RayWiki, a free wiki encyclopedia about Rayman [2]
- Rayman Fanpage [3] (in bilingual German and English)

List of minor Hollyoaks characters (1995–96)

List of minor Hollyoaks characters (1995–96)

Hollyoaks minor characters				
95-96	1997	1998	1999	2000
2001	2002	2003	2004	2005
2006	2007	2008	2009	2010

The following is a list of minor characters that first appeared in the Channel 4 soap opera *Hollyoaks* between 1995 and 1996, by order of first appearance.

Jane Andersen

Jane Andersen	
Hollyoaks character	
Portrayed by	Sally Faulkner
Created by	Phil Redmond
Duration	1995–96
First appearance	1995
Last appearance	1996
Profile	
Home	United States
Occupation	Landlady

Family	
Husband	Greg Andersen
Daughters	Natasha Andersen
	Sarah Andersen

Jane Anderson is a fictional character from the long-running Channel 4 soap opera *Hollyoaks*, played by Sally Faulkner. Jane first appeared as the mother of Natasha and Sarah and wife of Greg Andersen.

Greg Andersen

Greg Andersen	
Hollyoaks **character**	
Portrayed by	Alvin Stardust
Created by	Phil Redmond
Duration	1995–96
First appearance	23 October 1995
Last appearance	1996
Profile	
Date of birth	1952
Home	United States
Occupation	Landlord

Family	
Wife	Jane Andersen
Father	Bert Andersen
Mother	Beryl Andersen
Sisters	Celia Osborne
Daughters	Natasha Andersen Sarah Andersen
Nephews	Darren Osborne
Nieces	Ruth Osborne

Greg Andersen is a fictional character from the long-running Channel 4 soap opera *Hollyoaks*, played by Alvin Stardust, he is the father of Natasha and Sarah, husband of Jane Andersen and brother of Celia Osborne. He first appeared in 1995 as the landlord of The Dog in the Pond. After Natasha died he sold the pub to his sister Celia and brother-in-law Jack.

Sarah Andersen

Sarah Andersen	
Hollyoaks character	
Portrayed by	Anna Martland
Created by	Phil Redmond
Duration	1995–96
First appearance	1995
Last appearance	1996
Profile	
Date of birth	1980
Home	United States
Occupation	Barmaid

Family	
Father	Greg Andersen
Mother	Jane Andersen
Sisters	Natasha Andersen
Grandfathers	Bert Andersen
Grandmothers	Beryl Andersen
Aunts	Celia Osborne
Cousins	Ruth Osborne Darren Osborne

Sarah Andersen is a fictional character from the long-running Channel 4 soap opera *Hollyoaks*, played by Anna Martland. She is the sister of Natasha and daughter of Jane and Greg Andersen.

Juliette Benson

Juliette Benson	
Hollyoaks character	
Portrayed by	Martine Brown
Created by	Phil Redmond
Duration	1995–99
First appearance	23 October 1995
Last appearance	May 1999
Family	
Husband	Kirk Benson
Sons	Kurt Benson Ollie Benson
Daughters	Lucy Benson

Juliette Benson is a fictional character from the long-running Channel 4 soap opera *Hollyoaks*, played by Martine Brown. She is the mother of Kurt, Lucy and Ollie Benson, and wife of Kirk Benson. She left Hollyoaks with her husband, Kirk, after their children did not need them any more as Kurt and Lucy moved out.

Kirk Benson

Kirk Benson	
Hollyoaks character	
Portrayed by	James Quinn
Created by	Phil Redmond
Duration	1995–99
First appearance	23 October 1995
Last appearance	May 1999
Family	
Wife	Juliette Benson
Sons	Kurt Benson Ollie Benson
Daughters	Lucy Benson

Kirk Benson is a fictional character from the long-running Channel 4 soap opera *Hollyoaks*, played by James Quinn. He is the father of Kurt, Lucy and Ollie Benson, and husband of Juliette Benson. He owned his own computer business and left Hollyoaks with his wife Juliette, after their children did not need them any more, due to Kurt and Lucy moving out and Ollie's death.

Angela Cunningham

Angela Cunningham	
Hollyoaks character	
Portrayed by	Liz Stooke
Created by	Phil Redmond
Duration	1995–99, 2004, 2006, 2008
First appearance	23 October 1995

Last appearance	10 July 2008
Family	
Husband	Gordon Cunningham
Sons	Max Cunningham
Daughters	Dawn Cunningham Jude Cunningham Cindy Cunningham
Granddaughters	Bethany Cunningham Holly Cunningham

Angela Cunningham is a fictional character from the long-running Channel 4 soap opera *Hollyoaks*, played by Liz Stooke. Prior to her first and last appearances in 1995 and 1999, Angela has made several guest appearances in 2004, 2006 and 2008.

Angela was the ex-wife of Gordon, and mother of Max, Jude, Cindy and Dawn. When *Hollyoaks* began, Angela and Gordon were already divorced, but Angela tried to play a part in the complicated lives of her children, including Cindy's teenage pregnancy and Dawn's death from leukemia. Angela returned for Max's wedding to Clare Devine, and again for his wedding to Steph Dean. Sadly, Max was killed in a car accident soon after the ceremony, and Angela's last appearance was attending her son's funeral.

She was mentioned in February 2010 when her granddaughter Holly Hutchinson went missing however she did not come to support her daughter.

Lee Stanley

Lee Stanley	
Hollyoaks character	
Portrayed by	Nathan Valente
Created by	Phil Redmond
Duration	1996–97
First appearance	January 1996
Last appearance	October 1997

Family	
Daughters	Holly Cunningham

Lee "Stan" Stanley was a cafeteria worker at Hollyoaks Community College, who befriended teenager Ollie Benson.

Stan appeared as the sidekick of Ollie Benson in 1996. Stan's life took a dramatic change when he found out that he was the father of Cindy Cunningham's child, Holly, after the pair had a one night stand on her sixteenth birthday. Stan offered to stand by Cindy throughout the pregnancy but was cruelly rejected. Depressed, Stan began drinking heavily at The Dog. Ollie did his best to try to snap Stan out of his depression but it was no good, as Stan got in his car and started to drive at a dangerous speed. Ollie's warnings fell on deaf ears as the drunken Stan had careered into a reversing lorry, crashing and seriously injuring the pair. Both lay in a critical condition for a week in hospital, where they later died.

Celia Osborne

Celia Osborne	
Hollyoaks character	
Portrayed by	Carol Noakes
Duration	1996–97
First appearance	18 November 1996
Last appearance	June 1997
Profile	
Date of birth	1954
Home	United States

Family	
Husband	Jack Osborne (1974–97)
Father	Bert Andersen
Mother	Beryl Andersen
Brothers	Greg Andersen
Sons	Darren Osborne
Daughters	Ruth Osborne
Nieces	Natasha Andersen Sarah Andersen

Celia Osborne (née **Andersen**) is the mother of Ruth and Darren Osborne and former wife of Jack Osborne. Celia arrived in Hollyoaks with Jack and Darren where they joined daughter Ruth as Jack became the new landlord of The Dog in the Pond after Celia's brother Greg decided to sell the bar following the death of her niece Natasha. After the revelation of Jack's affair and impregnation of Dawn Cunningham, Celia moved to America with Darren, leaving Jack running The Dog. They later divorced.

Balto (character)

Balto (character)

Balto.	
First appearance	Balto (film)
Portrayed by	Kevin Bacon (Original) Maurice LaMarche (Sequels)
Nickname(s)	"Balto, the trouble dog"
Species	Wolf/Canine *(Canis lupus familiaris)*
Gender	Male
Family	Jenna (mate), Boris (adoptive father), Aniu (deceased mother), unnamed father, Aleu (daughter), Kodi (son), Dingo (son), various other puppies, unknown in-laws

Balto is the main protagonist and titular character of the "Balto film series". He is based on the real dog of the same name.

Personality

Despite his heritage and appearance, Balto always desired to be more like a dog than a wolf. He is deeply in love with Jenna. Balto has a lot of wisdom, patience, and perseverance that usually helps him save the day. He also cares a lot for others, and is willing to risk his own life to save someone else. Balto is also very humble (not letting fame go to his head). He appears to not have any interest in hunting, nor does he know how to do so. Balto was very insecure about being half-wolf (a trait Aleu later developed) but after the events the first movie learned pride for his species (although he still says being half-wolf can be painful, and that some of the other dogs *still* make fun of him, and he was ashamed when he admitted to Aleu that he was half-wolf). By the 3rd film, all teasing stops and he is officially considered the hero of Nome. Balto also loves sled-dog racing, and would become very excited when watching a race.

He also developed a fascination about flying in the 3rd film. This dream came true when Duke took Balto for a ride in his new plane, which he named the Balto Flyer in his honor and out of gratitude for having saved his life. Balto often acts as a peacemaker breaking up fights and trying to prevent them by saying "we don't want any trouble", though this usually doesn't work. He often avoids using force as much as possible, using his intellect to get out of tight spots, though when Steele insults his mother he would have most likely fought him and his cronies (Nikki, Kaltag and Star) if Boris hadn't intervened. So he does possess some outbursts of rage if prodded in the right manner. Despite this he refused to fight back against Steele in their showdown over the crate of serum in the first film out of fear of destroying the anti-toxin but manages to defeat Steele using his endurance, intelligence, and Steele's anger against him. This resulted in Steele falling off a cliff and Balto winning the fight without ever attacking once. He rarely get caught off guard, although whenever he is caught off guard, he recovers quickly.

Balto also has a soft spot for puppies, and was highly overprotective of Aleu, eventually having to let her go. Balto, despite his traumatic childhood, and being teased for several years, has a sense of humor. In the 1st film, Balto would often smile when around Boris, and would enjoy seeing Muk and Luk annoy Boris. In the 2nd film however, Balto has a more cynical personality. By the 3rd film, Balto starts to laugh more often, as well as starting to use sarcasm. When in search-and-rescue mode however, Balto's personality becomes dead serious, and uses a technique that he calls "marking the trail," in which he scratches various trees to set his path. He is also known to not deal well with extreme pressure panicking at the thought of letting Kodi down, and accidentally running off a cliff in the first film.

Balto is a fairly honest dog, continually recommending that Boris tell the truth to Stella throughout the 3rd film. But lied about Aleu's heritage in the 2nd film, to protect her feelings and hide his shame, which she found out the truth shortly after and ran away.

In the second film, we find out that Balto is ticklish.

Biography

Born to a wild Arctic wolf mother and a domestic Siberian Husky father, Balto was separated from his mother at an early age, and never found his father, wandering around for days, until he was adopted by Boris, a snow goose. Part of his family is Siberian Husky and part wolf, which means he is both American and Russian..

Balto was then an outcast, a creature that every one hated. The majority of dogs and humans of Nome reject him because of his wolf heritage, and he rejects the wolves because he himself also despised his wolf heritage, as he showed no interest in being a predator. Thus, he eventually ended up living a life that was somewhere between wild and domestic, although he always desired to eventually become fully domestic. Balto then developed a crush on Jenna, a local purebred female husky. However, the town was being under siege from an outbreak of Diphtheria, and Steele was chosen to lead the sled dogs with the medicine. Steele soon got them lost and stuck in a blizzard. Balto later went to rescue the team of sled dogs from a blizzard by "marking the trail," in which he scratches various trees to form a route, and got the medicine to the village in time to save the town. Balto became famous and became

Jenna's mate. Although some dogs still had their doubts .

A few years later, Jenna gave birth to a litter of pups who were all adopted except for one named Aleu. When Aleu discovers that she's half wolf she runs away. When Balto goes to find her he rescues her from a bear and they discover that Aleu's destiny is to lead a pack of wolves across the sea to where they can find food. Aleu later left with the wolf pack while Balto stayed behind with Jenna.

Another few years later, Balto is officially retired from sledding, but later helps his son Kodi keep his job as mail-dog. Balto later rescued a pilot and Boris from a bad plane accident and was rewarded with a trip in an airplane.

Age

Physical Appearance

Balto has unusually big paws, due to being half-wolf, that he says runs in one side of his family. He also has a long bushy tail. Balto has light and dark brown fur. Balto's eyes are yellow and red. Even though Balto is half wolf and half dog, he bears greater resemblance to a wolf, being teased about it for most of his life by other dogs and humans, particularly about his large, sharp teeth, as wolves have larger and sharper teeth (as well as stronger jaws) than dogs.

Abnormalties

At night, Balto's brown fur appears gray. In "Balto: The Junior Novelization", Balto's fur was described as gray. In *Balto II: Wolf Quest*, Balto's eyes were a very light shade of yellow, but in *Balto III: Wings of Change*, his eyes are a darker shade of yellow.

Physical Traits

As a wolf-dog hybrid, Balto possesses strength, speed and agility greater than that of a regular domestic dog. Balto has a highly developed sense of smell. He was also capable of hearing the bush plane when no other dog could, suggesting he has a heightened sense of hearing. Balto is highly intelligent, often coming up with plans and tactics to help aid others. In the 2nd installment, he had recurring dreams that were a visions of things to come, hinting that Balto may have the gift of prophecy.

While he does not possess predatory instincts, nor a strong prey drive (the desire for hunting), Balto is capable of holding his own against other dogs and wolves; but when he faces other creatures of the forest (bears, moose, etc.), he usually has to outsmart them, or flee from them due to their greater size. He also outsmarted Steele to defeat him without fighting back. He also has a great deal of durability, shown when he got up from the beating he received from the bear in the first film without much harm and later on in the film continuing on despite receiving a number of heavy hits from Steele, including being brutally thrown head first into a rock.

Relationships

- Aniu – Aniu was Balto's mother who died when Balto was a pup. Aniu's spirit later returned to guide Balto several times. At the end of the second film Balto realizes that Aniu has been with him the whole time as the raven, and that she is his mother.
- Boris Goosinov – After Balto was separated from his mother, he was adopted by Boris Goosinov, a goose from Russia. Boris raised Balto from a pup, and stayed with him as an adult claiming "I'm sticking here until I'm sure that you can stand on all four feet".
- Jenna – During the events of the first film (and possibly before that), Balto had a crush on local husky Jenna, which was returned. They first met after Balto saved Rosy's hat from being trampled. After the events of the first film, they became mates for life.
- Aleu – Balto's only pup who resembles him. Their relationship is explored further in *Balto: Wolf Quest*, where the two journey to the ocean to find Aleu's destiny. Their relationship is initially rocky, due to Balto not telling Aleu about her wolf appearance and heritage until she was almost killed by a hunter, and Aleu's inability to accept that she is half-wolf. However, by the end of *Wolf Quest*, the two have genuinely gained respect and love for each other. Their relationship ends on a good note, with Aleu howling goodbye to Balto as she and the pack drift away on an ice floe.
- Rosy – Jenna's owner. She is possibly the only human in Nome (in the beginning of the first film) to like Balto for who he is; even her own parents feared Balto because of his wolf heritage.
- Kodiak – Balto's pup. Their relationship is explored in *Balto III: Wings of Change*.

See also

- Balto
- 1925 Nome Serum Run
- Balto (film)
- Balto II: Wolf Quest
- Balto III: Wings of Change
- List of Balto characters

E127 series

E127 series

E127 series	
 E127 series at Niigata Station, May 2008	
In service	1995–Present
Manufacturer	JR East, Kawasaki Heavy Industries, Tokyu Car Corporation
Constructed	1995–1998
Number built	50 vehicles
Number in service	50 vehicles (25 sets)
Formation	2 cars per trainset
Operator	JR East
Depot(s)	Niigata, Matsumoto
Specifications	
Car body construction	Stainless steel
Car length	20,000 mm
Width	2,800 mm
Doors	3 pairs per side
Maximum speed	110 km/h
Electric system(s)	1,500 V DC

Current collection method	Overhead catenary
Safety system(s)	ATS-P, ATS-Ps
Gauge	1,067 mm

The **E127 series** is a DC EMU operated on local services by East Japan Railway Company (JR East) in Japan. The design is derived from the 209 series commuter EMU.

Variants

E127-0 series

Thirteen 2-car sets were delivered to Niigata Depot in March 1995 (sets V1 to V6) and November 1996 (sets V7 to V13) for use on Echigo Line, Hakushin Line, and Uetsu Main Line local services. They entered service on 8 May 1995.

Formation

1. KuMoHa E127 (with one PS30 pantograph)
2. KuHa E126 (with toilet)

E127-100 series

Twelve 2-car sets were delivered to Matsumoto Depot in November and December 1998 for use on Ōito Line and Shinonoi Line local services. They entered service on 8 December 1998. The external styling differs from the earlier E127-0 series, resembling the 701 series design. Sets A7 to A12 have a second de-icing pantograph on the KuHa trailer car.

Matsumoto-based E127-100 series at Matsumoto Station, March 2009

Formation

1. KuMoHa E127 (with one PS34 pantograph)
2. KuHa E126 (with toilet)

See also

- ⚭ Media related to E127 series at Wikimedia Commons

External links

- JR East E127 series [1] (Japanese)

Interior view of E127-100 series set
showing mixed longitudinal/transverse
seating and driver-only-operation ticket
issuing machine

E501 series

E501 series

E501 series	
 E501 series on Jōban Line service, April 2003	
In service	1995–Present
Manufacturer	Kawasaki Heavy Industries, Tokyu Car Corporation
Constructed	1995–1997
Refurbishment	2006–2007
Number built	60 vehicles
Number in service	60 vehicles (8 sets)
Formation	5/10 cars per trainset
Fleet numbers	K701–K704, K751–K754
Operator	JR East
Depot(s)	Katsuta
Line(s) served	Jōban Line, Mito Line
Specifications	
Car body construction	Stainless steel
Car length	20,420 mm (end cars), 20,000 mm (intermediate cars)
Width	2,890 mm
Doors	4 pairs per side

Maximum speed	120 km/h
Electric system(s)	1,500 V DC / 20 kV AC (50Hz)
Current collection method	Overhead catenary
Safety system(s)	ATS-P, ATS-SN
Gauge	1,067 mm

The **E501 series** is an AC/DC dual-voltage EMU operated on local services by East Japan Railway Company (JR East) in Japan. The design is derived from the 209 series commuter EMU, and were initially operated as 10+5-car formations on Jōban Line services out of Ueno in Tokyo, but were modified with the addition of toilets and transferred to Jōban Line and Mito Line local services in the Mito area from 2007.

See also

- ⬧ Media related to E501 series at Wikimedia Commons

External links

- JR East E501 series [1] (**Japanese**)

Cunningham family

Cunningham family

The **Cunningham family** are a fictional family in the long-running Channel 4 soap opera, *Hollyoaks*

The family was one of the original families introduced in 1995, the first airing of *Hollyoaks*. Subsequently, the family has seen more tragedy than happiness, with four members of the family being killed since the start of the show.

History

Gordon was an only child. He had a cousin, Benny, who was a criminal and bad influence. Gordon married Angela, the pair had three daughters, Dawn, Cindy and Jude and one son, Max. Gordon and Angela split up before 1995. Gordon then found love in Helen Richardson, the pair married in 1999 and Helen gave birth to Tom Cunningham. The family, over the years, has been surrounded by death and heartbreak, Dawn died of leukaemia in 1997, Lee Stanley, father of Holly, also died in 1997. In 2004, Gordon suffered a heart attack whilst driving Helen and Tom. He crashed the car, which killed himself and Helen. In 2008, Max was run over and killed moments after marrying Steph Dean. Other relatives have also died. Grace Hutchinson, step-granddaughter of Gordon, died in 2006 of SIDS. Gordon's stepson, Lewis committed suicide in 2001. The Cunningham family have also owned several businesses since the beginning of *Hollyoaks*. Gordon became the owner of video shop, Got it Taped and later supermarket, Drive 'n' Buy. Gordon also became Councillor of Chester. After Gordon's death, Max inherited Drive 'n' Buy, which he sold to Neville Ashworth. Got it Taped was then sold to Tony Hutchinson. Max also owned part of The Loft before selling it to Clare Devine and also opened juice bar, MOB's (short for Max and OB's) with OB. After Max's death, Steph took over Max's half of MOB's and ran it with Cindy.

In *Hollyoaks*

Before 1995, Dawn had begun an affair with best friend Ruth Osborne's father, Jack. Dawn got pregnant and gave baby Beth up for adoption. When Ruth found out, she did not want to see Dawn again. On her sixteenth birthday, Cindy slept with Lee Stanley, she then discovered she was pregnant. Max had struck a double act with Sam "OB" O'Brien. The pair were always involved in money making schemes. Dawn and James "Jambo" Bolton discovered Beth needed a kidney transplant. After a number of failed donors, Dawn told Jack of his illegitimate daughter. Jack was found to be a match and saved Beth's life. Dawn and Jambo then kissed after realising their feelings Dawn began feeling unwell and, with Jambo, she visited the doctor, who diagnosed her with leukaemia. On Christmas 1997, Jambo proposed to Dawn, who then died after her battle with leukaemia, the same day Cindy gave birth to Holly.

Cindy became depressed at being a 16-year-old mother and contemplated smothering her baby, however she could not go through with it and realised she did love Holly after all. She found love with Sean Tate; however, he hated Holly and began hurting her. After social services found out Holly was being abused, Cindy decided to leave Britain for abroad. On her way to the airport, she ran over Anna Green and left her for dead. A debt-ridden Jude began stealing cars with her father's cousin Benny to pay off the debts. After months of stealing, the police came after Jude. Realising she could not go to jail, Jude donned a dark wig and used Dawn's passport to flee the country. Gordon began a relationship with Helen Richardson, who discovered she was pregnant. Gordon then proposed and the pair married. She then gave birth to Tom

Max became depressed over his stepbrother Lewis's death and decided to make the most of his life, which separated himself from OB. On a cliff trip, Max, OB, Ben Davies, Kristian Hargreaves, Jamie Nash and Theo Sankofa were climbing when more tragedy struck, leaving Jamie and Theo dead. Cindy returned with Holly in 2002, where she scammed Max and OB out of money before leaving once again. OB found out Helen was having an affair with Tony Hutchinson. He told Gordon who was heartbroken. Helen left Gordon but eventually returned to him. 2004 seen the deaths of Gordon and Helen, who died after Gordon had a heart attack at the wheel of a car and crashed it. Five-year-old Tom was put to stay with sister, Mandy, however, he soon moved in with Max and OB. At the funeral, Cindy returned for a brief stint, however, Jude did not.

Max bought part of The Loft nightclub. He made OB a co-manager. They hired an events organiser named Clare Devine, both Max and OB fell for her. Max began a relationship with Clare and asked her to move in. Mel Burton caught Clare sleeping with Sean Kennedy. OB told Max of this but Max took Clare's side and refused to believe it. He then proposed to Clare. Clare poisoned Max's mind into him believing that OB could not accept their relationship. As a result, Max and OB's friendship was over. As Clare planned to leave with Max's money, OB burst into the church and told him so. Max did not believe him and ended up marrying Clare, who thought up a new plan to kill Max and inherit the money. Max had a heart attack and Clare began to tamper with his medication in the hope he would have another and die. For Christmas, Clare took Max and Tom to a secluded cottage near a lake, there she put Tom's coat in the lake, which made Max jump in. Max then realised Tom was not in the lake. As he began to drown, OB turned up. Clare tried to tell him it was an accident, however, OB punched her and rescued Max. Clare was arrested, however was released. She then threatened to kill Max if he did not sign over The Loft. Realising Tom would be left alone, Max agreed and signed the deed.

Max became one of five named suspects for the attempted murder of Clare. Max was questioned but the police released him. Tom was put into foster care after Clare manipulated both Tom and social services. On the night she was pushed, Max had run into The Loft and publicly threatened to kill Clare.

When Clare returned from the hospital, Max went into her house and poisoned her food as revenge, however she did not eat it. Max threatened her to tell the social services the truth, which she did. Clare supposedly left Hollyoaks but secretly kidnapped Katy Fox. Max, Warren and Justin went after her. Clare ordered Warren to kill Justin after it was revealed he had pushed her. They pretended to do so. Clare then ordered Max to kick "Justin's body", however, he could not because he was too nice. Clare sped off in the car with Katy and ended up going over a quarry, Max jumped in to save her but she disappeared beneath the water. Max confided in Steph over his guilt of letting Clare "die". The pair started a relationship and finally got engaged. At this time, Cindy returned to Hollyoaks with Holly after escaping her abusive ex-boyfriend. She began staying with Max, Tom and Steph. After marrying Steph, Max, along with OB and Tom went to get a present for Steph. On their way, Max saw Tom playing on the road and then Niall Rafferty, who then drove off, in his car. Max pushed Tom out of the way of the car, but was hit himself. OB and Tom held Max as he began to die, Steph came running over in her wedding dress just as he died.

Mandy decided to let Tom stay with OB, who was moving to London to be with his girlfriend Summer. However, Tom realised Steph would be on her own if he left and decided to stay with her, she then became his legal guardian. Steph began a relationship with Niall, which Cindy and Mandy frowned upon, however their relationship ended after Steph realised she was not over Max. Cindy discovered Mandy was having an affair with Warren and threatened to tell his fiancée, Louise Summers. Warren told Cindy that if she did, he would hurt Holly. Cindy then started seeing Darren Osborne until he was sent to prison, where she started seeing Rhys Ashworth. Holly did not get along with Rhys to begin with but slowly they grew to like each other. Holly was then upset when Cindy split up from Rhys and returned to Darren, who had been released from prison. Steph took a holiday to Scotland with Craig Dean and Tom. There, Niall returned for revenge and kidnapped Tom. However, he ended up killing himself. Cindy split up with Darren after it was discovered he got Jake Dean to confess to Sean Kennedy's murder. Cindy then fell for Tony Hutchinson and they started going out. Cindy became jealous when she discovered Darren had drunkenly married Hannah Ashworth. She and Darren then decided to con both Tony and Hannah by stealing money from Tony and getting their hands on The Dog from Hannah.

Generations

- Unknown
  - Gordon Cunningham; son of unknown, married Angela Cunningham, then Helen Cunningham (1999–2004)
    - Max Cunningham; son of Gordon and Angela, married Clare Devine (2006–2007), then Steph Cunningham (2008)
    - Dawn Cunningham; daughter of Gordon and Angela
      - Bethany Cunningham; daughter of Dawn and Jack Osborne

- Jude Cunningham; daughter of Gordon and Angela
- Cindy Longford; daughter of Gordon and Angela, married Tony Hutchinson (2009–2010), then Alistair Longford (2010—)
    - Holly Hutchinson; daughter of Cindy and Lee Stanley
- Tom Cunningham; son of Gordon and Helen
- Benny Cunningham; cousin of Gordon

Reception

Due to being seen as the *Hollyoaks* original family, members of the Cunninghams have been popular, especially Max and Gordon. In 1997, Davinia Taylor was axed from her role as Jude for time-keeping issues. She departed in 1998. In 2008, it was reported that Taylor was to return to the show.

On 9 May 2008, it was announced that Matt Littler had quit his role as Max and would leave in the late Summer after almost 13 years of playing the character. In a 2008 episode of *T4*, Littler reprised his role as Max in a dream sequence that seen him reunited with on-screen father, Bernard Latham (Gordon) in heaven.

External links

- Max Cunningham [1] on the E4 website [2]
- Cindy Hutchinson [1] on the E4 website [2]
- Holly Hutchinson [2] on the E4 website [2]
- Tom Cunningham [3] on the E4 website [2]
- Mandy Richardson [4] on the E4 website [2]
- Clare Devine [5] on the E4 website [2]
- Steph Cunningham [6] on the E4 website [2]
- Tony Hutchinson [1] on the E4 website [2]
- Jack Osborne [7] on the E4 website [2]

Bhopal – Indore Intercity Express

Bhopal – Indore Intercity Express

The **Bhopal - Indore Intercity Express** is a daily intercity express train which runs between Bhopal Habibganj, the sub-urban railway station of Bhopal, the capital city of Central Indian state Madhya Pradesh and Indore Junction railway station of Indore, the largest city & commercial hub of Madhya Pradesh.

Bhopal-Indore Intercity Express, about to depart for Indore from platform no. 1, Habibganj Railway Station, Bhopal

Number and nomenclature

The number allowted for the train :

*   9324 - Habibganj to Indore
*   9323 - Indore to Habibganj

The name "Intercity Express" refers to the mail express passenger train service between two important cities.

Arrival and departure

Train no.9324 departs from Bhopal Habibganj daily at 17:20 hrs., reaching Indore the same day at 21:30 hrs. Train no.9323 departs from Indore daily at 06:55 hrs. from platform no.3 reaching Bhopal Habibganj the same day at 10:40 hrs.

Route and halts

The train goes via. Maksi & Dewas. The important halt of the train are :

*   **BHOPAL HABIBGANJ**
*   **Bhopal Junction**
*   Bhopal Bairagarh
*   **Shajapur**
*   Maksi
*   Dewas
*   **INDORE JUNCTION**

Coach composite

The train consist of 11 Chair Car Coaches :

- 1 AC Chair Car
- 6 Reserved Chair Car
- 4 Second Class Chair Car

Average speed and frequency

The train runs with an average speed of 50 km/hr to cover more than 220 kms stretch of Bhopal to Indore route in 5 - 6 hours. While its reverse service Indore - Bhopal Intercity Express runs with an average speed of 70 km/hr. This train is the first choice of the Bhopal people to reach Indore as it has few halts. The train runs on daily basis.

Loco link

The train is hauled by Ratlam RTM WDM-3 Diesel engine.

Rake maintenance & sharing

The train is maintained by the Habibganj Coaching Depot. The same rake is used for Bhopal-Dahod Express for one way which is altered by the second rake on the other way.

Bhopal-Dahod Passenger

The Bhopal-Dahod Passenger trains is a daily service which runs between Bhopal Habibganj railway station of Bhopal, the capital city of Madhya Pradesh and Dahod town in Gujarat. The train is numbered 287/288 and shares the same coaches of Bhopal-Indore Intercity Express. It halts at as many as 18 major-minor railway stations such as Bhopal Junction, Sehore, Shujalpur, Ujjain Junction, Ratlam Junction, Meghnagar, Anas, etc.

Other trains from Bhopal / Habibganj to Indore

- 2919/2920 Indore - Udhampur Malwa Express
- 9313/9314 Indore - Patna Express
- 9321/9322 Indore - Patna Express
- 1471/1472 Indore - Jabalpur Express
- 6325/6326 Indore - Trivendrum Ahilyanagari Express
- 8233/8234 Indore - Bilaspur Narmada Express
- 9305/9306 Indore - Howrah Shipra Express
- 2913/2914 Indore - Nagpur Express

• 0279/0280 Indore - Bhopal Passenger

Trivia

• It goes via. Dewas without touching Ujjain Junction
• Ratlam RTM-WDM 3 its regular loco link along with pale-yellow coloured livery coaches.

See also

• Indore - Bhopal Intercity Express
• Indore Junction
• Bhopal Junction
• Bhopal Habibganj

Indore - Bhopal Intercity Express

Indore - Bhopal Intercity Express

The **Indore - Bhopal Intercity Express** is a daily intercity express train which runs between Indore Junction railway station of Indore, the largest city & commercial hub of Central Indian state Madhya Pradesh and Bhopal Habibganj, the sub-urban railway station of Bhopal, the capital city of Madhya Pradesh.

Number and nomenclature

The number allowted for the train :

- 9323 - Indore to Habibganj
- 9324 - Habibganj to Indore

The name "Intercity Express" refers to the mail express passenger train service between two important cities.

Arrival and departure

Train no.9323 departs from Indore daily at 06:55 hrs. from platform no.3 reaching Bhopal Habibganj the same day at 10:40 hrs. Train no.9324 departs from Bhopal Habibganj daily at 17:20 hrs., reaching Indore the same day at 21:30 hrs.

Route and halts

The train goes via. Maksi & Dewas. The important halts of the train are :

- **INDORE JUNCTION**
- Dewas
- Maksi
- **Shajapur**
- Bhopal Bairagarh
- **Bhopal Junction**
- **BHOPAL HABIBGANJ**

Coach composite

The train consist of 11 Chair Car Coaches :

- 1 AC Chair Car
- 6 Reserved Chair Car
- 4 Second Class Chair Car

Average speed and frequency

The train runs with an average speed of 63 km/hr which makes it really the fastest to cover more than 220 km stretch of Indore to Bhopal route in less than 4 hours. Hence this train is the first choice of the Indore people to reach Bhopal as it also has few halts. The train runs on daily basis.

Loco link

The train is hauled by Ratlam RTM WDM-3 Diesel engine.

Rake maintenance & sharing

The train is maintained by the Habibganj Coaching Depot. The same rake is used for Bhopal - Dahod Express for one way which is altered by the second rake on the other way.

Bhopal-Dahod Passenger

The Bhopal-Dahod Passenger trains is a daily service which runs between Bhopal Habibganj railway station of Bhopal, the capital city of Madhya Pradesh and Dahod town in Gujarat. The train is numbered 287/288 and shares the same coaches of Bhopal-Indore Intercity Express. It halts as many as 18 major-minor railway stations such as Bhopal Junction, Sehore, Shujalpur, Ujjain Junction, Ratlam Junction, Meghnagar, Anas, etc.

Other trains from Indore to Bhopal / Habibganj

- 2919/2920 Indore - Udhampur Malwa Express
- 9313/9314 Indore - Patna Express
- 9321/9322 Indore - Patna Express
- 1471/1472 Indore - Jabalpur Express
- 6325/6326 Indore - Trivendrum Ahilyanagari Express
- 8233/8234 Indore - Bilaspur Narmada Express
- 9305/9306 Indore - Howrah Shipra Express
- 2913/2914 Indore - Nagpur Express
- 0279/0280 Indore - Bhopal Passenger

Trivia

- This train is the fastest connection of Indore with Bhopal despite of being an express train. The super fast Malwa Express takes more then 5.2 hours while this train takes less then 4 hours to reach Bhopal. Hence it is the most busiest train of the route.
- It goes via. Dewas without touching Ujjain Junction
- Ratlam RTM-WDM 3 its regular loco link along with pale-yellow coloured livery coaches.

See also

- Bhopal - Indore Intercity Express
- Indore Junction
- Bhopal Junction

External links

- 9323 Indore - Bhopal Intercity Express timings [1]

Piedmont (train)

Piedmont (train)

Piedmont	
Overview	
Service type	Inter-city rail
Status	Active
Locale	North Carolina
First service	May 26, 1995
Current operator(s)	Amtrak
Route	
Start	Raleigh, North Carolina
No. of intermediate stops	7
End	Charlotte, North Carolina
Distance travelled	173 miles (278 km)
Average journey time	3 hours 9 minutes
Service frequency	Twice daily
Train number(s)	(73/74/75/76)
Technical	
Gauge	4 ft 8 $\frac{1}{2}$ in (1435 mm)
Track owner(s)	NCRR

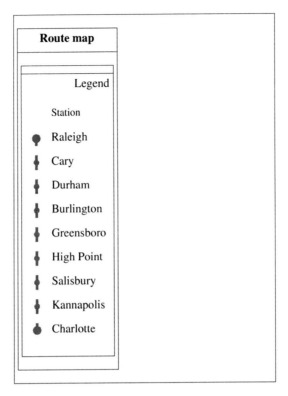

The ***Piedmont*** is a twice daily passenger train that travels between Raleigh and Charlotte with a run time of 3 hours and 9 minutes, including intermediate stops at Cary, Durham, Burlington, Greensboro, High Point, Salisbury, and Kannapolis. Started in 1995, the train is jointly funded and operated by Amtrak and the North Carolina Department of Transportation. Uniquely for such partnerships, North Carolina owns the rolling stock.

History

North Carolina developed the *Piedmont* as a follow-on to the successful *Carolinian*, which entered service in early 1990. Officials sought to add a second daily round-trip between Charlotte and Raleigh. In the fall of 1990, the board of transportation approved the acquisition of five used passenger cars and the leasing of two diesel locomotives. The board planned to have the second train enter service in "early 1992."

The *Piedmont* (as the train came to be called) faced numerous delays. The Norfolk Southern Railway, which leased the track, insisted that the state construct a wye in Charlotte for turning the two trains around. (The *Carolinian* had continued 10 miles (16 km) south to Pineville and turned around there). In 1993 the cost of the wye plus land purchase was estimated at $200,000; by late 1994 this grew to $695,000, plus $1.5 million for a maintenance facility in Raleigh.

The *Piedmont* finally entered service on May 26, 1995.

In early 2010, Amtrak announced that a second daily *Piedmont* train would enter service, after delays encountered in refurbishing motive power and passenger cars for the new train. The second frequency began on June 5, 2010, and is expected to carry around 43,000 people during its first year of service.

After the second train entered service, Amtrak renamed the route *Piedmont Service* to reflect the multiple daily frequencies.

Incidents

On May 13, 2010, a northbound *Piedmont* collided with a truck in Mebane, North Carolina and derailed. The collision derailed the locomotive and 3 cars, and also ruptured the locomotive's fuel tank, causing a fire. As a result, 13 people were injured.

Route details

The *Piedmont* operates over North Carolina Railroad (leased to Norfolk Southern Railway) trackage:

- Charlotte District, Charlotte to Linwood
- Danville District, Linwood to Greensboro
- Raleigh District, Greensboro to Raleigh

Rolling stock

The motive power for the *Piedmont* is provided by five state-owned locomotives, of which two are EMD F59PHIs, numbered 1755 (City of Salisbury) and 1797 (City of Asheville); two are EMD F59PHs, numbered 1810 (City of Greensboro) and 1859 (City of High Point); and one is a rebuilt GP40PH-2, numbered 1792 (City of Raleigh), and originally used in the 1960s by the L&N.

State-owned passenger cars on the *Piedmont* are refurbished coach cars originally built by Pullman-Standard and the St. Louis Car Company in the 1960s for the Kansas City Southern and Union Pacific. There are two lounge cars and one combination car originally built by the St. Louis Car Company in the 1950s and used by the United States Army.

All rolling stock is painted in special North Carolina livery (different from the national Amtrak livery). The color scheme is blue and silver with red accents.

Station stops

State	Town/City	Station	Connections
North Carolina	Raleigh	Raleigh	**Amtrak:** *Silver Star, Carolinian* CAT Buses
	Cary	Cary	**Amtrak:** *Silver Star, Carolinian* C-Tran Buses
	Durham	Durham	**Amtrak:** *Carolinian* Future link to DATA's Durham Station Transportation Center
	Burlington	Burlington	**Amtrak:** *Carolinian*
	Greensboro	Greensboro	**Amtrak:** *Crescent, Carolinain* GTA, PART, and Greyhound Buses
	High Point	High Point	**Amtrak:** *Crescent, Carolinian* Thruway Motorcoach to Winston-Salem, North Carolina Hi tran(Broad Avenue Terminal)
	Salisbury	Salisbury	**Amtrak:** *Crescent, Carolinian*
	Kannapolis	Kannapolis	**Amtrak:** *Carolinian*
	Charlotte	Charlotte	**Amtrak:** *Crescent, Carolinian* **CATS**: 11

External links

- Amtrak - *Piedmont and Carolinian* [1]
- NCDOT Rail Division [2]

The Harbingers

The Harbingers

The Harbingers game board.	
Designer	Brett Clements Phillip Tanner
Illustrator	Richard McKenna Carmen Delprat Daniel Burns
Actor	**The Gatekeeper:** Wenanty Nosul
Publisher	Mattel
Publication date	1995
Genre(s)	Horror and terror
Players	3–6
Age range	12+
Setup time	15 minutes
Playing time	up to 60 minutes
Skills required	Dice rolling Strategy

The Harbingers is an Australian video board game designed by Brett Clements and Phillip Tanner and published by Mattel as a major update to the Atmosfear series. The object of the game is to collect six different coloured "Keystones" and thus beat the "Gatekeeper". Before players can start collecting Keystones they race each other, each seeking to become a "Harbinger". Players who fail to become Harbingers within ten minutes must play the main game as "Soul Rangers"—miserable scavengers who obey their own rules. To beat the Gatekeeper, players must face their worst fear. If none of players is able to win the game within sixty minutes, the Gatekeeper is the winner.

The game is set in a place known as "The Other Side". This place has six Harbingers, each of whom has authority over a Province. To play the game, each player adopts the persona of one of the

Harbingers: Gevaudan the werewolf; Hellin the poltergeist; Khufu the mummy; Baron Samedi the zombie; Anne de Chantraine the witch, and Elizabeth Bathory the vampire. The final character in the game is the Gatekeeper, whose job is to ensure that the other characters do not escape from The Other Side.

The game board is made up of a central hub and six two-sided interchangeable "Provinces" which fit together, creating a hexagon. A videotape is included with the game, and acts as a game clock. The videotape stars Wenanty Nosul as The Gatekeeper, who appears throughout the tape giving instructions to players. At the end of the videotape there is a fifteen-minute presentation in which a voice-over, along with the Gatekeeper, explains how to play the game.

The Harbingers became one of the top ten best selling games in America and UK, within months of its release. Following this release, two booster tapes and the Soul Rangers add-on were released. The booster tapes provide a more challenging experience for experienced players, while the add-on allows players to play only as Soul Rangers. The add-on was released because the creators found that players enjoyed the Soul Ranger role.

Gameplay

It is recommended by the voice-over that players find or create a perfect *Atmosfear* (atmosphere), before starting the game: "Turn the lights down and volume up, and welcome to the Other Side." When they are ready, players roll the dice in turn, the one who rolls highest becoming the "Chosen One" who assembles the game board by connecting the Provinces to the central hub, creating a hexagon shape. The players write down their greatest fear on a slip of paper which is placed in the "well of fears" by the Chosen One. The Gatekeeper then starts the game, and the players, using their *Numb Skulls*, race to become a Harbinger by landing on the Harbinger's headstone located in each province. If a player fails to make it to a headstone within ten minutes, they become Soul Rangers for the rest of the game. They must remain in the sewers until either they are released by the Gatekeeper, or collect the Keystone which allows them to release themselves.

Players who become Harbingers start collecting Keystones either by landing on them on the game board, or by taking them from other players by dueling. Soul Rangers cannot collect Keystones by landing on them; instead, they chase down other players and steal their Keystones. Players must collect the six Keystones of different colour to win. Although players only need one keystone per colour, players can collect more than one which can prevent other players from completing the game. Each Keystone gives players different powers, depending on which Harbinger they are, the list of powers being described on the back of the character's card. When players have collected the Keystones, they can win the game by returning home to the central hub. Then they must roll a six on the dice; a fear is picked from the well of fears, and if it does not correspond to the player's earlier expressed "greatest fear", that player wins the game. Otherwise, players must return to their headstone and try again. If none of players is able to win the game within sixty minutes, the Gatekeeper is the winner.

Characters

The six Harbingers in the game are: Gevaudan the werewolf; Hellin the poltergeist; Khufu the mummy; Baron Samedi the zombie; Anne de Chantraine the witch; and Elizabeth Bathory, the vampire. Each of the Harbingers is based on either a real person or a myth, except for Hellin. Hellin is the only Harbinger entirely created by Brett Clements. Hellin is evil infant trouble-maker who gets very angry when things don't go her way. Baron Samedi got his name from the ancient Arawak Indian God of the Dead. Anne de Chantraine is based on the first "official" witch who was burned at the stake. Elizabeth Bathory is based on a serial killer who is believed to have murdered and drunk the blood of about six hundred and fifty virgin girls. Khufu is based on an Fourth Dynasty Egyptian Pharaoh. Gevaudan is based around a man who was hunted by armies of people for supposedly carrying the sickness of lycanthropy.

Soul Rangers, players who have failed to become Harbingers, are described as miserable, skeletal scavengers, the scourge of The Other Side. Soul Rangers hunt down other players and steal their keystones. Soul Rangers were created during the game's development. Brett Clements wanted to introduce characters that players did not want to become, but he later found that players enjoyed the anarchic role of the Soul Ranger. The final character in the game is the Gatekeeper, whose job is to make sure the other characters cannot escape from The Other Side to the real world. The Gatekeeper's character is based on the old cemetery gatekeepers, whose job was to guard cemeteries from grave robbers.

Layout

The game board is made up of the Central Hub and six two-sided Provinces which fit together creating a hexagon. The Central Hub is made up of the Well of Fears, the home positions and the Ring Road. The Well of Fears is a cup with a lid that fits inside the hole in the middle of the Central Hub. Located around the Well of Fears are six numbered grooves, called "Home"; players must start from and return to Home. The Home positions are connected to the Ring Road, a path that runs around the Central Hub. The Ring Road give players access to all the Provinces.

Each Province is a two-sided interchangeable board, on one side of which is a Harbinger's province while on the other are the sewers. The Provinces can be assembled in any order, which can allow different game experiences when the Provinces are changed. Each Province has its own headstone and is in the Harbinger's colours. Both sides of the Province board have paths used by the players to move around the board. Located along the paths are the six Keystones for that colour Province, and three different game symbols: the black holes, the lighting bolts and the compasses.

The game includes six boomerang-shaped slabs which allow players to store their character card, Numb Skull and collected Keystones. The character card has a photograph of the character on the front, and on the back a list of powers each keystone gives to the player. To move around the game board, players use their own character's playing pieces: a vampire bat for Elizabeth Bathory, a cobra for Khufu, a top hat for Baron Samedi, an "H" building block for Hellin, a fang for Gevaudan, a cauldron for Anne de Chantraine. and a Numb skull for Soul Rangers. The Numb skull is also used at the beginning of the game, before players become Harbingers.

Video

A VHS videotape is included with The Harbingers which is played during the game. The videotape begins with The Gatekeeper – played by Wenanty Nosul – starting the game with "On your marks...Get ready...Get set...Go!". As the game begins the game clock appears in the right-hand corner of the screen, counting down from sixty minutes; unless the game is won by a player within one hour the Gatekeeper is declared the winner. During the sixty minutes the Gatekeeper will appear on screen, to give players instructions or a choice between receiving a prize or imposing a penalty on an opponent. Players must carry out all instructions given by the Gatekeeper. When the Gatekeeper appears he demands that players stop and listen to him. He will not hold back from insulting players and is reluctant to reward or help players. During the game a computer-generated storm can be seen in the background; sometimes the storm partly covers the game clock. Along with the storm, spooky sounds and sometimes the Gatekeeper's laughter can be heard.

During development there was a concern that the game might initially seem too complicated. At the end of the videotape there is a special fifteen minute presentation called the *rules presentation* in which a voice-over along with the Gatekeeper explains the game, the characters and how to play. The rules presentation was created to help explain the game to new players. The videotape can be forwarded to the start of the instructions. During the rules presentation a game is played by actors who are dressed as three Harbingers – Baron Samedi, Anne de Chantraine and Elizabeth Bathory – and three Soul Rangers. The demonstraion game is used throughout the rules presentation to help explain how to play the game.

Development and reception

With the feedback received from players after the release of Nightmare, Brett Clements and Phillip Tanner started work on the major update to the series. They struck a deal with J. W. Spear & Sons, to use publishing experience and market research with Nightmare to help create the new game. The deal allowed J. W. Spear & Sons to have input into how the game was developed, which was not the case with Nightmare. Village Roadshow was also involved with the game's development and with its release in the United States.

The development ended six years after it started, with about six million dollars invested in the development of the game. The Harbingers became one of the top ten best selling games in America and UK, within months of its release. On the game's release, Mattel launched a marketing campaign with a spot on MTV, cross-promotions with soft drinks and a website for the game.

Expansions

Following the release of The Harbingers, two booster tapes was released. The tapes provide a challenging experience to The Harbingers for experienced players. The booster tapes run for forty-five minutes instead of the sixty minutes of the original, and come with a new rule to limit the number of Keystones added to each province based on the number of players. Other than this limit the normal rules apply. Following the booster tapes, an add-on called Soul Rangers was released. The add-on allows players to play only as Soul Rangers. The add-on was released because the creators found out that players enjoy causing damage as Soul Rangers.

See also

- List of Australian inventions
- List of board games

External links

- Atmosfear: The Harbingers [1] at BoardGameGeek
- Atmosfear: Booster Game Tape Set [2] at BoardGameGeek
- Atmosfear: The Soul Rangers [3] at BoardGameGeek
- Atmosfear: The Card Game [4] at BoardGameGeek
- Nightmare series [5] and Atmosfear series [6] at BoardGameGeek

Article Sources and Contributors

BeBox *Source*: http://en.wikipedia.org/?oldid=386823520 *Contributors*:

JavaScript *Source*: http://en.wikipedia.org/?oldid=390682838 *Contributors*: Nigelj

Virtual Boy *Source*: http://en.wikipedia.org/?oldid=390572813 *Contributors*: Martin IIIa

Xena *Source*: http://en.wikipedia.org/?oldid=389489308 *Contributors*: Cameron Scott

Microsoft Bob *Source*: http://en.wikipedia.org/?oldid=387129626 *Contributors*:

Pentium Pro *Source*: http://en.wikipedia.org/?oldid=389967349 *Contributors*: CommonsDelinker

Sega Nomad *Source*: http://en.wikipedia.org/?oldid=373194521 *Contributors*: Martin IIIa

IS-95 *Source*: http://en.wikipedia.org/?oldid=387069867 *Contributors*: 1 anonymous edits

Microsoft Agent *Source*: http://en.wikipedia.org/?oldid=389762693 *Contributors*: Angel Emfrbl

Frappuccino *Source*: http://en.wikipedia.org/?oldid=389823967 *Contributors*: Macrakis

Apple Bandai Pippin *Source*: http://en.wikipedia.org/?oldid=388295085 *Contributors*: Frenard

Initial D *Source*: http://en.wikipedia.org/?oldid=390550929 *Contributors*: 1 anonymous edits

Dan Hibiki *Source*: http://en.wikipedia.org/?oldid=389747539 *Contributors*: 1 anonymous edits

SmartMedia *Source*: http://en.wikipedia.org/?oldid=382757312 *Contributors*:

System Management Bus *Source*: http://en.wikipedia.org/?oldid=381740718 *Contributors*: 1 anonymous edits

3D Movie Maker *Source*: http://en.wikipedia.org/?oldid=389332730 *Contributors*: Willdasmiffking

Rapi:t *Source*: http://en.wikipedia.org/?oldid=367895560 *Contributors*:

Cheese-eating surrender monkeys *Source*: http://en.wikipedia.org/?oldid=385850534 *Contributors*: 1 anonymous edits

Iori Yagami *Source*: http://en.wikipedia.org/?oldid=389034259 *Contributors*: Tbhotch

Josta *Source*: http://en.wikipedia.org/?oldid=386530123 *Contributors*: 1 anonymous edits

Ryuji Yamazaki *Source*: http://en.wikipedia.org/?oldid=386923268 *Contributors*: 1 anonymous edits

French Toast Crunch *Source*: http://en.wikipedia.org/?oldid=386852646 *Contributors*: Miacix

.ci *Source*: http://en.wikipedia.org/?oldid=381918172 *Contributors*: Cesium 133

Dippin' Dots *Source*: http://en.wikipedia.org/?oldid=390557499 *Contributors*: Spamelgoog

NV1 *Source*: http://en.wikipedia.org/?oldid=379209650 *Contributors*: Hyins

Alec Trevelyan *Source*: http://en.wikipedia.org/?oldid=384898458 *Contributors*: Imladros

Max Cunningham *Source*: http://en.wikipedia.org/?oldid=390593647 *Contributors*: Raintheone

Sun Ultra series *Source*: http://en.wikipedia.org/?oldid=373078573 *Contributors*: ChristTrekker

Security Administrator Tool for Analyzing Networks *Source*: http://en.wikipedia.org/?oldid=375354431 *Contributors*:

Blue Mary *Source*: http://en.wikipedia.org/?oldid=390499411 *Contributors*: DarkGhostMikel

Cray T3E *Source*: http://en.wikipedia.org/?oldid=346583572 *Contributors*:

Jack (mascot) *Source*: http://en.wikipedia.org/?oldid=382184315 *Contributors*: 1 anonymous edits

Tony Hutchinson *Source*: http://en.wikipedia.org/?oldid=387980604 *Contributors*: Raintheone

Curlz *Source*: http://en.wikipedia.org/?oldid=323375962 *Contributors*: 1 anonymous edits

Hayley Smith (American Dad!) *Source*: http://en.wikipedia.org/?oldid=389135811 *Contributors*: The Man in Question

ICE 2 *Source*: http://en.wikipedia.org/?oldid=388763879 *Contributors*: Rontombontom

Area code 360 *Source*: http://en.wikipedia.org/?oldid=368690375 *Contributors*: Salvio giuliano

RIM-900 *Source*: http://en.wikipedia.org/?oldid=332247267 *Contributors*:

Inter@ctive Pager *Source*: http://en.wikipedia.org/?oldid=379221974 *Contributors*: Urbanrenewal

Rayman *Source*: http://en.wikipedia.org/?oldid=388980879 *Contributors*: Pwlodi

Everson Mono *Source*: http://en.wikipedia.org/?oldid=390186049 *Contributors*: 1 anonymous edits

Canon PowerShot *Source*: http://en.wikipedia.org/?oldid=383445834 *Contributors*: Billwhittaker

Cray T90 *Source*: http://en.wikipedia.org/?oldid=346384792 *Contributors*:

Time Out (confectionery) *Source*: http://en.wikipedia.org/?oldid=374200621 *Contributors*: 1 anonymous edits

Digital-S *Source*: http://en.wikipedia.org/?oldid=379265809 *Contributors*: R'n'B

Gene Marshall *Source*: http://en.wikipedia.org/?oldid=385872156 *Contributors*: Siawase

Super A'Can *Source*: http://en.wikipedia.org/?oldid=390319415 *Contributors*:

R-Zone *Source*: http://en.wikipedia.org/?oldid=381760884 *Contributors*: 1 anonymous edits

Gerald "T-Bones" Tibbons *Source*: http://en.wikipedia.org/?oldid=380851031 *Contributors*: Caleson

Jambo Bolton *Source*: http://en.wikipedia.org/?oldid=379844094 *Contributors*: Raintheone

350 nanometer *Source*: http://en.wikipedia.org/?oldid=376620735 *Contributors*: Abduallah mohammed

Gordon Cunningham *Source*: http://en.wikipedia.org/?oldid=390093918 *Contributors*: Ooh, Fruity

Cindy Longford *Source*: http://en.wikipedia.org/?oldid=390073828 *Contributors*: LostHavoc

Ruth Osborne *Source*: http://en.wikipedia.org/?oldid=385768450 *Contributors*: AcidBrights

Maddie Parker *Source*: http://en.wikipedia.org/?oldid=389355165 *Contributors*: WOSlinker

Threatened Species Protection Act 1995 *Source*: http://en.wikipedia.org/?oldid=388237200 *Contributors*:

Tōyō Rapid 1000 series *Source*: http://en.wikipedia.org/?oldid=364235136 *Contributors*: DAJF

DVD *Source*: http://en.wikipedia.org/?oldid=390682100 *Contributors*: 1 anonymous edits

Keiō 1000 series *Source*: http://en.wikipedia.org/?oldid=372997191 *Contributors*: DAJF

Odakyū 2000 series *Source*: http://en.wikipedia.org/?oldid=364489640 *Contributors*: DAJF

Spatial twist continuum *Source*: http://en.wikipedia.org/?oldid=366220287 *Contributors*: SchuminWeb

Major League Baseball Wild Card *Source*: http://en.wikipedia.org/?oldid=389472745 *Contributors*: 1 anonymous edits

Big Hardee *Source*: http://en.wikipedia.org/?oldid=387008773 *Contributors*:

Lone Star Card *Source*: http://en.wikipedia.org/?oldid=348552317 *Contributors*: Bovineone

Fender Roscoe Beck Bass *Source*: http://en.wikipedia.org/?oldid=389348002 *Contributors*: Peterdjones

Charlie Schneider *Source*: http://en.wikipedia.org/?oldid=350789033 *Contributors*: Lucaslovespeyton

Sentricon *Source*: http://en.wikipedia.org/?oldid=385225022 *Contributors*: Crs20smo

Hunter Van Pelt *Source*: http://en.wikipedia.org/?oldid=387150053 *Contributors*: Visokor

10 Złotych *Source*: http://en.wikipedia.org/?oldid=369312274 *Contributors*: Kgbo

20 Złotych *Source*: http://en.wikipedia.org/?oldid=369312330 *Contributors*: Kgbo

50 Złotych *Source*: http://en.wikipedia.org/?oldid=369312375 *Contributors*: Kgbo

100 Złotych *Source*: http://en.wikipedia.org/?oldid=369312457 *Contributors*: Kgbo

200 Złotych *Source*: http://en.wikipedia.org/?oldid=369314052 *Contributors*: Kgbo

Rayman (character) *Source*: http://en.wikipedia.org/?oldid=390270727 *Contributors*: Legitimus

List of minor Hollyoaks characters (1995–96) *Source*: http://en.wikipedia.org/?oldid=390210885 *Contributors*:

Balto (character) *Source*: http://en.wikipedia.org/?oldid=387053709 *Contributors*: 1 anonymous edits

E127 series *Source*: http://en.wikipedia.org/?oldid=363898258 *Contributors*: DAJF

E501 series *Source*: http://en.wikipedia.org/?oldid=378830591 *Contributors*: Rpyle731

Cunningham family *Source*: http://en.wikipedia.org/?oldid=389885977 *Contributors*: Whoniverse93

Bhopal – Indore Intercity Express *Source*: http://en.wikipedia.org/?oldid=390000524 *Contributors*: 1 anonymous edits

Indore - Bhopal Intercity Express *Source*: http://en.wikipedia.org/?oldid=390000375 *Contributors*: 1 anonymous edits

Piedmont (train) *Source*: http://en.wikipedia.org/?oldid=379099259 *Contributors*: Murjax

The Harbingers *Source*: http://en.wikipedia.org/?oldid=386473384 *Contributors*: Rich Farmbrough

Image Sources, Licenses and Contributors

Image:Pc_005.jpg *Source*: http://en.wikipedia.org/w/index.php?title=File:Pc_005.jpg *License*: Creative Commons Attribution-Sharealike 3.0 *Contributors*: User:Mazzmn

File:Wikibooks-logo-en.svg *Source*: http://en.wikipedia.org/w/index.php?title=File:Wikibooks-logo-en.svg *License*: unknown *Contributors*: -

Image:VIRTUAL BOY sistem.png *Source*: http://en.wikipedia.org/w/index.php?title=File:VIRTUAL_BOY_sistem.png *License*: Public Domain *Contributors*: Bayo, JohnnyMrNinja, Lenin and McCarthy, METROID

File:Virtual Boy controller.jpg *Source*: http://en.wikipedia.org/w/index.php?title=File:Virtual_Boy_controller.jpg *License*: Creative Commons Attribution-Sharealike 3.0 *Contributors*: User:Sesu Prime

Image:Ppro512K.jpg *Source*: http://en.wikipedia.org/w/index.php?title=File:Ppro512K.jpg *License*: GNU Free Documentation License *Contributors*: Edwtie, Mike.lifeguard, Qurren, Testus, Ureaters, Павел Корниенко

File:Pentium Pro Black Edition Front.jpg *Source*: http://en.wikipedia.org/w/index.php?title=File:Pentium_Pro_Black_Edition_Front.jpg *License*: Creative Commons Attribution-Sharealike 3.0 *Contributors*: User:Kyro

Image:Pentiumpro moshen.jpg *Source*: http://en.wikipedia.org/w/index.php?title=File:Pentiumpro_moshen.jpg *License*: Creative Commons Attribution-Sharealike 2.5 *Contributors*: w:en:User:MoshenMoshen

Image:KL Intel PPro Overdrive P6T Top.jpg *Source*: http://en.wikipedia.org/w/index.php?title=File:KL_Intel_PPro_Overdrive_P6T_Top.jpg *License*: GNU Free Documentation License *Contributors*: Konstantin Lanzet

Image:Genesis Nomad.jpg *Source*: http://en.wikipedia.org/w/index.php?title=File:Genesis_Nomad.jpg *License*: unknown *Contributors*: -

Image:StarbucksVentiMintMochaChipFrappuccino.jpg *Source*: http://en.wikipedia.org/w/index.php?title=File:StarbucksVentiMintMochaChipFrappuccino.jpg *License*: Trademarked *Contributors*: Douglas Whitaker at the English Wikipedia.

Image:Frappucino.jpg *Source*: http://en.wikipedia.org/w/index.php?title=File:Frappucino.jpg *License*: Creative Commons Attribution-Sharealike 3.0 *Contributors*: User:RandomGuy666

Image:Pippinfront.jpg *Source*: http://en.wikipedia.org/w/index.php?title=File:Pippinfront.jpg *License*: unknown *Contributors*: -

Image:Pippinrear.jpg *Source*: http://en.wikipedia.org/w/index.php?title=File:Pippinrear.jpg *License*: GNU Free Documentation License *Contributors*: Beavis, Hellisp

File:Flag of Canada.svg *Source*: http://en.wikipedia.org/w/index.php?title=File:Flag_of_Canada.svg *License*: unknown *Contributors*: -

Image:Pippin-atmark-bios.jpg *Source*: http://en.wikipedia.org/w/index.php?title=File:Pippin-atmark-bios.jpg *License*: Creative Commons Attribution-Sharealike 3.0 *Contributors*: User:Incog88

Image:Pippinpaddle.jpg *Source*: http://en.wikipedia.org/w/index.php?title=File:Pippinpaddle.jpg *License*: GNU Free Documentation License *Contributors*: Museo8bits, Suimasentyottohensyuushimasuyo

Image:Smartmedia.svg *Source*: http://en.wikipedia.org/w/index.php?title=File:Smartmedia.svg *License*: unknown *Contributors*: -

Image:Smartmedia on keyboard.jpg *Source*: http://en.wikipedia.org/w/index.php?title=File:Smartmedia_on_keyboard.jpg *License*: unknown *Contributors*: -

Image:Smart Media X-ray.jpg *Source*: http://en.wikipedia.org/w/index.php?title=File:Smart_Media_X-ray.jpg *License*: unknown *Contributors*: -

Image:Kansai Airport Expressway.JPG *Source*: http://en.wikipedia.org/w/index.php?title=File:Kansai_Airport_Expressway.JPG *License*: unknown *Contributors*: -

Image:Jostalogo.gif *Source*: http://en.wikipedia.org/w/index.php?title=File:Jostalogo.gif *License*: Creative Commons Attribution 3.0 *Contributors*: KDanieli

File:Flag of Cote d'Ivoire.svg *Source*: http://en.wikipedia.org/w/index.php?title=File:Flag_of_Cote_d'Ivoire.svg *License*: unknown *Contributors*: -

Image:Dippin' Dots Rainbow Flavored Ice.jpg *Source*: http://en.wikipedia.org/w/index.php?title=File:Dippin'_Dots_Rainbow_Flavored_Ice.jpg *License*: Public Domain *Contributors*: Hohum, RadioActive

Image:Valleyfair MN Jun2006 DippingDotsStand DSCN8325.JPG *Source*: http://en.wikipedia.org/w/index.php?title=File:Valleyfair_MN_Jun2006_DippingDotsStand_DSCN8325.JPG *License*: Creative Commons Attribution 2.5 *Contributors*: User:Lar

Image:Dippindots cedarpoint.jpg *Source*: http://en.wikipedia.org/w/index.php?title=File:Dippindots_cedarpoint.jpg *License*: Creative Commons Attribution-Sharealike 3.0 *Contributors*: User:Ricknightcrawler

Image:Diamond EDGE 3400 NV1.png *Source*: http://en.wikipedia.org/w/index.php?title=File:Diamond_EDGE_3400_NV1.png *License*: unknown *Contributors*: -

Image:Dedge3d.jpg *Source*: http://en.wikipedia.org/w/index.php?title=File:Dedge3d.jpg *License*: unknown *Contributors*: -

Image:Yuan3DS.jpg *Source*: http://en.wikipedia.org/w/index.php?title=File:Yuan3DS.jpg *License*: unknown *Contributors*: -

Image:Sun ultra 1.jpg *Source*: http://en.wikipedia.org/w/index.php?title=File:Sun_ultra_1.jpg *License*: unknown *Contributors*: -

Image:Sun Ultra 5 front.jpg *Source*: http://en.wikipedia.org/w/index.php?title=File:Sun_Ultra_5_front.jpg *License*: unknown *Contributors*: -

Image:Processor_board_cray-2_hg.jpg *Source*: http://en.wikipedia.org/w/index.php?title=File:Processor_board_cray-2_hg.jpg *License*: unknown *Contributors*: -

File:CurlzSpec.svg *Source*: http://en.wikipedia.org/w/index.php?title=File:CurlzSpec.svg *License*: unknown *Contributors*: -

File:Db-402009-01.jpg *Source*: http://en.wikipedia.org/w/index.php?title=File:Db-402009-01.jpg *License*: unknown *Contributors*: -

File:402039-2.jpg *Source*: http://en.wikipedia.org/w/index.php?title=File:402039-2.jpg *License*: GNU Free Documentation License *Contributors*: MB-one, Qualle

File:ICE2 Hilpodrom.jpg *Source*: http://en.wikipedia.org/w/index.php?title=File:ICE2_Hilpodrom.jpg *License*: unknown *Contributors*: -

File:Ice2 mfa on lzb.jpg *Source*: http://en.wikipedia.org/w/index.php?title=File:Ice2_mfa_on_lzb.jpg *License*: Creative Commons Attribution-Sharealike 2.5 *Contributors*: Own work

File:Rabbid cosplay (edit).jpg *Source*: http://en.wikipedia.org/w/index.php?title=File:Rabbid_cosplay_(edit).jpg *License*: Creative Commons Attribution 2.0 *Contributors*: User:Cousin Kevin

File:Eversonmono.png *Source*: http://en.wikipedia.org/w/index.php?title=File:Eversonmono.png *License*: Public Domain *Contributors*: User:Evertype

Image:Everson-mono-sample.png *Source*: http://en.wikipedia.org/w/index.php?title=File:Everson-mono-sample.png *License*: Public Domain *Contributors*: User:Evertype

Image:Powershot A720is.jpg *Source*: http://en.wikipedia.org/w/index.php?title=File:Powershot_A720is.jpg *License*: unknown *Contributors*: -

File:D9 tape.jpg *Source*: http://en.wikipedia.org/w/index.php?title=File:D9_tape.jpg *License*: unknown *Contributors*: -

CPSIA information can be obtained at www.ICGtesting.com
Printed in the USA
LVOW131535161211

259788LV00004B/150/P